℥ *The Humanities in the*
Age of Technology

Ciriaco Morón Arroyo

The Humanities in the Age of Technology

The Catholic University of America Press
Washington, D.C.

First published as *Las humanidades en la era tecnológica* by Ediciones Nobel, 1998.

Copyright © 2002
The Catholic University of America Press
All rights reserved
Printed in the United States of America

The paper used in this publication meets the minimum requirements of American National Standards for Information Science—Permanence of Paper for Printed Library materials, ANSI Z39.48-1984.
∞

LIBRARY OF CONGRESS CATALOGING-IN-PUBLICATION DATA
Morón Arroyo, Ciriaco.
    [Humanidades en la era tecnológica. English]
    The humanities in the age of technology / Ciriaco Morón Arroyo.
        p. cm.
    Originally published: Las humanidades en la era tecnológica.
    Ovideo: Ediciones Nobel, 1998, in series : Colección Jovellanos de ensayo.
    Includes bibliographical references and index.
    ISBN 0-8132-1074-7 (alk. paper)
    1. Humanities. 2. Science and the humanities. I. Title.
    AZ228.S63 M6713 2001
    001.3—dc21

ᘓ *For Maria*

Juan Manuel

José Carlos

Francisco Javier

Ricardo

Elisa

Andrés

Pedro

ᘓ Contents

ᘓ Acknowledgments

The first draft of this book was written in English in 1975–76, when I was a Senior Faculty Fellow at The Society for the Humanities at Cornell University. That version was read by the outstanding scholar and admired colleague in Comparative Literature, Professor Wolfgang Holdheim, now emeritus, who wrote long and inspiring comments on each chapter. My colleague in Romance Studies, Professor John Kronik, also read the manuscript and made useful observations, as did Professors Rolena and David Adorno, who encouraged me to publish one of the drafts they read. Although the present version is very different from the previous ones, the comments of the above-mentioned scholars continued to be helpful.

In the Spring Semester of 1996, I presented what is basically the content of this book in eight lectures at the University of Salamanca, as holder of The Miguel de Unamuno Chair. My appreciation goes out to the students and faculty who honored me with their presence and enthusiasm. A summary of my idea of the humanities was presented at a gathering of humanists in Santiago de Compostela in the summer of 1998. Professor Virgil Nemoianu (Catholic University of America) had a most generous reaction. Subsequently he read the manuscript of the book in English and, again most generously, recommended its publication.

The book was published in Spanish in 1998. I am grateful to the scholars who wrote insightful reviews, and to Ediciones Nobel (Oviedo) for permission to publish this translation. Conversations with Prof. Javier Bengoa (Universidad de Deusto, Bilbao) have led to some refinements on questions of language and cognitive psychology, which have been introduced in the translation.

Mrs. Susan Needham, Managing Editor of The Catholic University of America Press, has called my attention to several passages that needed clarification or improvement; to her, and to the director, Dr. David McGonagle, my sincere gratitude.

The translation is the work of my children, who are native speakers of English and gave it to me as a Christmas gift in 1998. The original idea came from their mother, and Juan Manuel, the oldest one, undertook the supervision of the project. Sometimes the translation is not literal, but the changes of words aim at a more precise formulation of the substance.

In the mystical tract *The Cloud of Unknowing* (ca. 1385) the soul is advised to overcome dispersion by condensing the whole world in a monosyllable: love. Inhabited by love, may I add another monosyllable: Thanks.

CB *The Humanities in the*
Age of Technology

Introduction

Ↄ *There are drivers in Madrid who earn fifteen hundred, and cooks who institute patrimonial estates; yet everyone knows that he will starve if he devotes himself to the sciences, except the ones* de pane lucrando, *the only ones that give enough to eat.*

(José Cadalso, 1789)

The humanities are in crisis. At least, this seems to be the consensus among many humanists, and certainly among natural scientists and society in general. The low value placed on the humanities by society discourages students from pursuing humanistic careers, and the few who defy the trend do it to the disappointment of their families. As a result of lower enrollments, universities and colleges cut back on scholarships and teaching positions. But there is also another side: the awareness of the crisis leads university administrators to pay special attention to humanities departments or to fund interdisciplinary programs; some foundations reserve special blocks of fellowships for projects in the humanities, and the government maintains agencies and institutions, such as The National Endowment for the Humanities, devoted to fostering these fields. The number of students majoring in literature may decrease, but the study of foreign languages is on the rise, interest in non-Western cultures is increasing, and the growing dissatisfaction with narrow specialization can only lead to sound interdisciplinary cooperation, if we find the appropriate topics and methods. The situation of the humanities is ambiguous, but in order to do justice to the complexity and importance of the subject we must set aside two prejudices: any nostalgia for a glorious past which never existed, and any obsession with waging a defensive war against technology and/or science.

The study of the humanities cannot be invoked as defense of something human opposed to technology that supposedly converts us into mere consumers or into victims of manipulation against our freedom. Except for the few who refuse to adapt, those who scorn technology as dehumanizing still take advantage of the computer, the fax, and electronic mail in order to better communicate with collaborators and friends, i.e., for their human needs. Words are a sublime gift that can even cure illnesses but, given a choice, as therapy we normally prefer an effective antibiotic to a sermon. In a computer we are merely names in a database; but this only proves the machine's inability to codify what is truly human. The lists of taxpayers in the Renaissance—supposedly the golden age of humanism—were at least as inhuman as modern databases. The goals and methods of the humanities and those of the sciences are so different from each other that an objective conflict between them is impossible. Many scientists are good pianists, read literature, and are concerned with the social impact of their disciplines; for them, however—and this reflects actual discussions with some prominent ones—scientific research is serious intellectual work, while the humanities are an elegant form of entertainment. Against this view I will try to demonstrate that the humanistic disciplines are fields of rigorous knowledge.

The anxiety about these disciplines is quite old; in Plato's dialogue *Gorgias,* Callicles tells Socrates that philosophy has a certain charm when studied in one's youth and in moderation, but that it is unworthy of a mature man. "You know perfectly well that philosophers know nothing about state laws and regulations. They are equally ignorant of the conversational standards that we have to adopt in dealing with our fellow men at home and abroad. Why, they are inexperienced even in human pleasures and desires! In a word, they are totally innocent of all human character" (484d). And on the next page Callicles says, "When I see an older man still into his philosophy and showing no sign of giving it up, he seems to me to be asking for some hard knocks!" (485d; trans., p. 293).[1]

Cadalso's text cited above as motto of this introduction is equally eloquent. But in Cadalso's time the sciences that let one earn his daily bread *(de pane lucrando)* were law and theology, which offered many career opportunities in both the state and the church. According to Cadalso, the Cinderellas in the eighteenth century were the exact and useful sciences: "The few who cultivate the others are like the adventurers in the armies, who do not get paid and put themselves in the line of fire. It is a pleasure to hear the scientists talk about mathematics, modern physics, natural history, public law, antiquities and humane letters, sometimes with greater shame than counterfeiters of money."[2] In this text, today's humanities—"antiquities and humane letters"—belonged with mathematics and physics in a mishmash of embarrassing occupations. As we can see, the crisis shows up in various ways in different periods of history.

When a certain motif in the history of civilization—here I refer exclusively to Western civilization—persists practically unchanged through the centuries, it ceases to be a historical event and becomes a sort of inherent feature of that civilization.[3] And this is indeed the case with the humanities, which in addition to asking specific questions about certain realities must ask about their status as fields of knowl-

1. Plato, *Gorgias*, part III. Trans. by W. C. Hembold, in *The Dialogues of Plato* (Toronto and New York: Bantam Books, 1986), p. 292.

2. J. Cadalso, *Cartas marruecas* (1789), VI, p. 24. See Gaspar M. de Jovellanos, "Moral theology, laws, and medicine ensure employment for their professors everywhere, and that is why they attract so many in untold numbers. The useful sciences, God help them, will not be so attractive, nor do they offer as many rewards" (*Informe sobre la ley agraria*, Clásicos Castellanos, vol. 110, p. 69).

3. The suspicion that I may postulate a fixed nature as opposed to history and therefore an "essentialistic view" of Western civilization would be out of place. I am only emphasizing that certain historical motifs have traversed the centuries since the time of the ancient Greeks, while others vanished after attracting attention for a while. This book is largely based on Heidegger's idea that "The essence of man lies in his existence," rephrased by Ortega y Gasset in his sentence: "Man has no nature, he has history." A book based on these premises can hardly be essentialistic.

edge and about their usefulness in comparison to other human pursuits. The need to repeat the search for the foundation makes clear that progress in these disciplines cannot be understood as a linear advancement from lesser to greater perfection. But if all progress is linear, then is human time linear? Is there any place left for the "a-temporal" classic? If the crisis brings us to some lucid analysis of concepts such as time, progress, and the classic, then the crisis offers at least a positive flank.

The term "humanities" implies a relation to man, but in a special way. Man is studied in biology, in psychology, and in the social sciences, often called the human sciences. And even though the natural sciences do not have man as the subject of their research, they possess a humanistic side insofar as they are a quest for knowledge and are cultivated for the sake of man. Humanities in the strict sense are language, literature, philosophy, and other disciplines that constitute the so-called "high culture." Culture is the spontaneous expression or articulation and use of the traditions, ideals, and resources of a collectivity, whereas "high culture" is the production of especially qualified individuals or groups.[4] Today this distinction is at the center of intellectual debate in America, for several reasons: first, it is difficult to establish the borders between the two. Shakespeare is an example of high culture become popular, while jazz music exemplifies the opposite process. But the border cases do not eliminate the basic difference. One particular poem may raise doubts as to whether it is learned or popular, and a mechanistic distinction between the two is impossible, but Eliot's *The Waste Land* is certainly not popular. Here, however, the second objection looms: today literary scholars venture into popular literature as a cultural manifestation that has been unduly neglected by academic scholars. This applies in particular to the products of minorities in past centuries, whose cultural contributions would not enter the white canon. And why have

4. For a stimulating discussion of the concept of culture see A. L. Kroeber and Clyde Kluckhohn, *Culture: A Critical Review of Concepts and Definitions*, who give one hundred and sixty-four definitions of this notion. See *Culture*, pages 291ff.

these products been neglected? Here we find the third reason for the doubts concerning high versus popular culture: many humanists today view the very distinction between the two as elitism, a shibboleth with which nobody wants to be identified.

As for the new attention to popular culture in academia, every manifestation that takes root in a society must become the subject of research in high culture. Cinema, the musical as a new theatrical genre, and children's books must be analyzed today as high and popular culture alike. All high culture is destined in one way or another to become popular, as proven by the avant-garde art of the 1920s. If a cubist painting looked outrageous back then, today it decorates the most conservative living rooms. The better educated a society is, the more products of high culture it can absorb. What is more, the music, literature, and art that in a certain moment look outrageous for their experimental character, eventually educate their own society and bring about reconciliation with it. The most obvious example is the spread of the computer from the most esoteric laboratories where it was invented to everyday use in supermarkets. Finally, with regard to elitism, it is reproachable only as an attitude of individuals or groups, not as the recognition of a hierarchy in the quality and value of different realities. Among human activities, science, which corrects our vague or erroneous knowledge of nature, is more valuable than intuitive impressions about natural phenomena.

High culture includes art, theology, literature, philosophy, the natural sciences, and the social sciences. What is common to all these fields of inquiry is that they are the result of an intellectual effort on the part of individuals and small groups, not the spontaneous expression of the habits, traditions and shared values of a society, as "popular culture" is. High culture is distinguished by being the product of mediated reflection; it implies surpassing the level of impressionistic perception of things into a better perception. And if we today appreciate popular culture, it is because we recognize how much intelligence and creativity, i.e., high culture, it exhibits. For this reason, the distinction between popular and high culture must highlight their common roots and features as much as their difference.[5]

Science is a valid approach to reality, but not the only valid one. For the sake of brevity and clarity, we look at water as an example of different possible approaches to a subject. In elementary school we learn that water consists of hydrogen and oxygen; eventually we learn about its actual composition and density; we may go deeper and study the nature of its components: hydrogen and oxygen in relation to the other elements in the chemical table. The scientific study may continue with attention to the microbes that populate water; the difference between fresh and salt water; its changes from gas to ice, etc. Nobody will deny the legitimacy of this knowledge. But water is also the element of survival for nature and man; it is a natural resource which becomes a subject of legal conflict among communities and nations; a beautiful object for contemplation and an awesome force of destruction. This human relationship to water, which ranges from the poetic to the legal, may be the subject of reflection, which is intellectually rigorous but not scientific, since it does not study its composition. Science is rigorous knowledge of reality but not all rigorous knowledge need be science, or at

---

5. "Culture" in this book means the systematic reflection on any reality—the natural, the social sciences, and the humanities—and the meta-reflection or philosophy. These levels of systematic reflection may take place in the western type of discourse (science), or in other types (symbolic thought). A rigorous definition of the concept must grapple with terms such as "high and low" culture; elitist versus popular; spontaneous expression of a society's identity versus intellectual reflection on reality; objective contents and values versus personal cultivation. These notions are inherited from the eighteenth century, when European societies were divided by strict social barriers which determined the degree of education each layer had access to—not to mention the distinction between the civilized European and the "savage" man of other continents. Something similar, though with different connotations, is valid for the distinction between elite and "popular" cultures. Suffice it to remember that in Kant's time the university had only four colleges: Arts and sciences (called by Kant the "inferior" college), Theology, Law, and Medicine. Anything not pertaining to the four lines of study was "popular." Today the universities put up no barriers to anyone who is willing and capable of study, and the curriculum encompasses any human endeavor that is susceptible to some sort of systematization. The difference between "high" and "low" today depends on the degree of systematization as opposed to pure empiricism and accumulation of data.

least not natural science, as evidenced by the legal and other aspects of man's relationship to water.

The humanities are not and should never pretend to be sciences, but they must be "rigorous knowledge" *(strenge Wissenschaft)*, as Husserl intimated for philosophy in his programmatic study of 1911.[6] Obviously, as subjects of study at the university the humanities deserve to survive only if they reveal sides of reality which are not accessible in other disciplines, and if they contribute in some way to improving human life. Some humanists consider the humanities an interesting game, and in a sort of desperate response to the social perception of their uselessness, proclaim the right to play, thus bringing the profession of the humanist dangerously close to the old role of court jester.

I have mentioned several times "rigorous knowledge" as the ideal for all knowledge worthy of the name. With regard to historical, philosophical, theological, and literary texts—which basically constitute the humanistic texts—rigor implies at least the following moments: (a) analysis; (b) classification; (c) relation; (d) context; (e) value and consequences. The steps enumerated follow this logic: one would start with a careful reading (analysis); then the text would be seen as a specimen within a certain genre (classification); the next step is the originality, dependence and connection of the text with other works (relationship and context), and finally, its artistic and social value (judgment). The actual order of these operations will of course be suggested by the text itself, and may vary in response to different circumstances.

The point of departure of this book is the crisis of the humanities in our time. But, as I have pointed out, with different names—especially philosophy and poetry—the humanities have always been in crisis. The main reason is that they are constituted by the search for their own foundation, therefore by self-criticism, and they do not lead to perceptible practical results. One aspect of the crisis is the doubt on the part of humanists themselves about the criteria of rigor and validity of the knowledge attained in these disciplines. This book tries both to explain

---

6. See "Philosophie als strenge Wissenschaft," in *Logos,* 1 (1910–1911), pp. 289–341.

and to dispel this persistent anxiety. But the crisis changes its character when legitimate doubts become skepticism. The word "skeptic" means etymologically the seeker, and refers to the person who carefully probes what he hears. The seeker may accept a truth with enthusiasm, but only after he has found it himself without accepting it dogmatically. I will not discuss dogmatism because I consider it childish. However, the battle in the humanities today is taking place not between dogmatists and skeptics, but between enthusiastic and relativistic skeptics.

Since about 1970 we have witnessed an array of theories that have marked the route of all humanistic disciplines, and to a great extent, of the social sciences: structuralism, post-structuralism or deconstruction, psychoanalysis, and the latest one, cultural studies. The rapid succession of theories, the difficulty of understanding some of them, and the frivolous results they have had in the mass of epigones, have led to equally frivolous rejections in the form of a "backlash against theory," or of a "return" to an imagined tradition. The return to the so-called tradition—just one?—would be a retreat from rigorous knowledge, as demanded by Husserl, to positivist research—useful but not strictly humanistic—or to subjective intuitions. For the so-called theory, which has influenced the social sciences and the humanities in the last thirty years is, particularly in the humanities, the mature reflection about their status as fields of knowledge. Since the ultimate reflection on theory belongs to philosophy, theory has been the work of professional philosophers, such as Foucault and Derrida, both under the influence of, and in dialogue with, Heidegger and Sartre. Psychologists and linguists have also contributed, but equally relying on classics who delved into the principles of their disciplines, such as Freud and Saussure. Literary critics entered the field belatedly, and in most cases they only applied mechanistically to literature what they had assimilated from the philosophers, especially from Derrida. In any case, the ubiquitous presence of theory and pseudo-theory in the last thirty years of the twentieth century has led literary scholars to a state of depressive relativism.

Relativists approach fragments of texts rather than the whole text or the complete works of an author. They claim equal rights for all readings of the same text. In teaching, they purport to stimulate the student by eliciting his personal reaction, and shunning any "dogmatic" intervention on their part. Recognizing some positive aspects of these views, especially the anti-dogmatic position, I maintain that serious study aims at a compelling interpretation of texts and, more importantly, at knowledge of the reality presented or analyzed in the text. The most interesting outcome of our work is the satisfaction of explaining the meaning of a text by analyzing the human experience evoked in it. If in addition this intellectual effort is imaginative and sophisticated, so much the better. But perception and reason should prevail over imagination.

An instance of the debate between the enthusiasts and the relativists is found in the book *Interpretation and Overinterpretation*. It consists of three lectures by Umberto Eco, responses by Richard Rorty, Jonathan Culler, and Christine Brooke-Rose, and a final reply by Eco. This author is associated with the notion of "Open Work," the *Semiotics* in which he rejects the dream of a final or comprehensive interpretation of any text, and with *The Name of the Rose,* the novel that displays the difficulty of establishing cohesive worlds of sense out of scattered data. These books emphasize the limitations of human understanding and thus some of their statements may seem to lean toward relativism. In *Interpretation and Overinterpretation* Eco, without renouncing his previous positions, denounces farfetched readings introduced into the texts by the interest of the reader. After adducing several examples of wild interpretations, he maintains that a text is a structure consisting of signs, some of which are more universal, and some more particular. Any attention to a certain sign that loses the perspective of the whole distorts the totality of the text. The approach to a text from methods that obey the interests of the reader must be incorporated into the approach suggested by the text itself. The question of whether we can dispense with the interests or the ideology of the reader in the name of an ideal objectivity will be discussed later (pp. 180–82).

The discussants in *Interpretation and Overinterpretation* advocate relativism, espousing the search for "the interesting," and warning against the intentional fallacy. In his reply Eco does not constrain the reader to searching for the intention of the author, because both author and reader are summoned by what Eco calls the intention of the text *(intentio operis)*. But where and how is that intention expressed? It is the text itself with its sense.[7]

An example may help to better understand Eco's position, with which I side. A feminist reader of *Hamlet* has every right to describe the two female characters in the play (Gertrude and Ophelia), and will probably discover that Shakespeare's view of woman reflects the stereotypes of his time and society ("Frailty, thy name is woman"). But unless that reader places his study of woman in relation to the other characters, to the structure and to the other signs of the text, the feminist study ends up in a distortion. Much criticism of *Hamlet* has focused on the main character; it is legitimate, but the text presents a story, that is, the interaction of many characters, which properly constitutes the drama. The text, therefore, forces the reader to consider the structure of the play and all its characters according to their role or significance in it. The significance of each character will in turn decide to what extent the study of women—or of the main character, the servants, lords, and clowns—would contribute to the understanding of the work as a whole.

Interpretation demands a holistic approach, which far from diminishing the value of the limited approaches enhances it because it puts those approaches in the proper perspective. But who decides about the proper perspective? We human beings are limited, and cannot aspire to exhaust the meaning of a text. But we know the ideal, and can grope for it. In any case, the consciousness of our limits does not justify relativism, because the texts mean something concrete, regardless of our success in ascertaining that meaning. The question of which interpretation is right or wrong admits only of an empirical decision, but we know empirically many distorted readings that are contradicted by the text.

The limited scope of every interpretation shows in another aspect

7. *Interpretation and Overinterpretation*, p. 19.

not touched upon in Eco's book. Let us postulate for a moment the best and most comprehensive interpretation of *Hamlet*. With its help the readers of the drama will finally understand the mysteries of the prince's character, the logic of the structure, whether Ophelia committed suicide for love of the prince or for love of her dead father, and all the other open questions. That masterpiece of criticism will in turn not be exhausted by its readers, and instead of closing the subject of *Hamlet* it will open countless questions never asked before. A comprehensive humanistic work opens a Pandora's box. The critical masterpiece will also reflect the language and interests of its own time and therefore will be only partially useful in a different social and intellectual environment. But this recognition of our limits does not justify the retreat from the most comprehensive approach we can muster.

This holistic view of a problem is apt to intimidate, and is easily dismissed as "grandiose" or even worse: totalitarian. I heard this once from a recognized scholar with regard to Eric Auerbach's *Mimesis,* and Ernst R. Curtius' *European Literature and the Latin Middle Ages.* This reaction makes no sense, unless we can accuse Auerbach and Curtius of making unfounded statements. But since this book is based on the "grandiose" tradition of Auerbach and Curtius, and, like most European philosophers since the 1930s—including of course Levinas, Derrida, and Lyotard—must recognize its debt to Heidegger, a few words on the holistic approach will not be superfluous. "Totalitarian" is just the Latin equivalent of Greek holistic, but after the fight of democracies against totalitarian Fascism in World War II the Latin word connotes historical conditions and behaviors that are far removed from the Greek word "holistic," and, as it is known, Heidegger had formal connections (the vagueness of my expressions reflects what is objectively known) with the Nazis for many years. But, as I see it, Heidegger's philosophy provides the best theoretical foundation against political totalitarianism and its historical offshoot, racism.

In philosophy Heidegger looked indeed for a foundation of all being and knowledge, for a sort of lever of the world. In this sense he is holistic, but he was in good company: all Western philosophy since Plato and Aristotle. Of course, medieval thought, guided by the presence of God as origin, holder, and goal of the universe, is totalitarian. Descartes posited the lever of the world in what he thought were the first experiences of man: sensitive knowledge. And modern philosophy belied Descartes by delving steadily into deeper and deeper foundations. Closer to Heidedgger, suffice it to remember that his original work was based on the key concepts of Husserl's phenomenology. Husserl was a German Jew who died in 1938, before the Auschwitz era, but had his share of suffering in the first five years of the Nazi regime. In a certain way, Heidegger's corrections of Husserl's phenomenology coincide with the idea of system that guided the Marburg School, whose most salient figure, the great Jewish philosopher Hermann Cohen, looked for the foundations of all knowledge, was obsessed with the ideal of the system, and called his own philosophy "constructivism." A key concept in Jaspers, who had to flee the Nazi threat, is "The Encompassing."

In his search for the ultimate foundation and comprehensive outlook into the real, Heidegger follows tradition. His shakeup of tradition takes place in his new way of approaching the relationship between life and reason, or life and cultural values. Before him philosophers conceived of human life as a biological phenomenon that eventually created culture. Georg Simmel portrays human life as the crossroads of biology and biography; in this sense he came at times very close to what Heidegger would later formulate. But what Simmel called "the tragedy of culture" derives from his conception of life in biological terms. Heidegger stands out for eliminating all references to biology in the understanding of human life. He calls the human being *Da-sein;* substitutes existence for life; and for him the defining note of the human being is projection, the future, not biological or even cultural heritage—the past. Thus, in his very terminology Heidegger precluded any biological approach to human existence and therefore any possibility of racism. As we shall see, Heidegger defines language as the call of truth to man. Anyone who embraces this idea of language will be an eager listener rather than a dictator.

Our holism is based on this idea of a humble discourse. It tries to display the spectrum of the humanities in order to see as many aspects of them as possible, and to look for their common core or foundation. This foundation is the difference as the ultimate structure of reality. The primordial reality and concept in traditional metaphysics was being. Heidegger defines it as the crossroads in which any particular entity receives its sense from being, while being is nothing outside of the particular entities. The mutual dependency and rejection is the difference. Applied to discourse, the difference is the border of language as a mirror that reflects the little we know, and language as the arrow that calls us to the dark labyrinth of what we do not know. Holism is an effort to penetrate into the essence and ramifications of the subject under study. It shuns fragmentary and partial approaches, but in the search for the whole it also shuns dogmatism; it is a friendly invitation to share both knowledge and ignorance with the sole aim of learning.

If the holistic ideal tempts us with the illusion of being comprehensive, we soon realize that the vision of the whole hangs on our ability to apprehend it. The following order has imposed itself on me as the most logical articulation of the book, but I would not claim that my perspective is the only valid one. The first chapter seeks a definition of the humanities; in it I refer to some notions inherited from the past, but only by way of perspective; this is not a book of history but of theory. Chapter II deals with the humanistic disciplines: linguistics, literature, history, philosophy, and theology. The disciplines lead logically to ask about the meaning of the interdisciplinary (Ch. III), and this to the human being as the nucleus from which all disciplines arise, in which all dwell, and on which they all converge (Ch. IV). The fifth chapter describes the crisis of the humanities, as I see it. The most conspicuous aspect of the crisis is doubt about the validity of the knowledge attained in the humanistic discourse, and the criteria for judging its validity. To this we devote three chapters with the respective titles: Reading (Ch. VI), Understanding (Ch. VII), and Knowing (Ch. VIII). Finally, the second aspect of the crisis concerns the usefulness of these studies in our society: chapters IX and X address this question.

Many thinkers have touched on the topics studied here, and between them they may have said all the important things that need to be said about the humanities. But some have conceived them too broadly, by including the social sciences. Others have written on hermeneutics or utilitarianism in philosophy, and for still others the discussion centers on rationalizing the need to keep alive some interest in Latin and ancient Greek. These partial analyses call for a systematic study in the sense outlined above, a sort of "first philosophy" with regard to the humanistic disciplines. This book is my response to that demand: a profession of faith in the humanities and, as such, a defense; but not a political defense with an eye to saving jobs or perpetuating beautiful lies. It is not a faith in search of understanding (*fides quaerens intellectum*), but the opposite, a faith based on the conviction that the humanities, cultivated at the proper intellectual level, can be rigorous knowledge of reality, and of greater practical value than the fax and e-mail. For these magnificent means of communication transmit messages, but before transmitting them, we need the desire and competence to create and express the message. The humanities may also serve to prevent violence and stress; but that role derives from their positive content: the intellectual rigor and the joy of living we can derive from the humanistic disciplines. The remedy against unhealthy situations is a secondary effect of the positive contribution. If religion makes sense, it is not primarily as consolation against poverty, ignorance and tyranny, but for its objective value in a situation of comfort, the highest level of education, and freedom.

I Toward a Definition

C3 'Tis evident, that all the sciences have a relation, greater or less, to human nature; and that however wide any of them may seem to run from it, they still return back by one passage or another.

(D. Hume, *A Treatise of Human Nature*, Introduction, p. XIX)

1. Thesis: Abstract definition

The humanities are the disciplines that study the human being in what is distinctly human, with the type of discourse required by this particular subject (human being) and approach (as human).

To describe the awareness of the crisis of the humanities already expressed by Plato, I have quoted Callicles' statements on philosophy. But humanities and philosophy are not synonymous terms; we rather associate the humanities with "Letters," which until the nineteenth century, when the vernacular languages and literatures were introduced as disciplines at the universities, meant basically Latin and Greek philology. The ambiguity increases when we confront the natural sciences with the "human sciences"—also called "moral and political sciences" or *Geisteswissenschaften* ("sciences of the spirit")—fields of knowledge whose subject of study is man in activities and forms of behavior that are distinctly human, but are not humanities in the strict sense. Thus, the term humanities refers to philosophy, classic letters, modern languages and literatures, and to some "human sciences," which are not called humanities but are more "humanistic" than physics or biology. In fact, when a bookstore window or a publisher's catalog has a section with the heading "Humanities," it usually gathers in it anything that crosses the boundaries of the traditional disciplines and resists classification. This vagueness, however, points to a positive aspect of the humanities: their interdisciplinary character.

To define a word is to unfold the reality that it denotes or evokes. In this sense, this whole book is an attempt to unfold the different meanings and connotations of the word "humanities." The result, if the project succeeds, will be the ideal definition, which comes always at the end, not at the beginning of research. Knowledge is an investigation that begins with a vague notion (thesis) in search of a clear and distinct idea or synthesis. The antithesis, i.e. the mid-term between thesis and synthesis in Hegel's popular formulation, would be the analysis of related concepts and background, which lead to the actual definition. But it would be simplistic to understand this dialectical process in a linear way. In the first place, when the philosopher introduces a preliminary definition at the beginning of his inquiry, he already knows the final one. But what is known to the author is not known to the reader. For the reader, the definition set forth at the beginning of a work is at best a description that marks off the field of study and raises questions; this chapter promises nothing more.

All the concepts that enter our mind can be grouped into four types: analogical, univocal, collective, and historico-cultural. Analogical concepts are the most universal ones that are taken for granted in all reasoning: being, truth, goodness. These concepts had in medieval philosophy a sort of nuclear meaning which applied properly to God, and then to creatures in the proportion in which they partook of God.[1] Univocal concepts are those whose features are found in all the individuals they encompass. Man is a rational animal; freedom is the ability to react in a

---

1. To be precise from the theological point of view, creatures are created by God out of nothing and therefore participate in God's being only as footprints or images of God. St. Thomas Aquinas gave the precise formulation that intended to affirm the participation while avoiding pantheism: "Deus est esse omnium effective et exemplariter, non autem per essentiam" (*Summa Theologica*, I, 3.8 ad 1) (God is the being of everything in the sense of being its effective and exemplary cause, not in the sense that things would share His essence. My translation.)

reflective way to a given situation. In spite of incidental variants, these definitions are valid for all men and for all the varieties of freedom. In a society that respects human rights, freedom is the reflective decision to do what must be done. In a prison, freedom is the acceptance or rejection of our condition in view of its justice or injustice. In both cases freedom is the ability to judge and take a position toward something.

Collective concepts designate groups and societies, and what is predicated of them does not apply to all its individuals. "The Americans," or "The Spaniard," are legitimate subjects of some general statements, but the content of those statements is not found in all Spaniards or Americans. The validity of these predicates is founded on statistics. Finally, historico-cultural concepts are the ones that describe cultural trends or social phenomena that act as background to concrete historical events. These concepts exhibit a nucleus of constant features, but those features take different forms in different societies, times, and fields of study. Terms such as "Baroque," "modernity," and "socialism," belong in this category. These concepts must be defined in their common nucleus, yet the common definition must be adapted to the diverse forms it has taken in the societies, times, and fields referred to above. The Baroque, for example, extends to literature, the visual arts, and music. However, since that style influenced also the way Europeans dressed, popular festivals, religious ceremonies, sermons, and ecclesiastical music in the seventeenth and the first half of the eighteenth centuries, some scholars have even spoken of the "Baroque man." Given the variety of its concrete forms, a definition of the term "Baroque" will have to explore both the core that justifies the common designation, and the specific shape it takes in each one of the arts.

"Humanities" is a historico-cultural term; its definition, therefore, involves delving into the underlying common core, while unfolding its main variables. To begin with, the humanities today cannot be identified with the Greek *paideia*. *Paideia* means nurture of the child, and included all the elements of the Greek citizen's education as opposed to that of the foreigner, the "barbarian." It was Cicero, the Roman rhetorician, who first introduced the term *humanitas* as the ideal to which all study or education aspires. "The arts that make us human"[2] was the comprehensive learning about all reality, including the fields now called sciences: grammar and rhetoric, the laws, Roman history, the nature of the gods, and astronomy. The same is valid for the medieval notion of liberal arts. The *trivium*—grammar, rhetoric, and logic—studied man's way of thinking and of expressing himself, while the *quadrivium*—arithmetic, geometry, astronomy, and music—was the ancestor of what eventually came to be modern science. Music was grouped with the sciences because it was based on rhythm and measurement, which made it a chapter of mathematics. The names "Philosophy," "Letters," "Human arts," and "Liberal arts" denote concrete historical forms of the humanities. A foray into history is always useful but not helpful for our purpose, since our intellectual situation and ideals are so different from the past. Indeed, it is only from our own definitions that we can make sense of the traditional concepts.

Fully aware of its abstract character and of the immediate need to explain its terms, I advanced my definition of humanities at the beginning of this chapter: The study of the human being in what is distinctively human, with the type of discourse required by this particular subject (human being) and approach (as human). The humanistic disciplines study man in what makes him different from all other entities. They study only man, but as a whole, in philosophy and history. Man is the "talking animal"; language is man as articulated coexistence, consciousness, and self-consciousness, and literature is a unique type of reference to language. And finally man as man is a conscious project. The search for the ultimate meaning of human life and of all reality is theology, as the reflective articulation of religion. The humanistic disciplines are therefore philosophy, history, language, literature, and theology. This definition calls for an investigation of how the humanities relate to the social or "human" sciences, and to the humanistic aspects of the natural sciences. But before engaging in this analysis, a possible objec-

2. "Artes quae ad humanitatem pertinent" (*Pro Archia poeta,* 5). See also in Cicero: "In omni genere sermonis, in omni parte humanitatis dixerim oratorem perfectum esse debere" (*De oratore,* I, 16, 71).

tion must be cleared up, since our definition does not mention the classical literatures and the humanism of the Renaissance, which are still spontaneously associated with the very idea of the humanities.

2. *Renaissance humanism*

Italian humanism, which defines an entire cultural age, not only in Europe but in the whole world, can be divided into three periods, each one with special characteristics: from Petrarch (1304–74) to Lorenzo Valla; from Valla (1407–57) to 1548; and from 1548 on, to the extent that one date can serve as symbol for a turning point in history. We can call these three periods early humanism, humanism proper, and mannerism.

Petrarch's humanism stems from his awareness of Italian identity as opposed to the barbarian invaders who dominated Italy and kept it divided. The inspiring landmark and source of his pride is the Rome of the Republic and the Empire, with its literature and art; hence Petrarch's attention to the Latin authors and his devotion to the relics of ancient Rome. He does not study the classics as models of literary form, but as examples of moral guidance; hence his concentration on Cicero and Seneca. Nevertheless, his literary taste confronts Petrarch with the bad Latin of the scholastics, and this prompts his polemics against the representatives of medieval theology. Moreover, his own creative work, especially the poems of the *Canzoniere,* have a modern flavor, because in them Petrarch expresses his own feelings, or at least gives the impression of doing so. This presence of the author in his text contrasts with the medieval style in which authors adhere to inherited themes, stylistic formulas, and generic structures (Curtius' *topoi*). Petrarch revives dialogue as the appropriate genre for intellectual discussion, and introduces the "letter," which is sometimes a true letter but may also be an essay, though with the personal touch of the letter.

Contemporary with Petrarch, new forms of art emerge in Giotto's painting, Boccaccio's ironic subversion in *Fiammetta* (1342) and the *Decameron* (1349–53), a new architecture, and the voracious unearthing of texts and ruins from ancient Rome. However, all the innovations introduced by Petrarch and his contemporaries do not change the prevailing way of thinking: scholasticism. In spite of his originality and his criticism of the scholastic Latin, Petrarch is himself a scholastic thinker. Scholasticism is basically the reading of the Bible from the standpoint and within the framework of Aristotle's philosophy. The God of the Bible is identified with Aristotle's "subsistent being"—an identification that was considered sanctioned by God himself in his self-definition "I am who I am" (Exodus 3:14). Man consists of three layers of faculties: vegetative, sensitive, and rational. Understanding and will, which are the rational faculties, constitute the spirit or superior layer, while the vegetative and sensitive form the inferior level of impulses and sensitivity: impressions of the senses and spontaneous inclinations, which must always be governed by the spirit. Petrarch's *Secretum,* a dialogue between reason and sensitivity, is based on the medieval image of man. The pagan authors who are most widely studied in that period are the moralists Cicero and Seneca, who are placed in harmony with Christianity and with Aristotle, the ethical authority par excellence.[3]

Petrarch criticizes the lack of formal elegance in the use of Latin by the scholastic theologians, yet the bitter confrontation between the scholastic friars and the humanists, which led to the breakup of the Medieval world outlook, did not originate in disputes over linguistic elegance but in the idea of the religious profession and its implications for reading the Bible. According to the Scholastics, the religious vows of poverty, chastity and obedience placed the Christian individual in a state of perfection that was objectively superior to that of the layman regardless of the individual's behavior. In his book, *On religion,* the humanist Coluccio Salutati, who died in 1408, does not question this doctrine. Lorenzo Valla, on the other hand, in his book *On the profession of the religious* (1440?) rejects this view. Erasmus repeats Valla's idea in his sentence *monachatus non est pietas:* being a monk or a friar is not more

3. Just one century later, Leonardo Bruni Aretino (1374?–1444) would produce a new translation of Aristotle's *Nicomachean Ethics,* distinct from the one used by St. Thomas Aquinas for his commentary.

perfect than being a layman; what matters is the subject, the conduct of the individual.

Lorenzo Valla was born in Rome in 1407. He began his career as a professor of Rhetoric at the University of Pavia (1429–1433). After 1437 he was secretary to King Alfonso V of Aragón, settling in Naples in 1442 after the conquest of this kingdom by Alfonso. From 1448 until his death in 1457, he lived in Rome as secretary to the Pope and professor at the University. Valla's main work is *Elegantiae linguae latinae* (1444). "Elegance" has in Valla a more precise meaning than in Petrarch: it means the pleasure of capturing the accurate sense of the Latin words when Latin was a living language. The study of that meaning is, therefore, the recovery of the realities expressed by those words, that is to say, of Latin culture. From this conception of language Valla confronts the Medieval philosophers and jurists, and scorns their misunderstanding of the Latin terms, and consequently of Roman law and the ideas of the classical authors.

Medieval logic, according to Valla, uses the dry language of pure reasoning, whereas language, in addition to conveying ideas, manifests feelings, possesses musical and pictorial qualities, and reveals possibilities of association based on the structure of the sentences. The field of rhetoric analyzes language in its fullness, i.e., in its four functions. Thus, rhetoric, which was traditionally understood as the art of persuading, is for Valla primarily the unfolding of language in its full potential of expression. Accordingly, Valla describes rhetoric as a radiant and bejeweled lady, and logic as a naked and skinny beggar.

A key term in scholastic thought was *ens* (being), the object of metaphysics. This philosophical discipline was defined as the knowledge of (a) beings that are immaterial and, consequently, the highest realities; (b) the most universal principles of knowledge; and (c) study of being as being, or *ens*, the ultimate reality and concept from which we confront every particular object. For Valla metaphysics is condemned at the outset because its basic concept, the word *ens*, active participle of the verb to be, is unknown in classical Latin and is a torture to the ear of any good Latinist. Today we can hardly imagine the subversive audacity involved in this rejection, but we may have a glimpse by remembering that the word *ens* was the subject of the "First philosophy," which the scholastics called the "Queen of the sciences." Valla did not bow before that Queen.

With prodigious learning and cruel irony, Valla exposed in 1440 the legend of the *Donatio Constantini,* according to which Emperor Constantine had transferred the government of the city of Rome to Pope Sylvester, thus giving its first title of legitimacy to the Papal State. Another legend exposed by Valla is that of the Pseudo-Dionysius. Some of the most influential texts in medieval theology and mysticism had been attributed to Saint Dionysius Areopagita, who converted to Christianity after listening to Saint Paul's sermon at the Areopagus of Athens (Acts 17:34). In large measure, the mystical language of the Middle Ages and of the following centuries was based on these writings, especially the division of the mystical experience into three stages: purification, illumination, and union. Valla maintains that those writings cannot belong to a disciple of Saint Paul, because they are more Platonic than Christian. And starting with the ideological decision as a hypothesis, he proves that they were never cited and, therefore, were unknown in the first five centuries of the Church. Historical criticism in the nineteenth century proved Valla right.

But Valla was most innovative and subversive in his reading of the New Testament. He analyzed the Latin of the Vulgate, compared it with the Greek, and noted the passages where the translation was not accurate, not sufficiently elegant, or could be more faithful to the original. In this way, he changed certain Latin formulas in which the theologians had found the scriptural basis of certain dogmas of faith, or of truths accepted practically as dogmas by the whole Church. Valla was not disputing the truth of the dogmas themselves; he only denied that the biblical sentences quoted by the theologians could serve as their foundation. But that was enough to ignite a revolution of far-reaching consequences in Christianity. The scholastic theologians were at a loss in the face of Valla's ideas, as we gather from these words of the Spanish mystic Francisco de Osuna: "Before the good letters came [the rebirth of Latin and Greek humanism] we were all obedient to our prelates, even to the wayward ones. But now, even if the prelates are saints, they will be told that their instructions cannot be found in the original Greek."[4] Obviously, Osuna attributed to the philological study of the Bible the breakdown of religious discipline. Now the novices in the monastery questioned the doctrine of their teachers, forcing them to re- alize that sometimes they did not have any basis in the original language of the New Testament.

The use of the printing press was just beginning when Valla died in 1457, and he never saw his works in print. But Erasmus discovered in 1504 the manuscript of Valla's *Annotationes in Novum Testamentum* (An- notations to The New Testament), printed it, and was so profoundly in- fluenced that he changed his intellectual project, and devoted the rest of his life to the purification of the biblical text and to the theological im- plications of the new reading of the Bible. Suffice it to recall the rela- tionship between Erasmus and Luther and the role of the Bible in the Protestant Reformation to properly assess the revolution aroused by Lorenzo Valla with his new conception of language and rhetoric.

If one can associate the dawn of a new historical era with a form of thinking that permeates all the expressions of that era, Valla may claim the right to be considered the father of European modernity. As op- posed to the scholastic way of reading, Valla concentrates on texts with their specific style and rhetoric, their concrete history, and the realities that the words denote and connote. Valla deconstructs scholasticism by reading the Bible as a new critic would. At the palace of King Alfonso V in Naples the friars taught that the Church's Creed consisted of twelve propositions because each one of the Apostles had contributed his own. Valla laughed at this imaginative but unsubstantiated belief; for him the Creed represented the apostolic faith, but nobody can claim that the Apostles wrote it, because it is not proven by documents.

With his direct attention to the text Valla inaugurates a new way of

---

4. Francisco de Osuna, *Abecedario espiritual,* p. 5ª (Burgos, 1541), ch. XXX, folio XXXVII.

reading the Bible. The scholastics extracted isolated passages to prove theses that were sometimes formulated in terms of Aristotle's pagan philosophy. For Valla, to read is to arrive at the most faithful text possible with the help of the best codices, and to study the text as completely as possible, unfolding its content by way of parallels within the same text and highlighting the nuances of each verse. The unfolding of the content of the text protects against allegories and moral or mystical applications to which readers resort when they are not competent for perceiving the literal meaning. And while Valla's intention was religious—to restore the Bible to its authentic meaning—his attack on the theologians' readings represented both the rebellion and the revelation of the lay intellectual and, therefore, a beginning of secularization.[5]

It sometimes appears that humanists limit their attention to grammatical details rather than to content. But the perspective of the humanists was far from formalistic. The work of recovering and editing classical texts was for them a return to the roots of their Latin identity after ten centuries of deviation. The humanists called themselves grammarians, but for them grammar was not purely formal, and much less a discipline for the grammar school; it was the exploration of how the mind works in its functions of reflection and expression. Humanism died when grammar became a school discipline.

The wars between Catholics and Protestants, the deaths of Erasmus and Luther in 1536 and 1545 respectively, the absorption and domestication of humanism by the theologians (Vitoria, Melchor Cano) who recognized the legitimacy of a "positive" theology (a philological study of the Bible) alongside the speculative one (scholastic method), and the expansion of education decreed by the Council of Trent for the Jesuit schools and the diocesan seminaries, brought about the purely formalist

---

5. This brief image of Valla summarizes studies that I began publishing in 1976 (*Nuevas meditaciones del Quijote*. Madrid: Gredos, pp. 74–95). See also "A historical revolution: Lorenzo Valla's attack on scholasticism," in *ACTA*, VIII (Binghamton, NY: CEMERS, 1981), pp. 23–45; and "Lorenzo Valla: nuevo discurso del método," in *Homenaje a Pedro Sainz Rodríguez* (Madrid: Fundación Universitaria Española, 1986), IV, pp. 319–34. On Erasmus: C. Morón Arroyo, "El sistema de Erasmo, origen, originalidad, vigencia," in M. Revuelta and C. Morón Arroyo, *El erasmismo en España*, pp. 41–52.

orientation of humanism in the second half of the sixteenth century. Giuseppe Toffanin calls this period "the end of humanism" and dates it from 1548, when Robertelli published the first commentary on Aristotle's *Poetics*.[6] Starting with Robertelli, speculation on literary theory began in Italy and spread all over Europe. Commentaries were made on the ancient as well as the modern classics, as El Brocense (1574) and Herrera (1580) did with Garcilaso de la Vega. Students began to learn the humanities in school; they no longer read the Bible, but rather the Greek and Latin authors appropriately expurgated. The son of the Knight of the Green Overcoat in the *Quijote* "wastes his time" on those studies, to the chagrin of his father, who sometimes regrets having engendered him, so aggravating can be the study of the humanities: "I have a son, that if I had not had him, I might think myself more blissful than I am" (*Quijote*, II, Ch. XVI). And the reason for this family misfortune is that "he spends the whole day studying if Homer was right or wrong in a verse of the Iliad; if Martial was dishonest or not in such and such an epigram; if Virgil's such and such verses must be understood in this way or that" (ibid.). This formalist humanism, devoid of ideological content and with the Bible off limits, is mannerism or the Baroque, and its most representative figure is Justus Lipsius (1547–1606), a prodigiously erudite grammarian and critic, but devoted to a field already marginal in the society of Montaigne, Francis Bacon, and Galileo.

In the second half of the sixteenth century Galileo codified the scientific method of looking at nature, and one begins to discern the outlines of "the two cultures": the humanities and the sciences. For the humanists of the Renaissance, until approximately 1550, the "human letters" encompassed all knowledge acquired by reason without the help of divine revelation. In fact, Luis de León (1528–91) calls them "profane letters" and opposes them to the sacred ones, *"sacra pagina,"* which are the Bible, and theology or divinity as the explanation of the Bible.[7] But the "profane letters" included the ethics inherited from Cicero and Seneca,

---

6. G. Toffanin, *La fine dell'umanesimo*, pp. 2, 29–45.

7. Luis de León, *La perfecta casada*, in *Obras completas castellanas*, edited by Félix García (Madrid: BAC, 1957), I, p. 244.

politics, aspects of the individual and society that can be analyzed in an empirical way in dialogues and banquets (symposia), the courtly way to behave in society, and mathematics and astronomy. In brief, the "human letters" included not only the humanities, but the areas of knowledge that eventually became the social and the natural sciences. In fifteenth century Florence an admirable fusion of geometry and art takes place when the painters make an effort to convey the third dimension according to the exact proportions of perspective as determined by geometry.

3. The three cultures

With his expression "The two cultures," the British physicist and novelist C. P. Snow expresses the lack of communication between scientists and humanists in today's university. Snow points to the lack of dialogue between the specialists in the two fields, although in his opinion scientists are usually more open to the humanities than the humanists are to science. The separation of the two cultures begins with the modern age, but at the beginning the institutions of higher learning were still dominated by the scholastics. That is why Cadalso said that whoever experimented with useful knowledge did it almost with embarrassment and without any expectation of reward.

Since scientific knowledge in the Renaissance was practically synonymous with mathematics and the "letters" inherited from antiquity, the meaning of "good letters" is spontaneously associated with the classics until the generation of Galileo (1564–1642). Thus, Covarrubias, who in his *Tesoro de la lengua castellana* (Thesaurus of the Castilian language, 1611) does not include the word "humanities," says under the term "Letter": "Man of good letters, the one who is versed in good authors, whose study is called by another name, letters of humanity."[8] But the scientific revolution that, initiated by Copernicus became entrenched with Galileo and Descartes, inaugurates the mathematical vision of the universe. Galileo's *Dialogues,* published in 1638 but anticipated in letters

8. S. de Covarrubias y Orozco, *Tesoro de la lengua castellana,* s. v. Letra.

dating from 1602, are a treasure of experiments on the behavior of bodies and of explanations that he calls "geometric." With these experiments and explanations he not only corrects Aristotle's physics, which he always treats with great respect, but applies to nature the method of observation, description, and explanation that Valla had applied before him to the study of the Bible. The "geometric" method found its main proponent in Descartes (1596–1650), who for some philosophers (the Neo-Kantians in particular) represents the leap into modernity. In the same vein Spinoza wrote his *Ethics* (1677), "demonstrated in the style of geometry." One century later, Condorcet wrote what would come to be the first application of statistics to the human sciences.[9]

As a response to the mathematical method, Giambattista Vico (1668–1744) published in 1725 his *magnum opus,* which is usually called the *Scienza nuova.* The definitive edition of 1744 bears the title *Principi di scienza nuova d'intorno alla comune natura delle nazioni* (Principles of a new science on the common nature of nations). Vico's work is a theory of humanistic knowledge, not on literature, history, or philosophy, but "on the nature of nations." Vico confronts Descartes, who founded all knowledge on the method of logical inference. It would be simplistic to say that Descartes built a geometric system; but it is clear that he subordinates all knowledge to the scientific method, that is to say, to observation by the senses, a broadening of the senses through instruments, and logical inference. Descartes describes knowledge as a process leading from premises to conclusions, the latter becoming in turn premises for other conclusions, and so on. This method can be called geometric as it seems to inadvertently identify logical reasoning with linear progress.

Vico, who was professor of Rhetoric at the University of Naples, transcended the formalist approach to rhetoric and poetics by uncover-

---

9. *Ethica more geometrico demonstrata* (1677). See Guillermo Fraile, *Historia de la filosofía,* III (Del Humanismo a la Ilustración) (Madrid: BAC, 1966), pp. 587–649. On Condorcet, see Keith M. Baker, *Condorcet: From Natural Philosophy to Social Mathematics.* Chicago: Chicago University Press, 1975.

ing the pristine meaning of the Greek and Latin words and the human experience from which those words—and ritual formulas and myths—emanated. According to Vico, the words of the classical languages preserved in their etymologies and in their archaic meanings the testimony of modes of life and thought that preceded the mental level of classical antiquity. Humanity, Vico says, has developed in three eras: savagery, barbarism, and reason. In the savage era men were immersed in the history of the gods and did not arrive at an independent expression of their relationship with them. The barbarian era, or the age of heroes, is characterized by consciousness vis-à-vis the gods, but in the form of a powerful imagination. In that stage all human knowledge is poetry, because observed phenomena are explained by histories that are myths, with gods and heroes as their main characters: the sunny wheat in the summer is the gift of the blond goddess Ceres. From the age of poetry man moved to science, when the same experience of the ripe wheat was no longer explained by the story of the goddess, but by the life cycle of the seeds. The mind here passed from the state of fantasy to the development of reason, from poetry to science. Vico opposed the illusion of a linear progress in history with his idea of the *corsi* and *ricorsi,* that is to say, the thesis that history periodically repeats its sequence. For that reason, Vico does not claim to have discovered the evolution of humanity as a simple fact, but rather the "common nature of nations": the law that governs the formation and evolution of societies.

Vico maintains that knowledge of human societies is possible by means of a well-documented exploration of their history, which is preserved not only in the events, but in the language of those societies. Language reflects constants that are deeper than the events, and the role of the humanist is to penetrate into the meaning of the words, and formulate the laws of the evolution of mankind in history. In my view Vico is the first to delimit the human sciences as a field where rigorous logic does not imply the linear progress of Descartes or the geometric style of Spinoza. Vico pinpoints with full lucidity what we will call humanistic discourse. But he applies this discourse to "the nature of nations"; he aptly highlights the social dimension of the humanities and the humanistic dimension of the modern social sciences.

In Spain, given the cultural situation of the country in the eighteenth century, the European movement of the two cultures appeared fundamentally as a struggle between the overwhelming dominance of scholasticism and a few thinkers open to the winds of modernity that blew from England and France. Gaspar Melchor de Jovellanos—who corresponded regularly with Lord Holland, the prestigious English intellectual—considers the "humanities" a field appropriate for secondary (high) school. Speaking of Fleury's *Historical Catechism* he says: "This catechism will be studied by the children who have passed from the first letters to the study of the humanities, which will form the second level."[10] Philology did not yet exist as a field of research, nor did most professors of cosmology practice research; but Jovellanos shows that he is aware of the different types of discourse when he distinguishes between "intellectual sciences" and "demonstrative sciences" (*op. cit.*, p. 102). He also proposes that French and English be studied in preference to Latin and Greek: "For those who would consecrate themselves to the exact or natural sciences, and even to the political and economic ones, I would give the first place to the study of the living languages, of English and French in particular."[11]

In the nineteenth century, the German universities introduced as fields of teaching and research classical philology, modern languages and literatures, history, philosophy, and theology as a humanistic science in response to the predominant materialism in the natural sciences, and from Germany these new fields of study spread to European

10. *Memoria sobre la educación pública*, p. 138.

11. *Memoria sobre la educación pública*, p. 90. On January 10, 1825, Goethe said to Eckermann: "No one can deny that he who knows German well can dispense with many other languages. Of the French, I do not speak; it is the language of conversation, and is indispensable in traveling. But as for Greek, Latin, Italian, and Spanish, we can read the best works of those nations in such excellent German translations, that, unless we have some particular object in view, we need not spend much time upon the toilsome study of those languages" (*Conversations with Eckermann*, p. 84).

and American universities. Meanwhile, the fields that today constitute the social or the human sciences were also codified: economics, ethnology, anthropology, sociology, and linguistics. The university curriculum proliferated with so many new disciplines that Goethe felt pity for the students of the future: "I am glad that I am not eighteen now. Germany stands so high in every department that we can scarcely survey all it has done; and now we must be Greeks and Latins, and English and French into the bargain. Not content with this, some have the madness of pointing to the East also; and surely this is enough to confuse a young man's head."[12]

The new human sciences, called "moral and political," studied man, but with the methods of the natural sciences. At that moment, between ca. 1830 and 1850, the problem of the humanities emerged as we have inherited it, which is no longer of two but of three cultures: the natural sciences, the social sciences, and the humanities in a strict sense. To dramatize the ambiguity of the term "humanities" and to open up clearer paths toward its definition, we will round out the historical outline with the views of two Spanish classics of our time.

4. Two humanists: Ortega y Gasset and Laín Entralgo

Ortega y Gasset (1833–1955) wrote on the humanities all throughout his life, but after 1946, given the situation of Spain—conservative dictatorship, and physical and intellectual indigence after the Spanish Civil War (1936–39) and World War II (1939–45)—and the philosopher's personal development, the humanities were his favorite topic.[13] Not only

12. Goethe to Eckermann, February 15, 1824; in *Conversations*, p. 55.

13. Wilhelm Dilthey (1833–1911) published in 1833 his classic work on the theory of the humanities: *Einleitung in die Geisteswissenschaften* (Introduction to the "Spiritual" Sciences). In this book Dilthey proposed his distinction between *Verstehen* (understanding), which he associates with the *Geisteswissenschaften* and *Erklären* (explanation), the aim of the natural sciences. For Dilthey, the "sciences of the spirit" are history, the social sciences and a "psychology" of history that serves as the unifying bond for all the others. This holistic psychology would eventually lead to the fundamental ontology of Heidegger. The influence of Dilthey has been profound, either by direct reading, or via Heidegger or Ortega y Gasset.

his theoretical writings, but his intellectual praxis make him a role model for any humanist. In 1948 Ortega and his disciple Julián Marías founded in Madrid the Institute for the Humanities.[14] To announce the inauguration of the Institute Ortega distributed a pamphlet whose first section was titled "The Meaning of the New Humanities." In the same way that teenage antics are the stuff of teenagers, the humanities are for Ortega the specifically human reality in its different aspects (hence the plural), and the disciplines that study that reality. Biological functions are not exclusively human, but biology as a science is. Science is, therefore, a topic for the humanities. In fact the courses announced by Ortega in the above-mentioned pamphlet are: the theory of language, classical philology (from a perspective that resembles Vico's), ethnology, the theory of history, and economics.

The Institute proposed to organize courses, colloquia, and concrete research on general topics, all related to Spanish cultural life. The following titles were announced for the first year (1948–49): "Socrates, and *The Clouds* by Aristophanes," "The Social Structures of Price," "On the Comparison Between Arabism and Classical Philology," and "An Essay on Idioms."[15] However, since economics, ethnology, and linguistics are also considered social sciences, their humanistic aspect in a strict sense is the reflection on the type of knowledge to which those disciplines can aspire and their status in the curriculum at any given moment in history. The humanities would be for Ortega what we call today meta-literature, meta-history, and meta-economics.

Pedro Laín Entralgo (1908–2001) was a brilliant humanist and a strenuous defender of the humanities in all levels of education. A professor of History of Medicine, he opened his discipline to the history of science in general, to the human dimension of illness, and to the philosophical study of man. His view of the humanities is best summarized

---

14. The project lasted only two years. By 1948 Franco's regime was already accepted by Western democracies, and it did not foster free humanistic research. The regime did not suppress Ortega's Institute, but the official journalists ridiculed it, and the majority of Spanish intellectuals at the time were more interested in the official line of thought than in liberal adventures. Ortega y Gasset abandoned the project in bitter disappointment.

15. *Obras completas,* op. cit., IX, 444.

in an article published in the Madrid daily ABC (July 9, 1996) with the title "Humanistic Education." In it, with the concision imposed by a newspaper column, Laín presented his ideas in the following words:

My formula starts with a distinction between two levels of humanism: a humanism "by extension," i.e. basic, and another "by intension," i.e. superior. Humanism by extension consists in knowing how to answer five questions with a minimum of precision: (1) what kind of world do I live in, as citizen of it? Beliefs, ideas, hopes, tensions, conflicts, and fears that are prevalent in it; most particularly in the part of it that we usually call "western." (2) While pursuing my life in the world I encounter things. What are things, from the original big-bang to the current universe, from the most elementary particle to the anthropoid? (3) While making my life in the world I also encounter other men, organized into human groups. What are these human beings? (4) What am I as a human being? What answers do the sciences and philosophy offer to this question? (5) In order for me to be what I am, what had to happen to the human species from its origin until today? After this basic humanism by extension, humanism by intension, or the one in-depth that the university professor should possess, implies the ability to respond to the following question: how does that which I know and teach have roots in man's reality and, therefore, how can it contribute to a precise knowledge of man's nature? In my opinion, this humanism requires intellectual consideration of the following five points: (1) the meaning of the discipline I know and teach. If this concern is serious, it will inevitably lead to the existence of a second or regional philosophy: philosophy of Physics, of Medicine, of Law, of Architecture, etc. (2) Concern with the 'why' of what is known and taught. (3) The history of what is known and taught. (4) The exoteric or popular presentation of that which is known and taught in specialized terminologies. The popular presentation aims at knowing, for instance, how medical, legal and economic knowledge, etc., have been expressed by the fine arts. (5) Concern with the way in which what is known and taught was expressed in the past and is expressed in our own time. Two fields of knowledge will in this regard attract the interest of the university professor, that of words (Philology) and that of literary expression (Literature).

Ortega and Laín Entralgo conceive of the humanities in a broad sense that also includes our social sciences as well as the philosophy and history of all the sciences, that is to say, justification of those sciences as an answer to man's needs or aspirations. The humanities are the metascientific side of science. We are going to work in the horizon opened by these masters, but we have to enlarge it on the one hand and limit it on the other. For example, neither Ortega nor Laín mentions ethics, although that may be because they include it in philosophy. Until the recent push for immigration from all over the world, Western Europe consisted of nations in which diverse peoples had melded through the centuries into very homogeneous societies. Christianity had also acted as a catalyst of unity, in spite of both civil and international wars in the name of orthodoxy. Both the ethnic homogeneity and the common Christian tradition made it possible for someone in Europe to take for granted a common ethics based on Christian theology. But in today's multiracial and multicultural societies we cannot assume common roots for anything. Consequently, today the ideal of an ethics that may claim validity for all men and women regardless of religious or cultural labels is an inevitable field of reflection for the humanist.

Ortega and Laín fail to remember the religious dimension of history. As an expression of love or hate, as an incitement to charity or to fanatical crimes, religion is a fundamental human fact and, consequently, it should be integrated into a theory of the humanities. At the same time, the two Spanish thinkers include in their view of the humanities the social and natural sciences, as human creations for the benefit of man. But such an inclusive idea sidetracks the strictly humanistic disciplines with regard to both their epistemological status and their practical usefulness.

5. Synthesis: Concrete definition

First, the humanities are certain disciplines: philosophy and history, which study man's being; linguistics and literature, which study man from the point of view of his expression, and theology as the inquiry into the ultimate meaning of everything. However, since language is the first discipline studied in elementary school, and language and literature are bonded in our most spontaneous expression, from now on we will refer to the humanistic disciplines in the usual order of the school curricula: language, literature, history, philosophy, and theology.

Second, the disciplines mentioned proceed with a type of discourse that distinguishes them from what is today called the social sciences.

Third, the natural sciences and technology are humanities in the following aspects: (A) Creativity. A scientist needs as much imagination as a poet. The difference lies in their distinct goals, and therefore in the type of discourse that constitutes poetry in contrast to science. (B) Aesthetics. Artistic creation and aesthetic enjoyment are usually associated with the humanities. But the beauty of certain complex molecules and the discovery of the greatness of the macro- or micro-cosmos produce the same effects of enjoyment and wonder that can be produced by the beautiful and the sublime in art. (C) Ethics. It is sometimes said that humanists study or cultivate values, while scientists study facts without reference to values. But no one is subject to greater demands of truthfulness (a supreme ethical value) than the scientist. The falsification of laboratory data is punished with the scientist's discredit for life. Besides demanding maximum honesty in all their procedures, ecological decisions have an immense impact on human life. (D) The theory of knowledge of each of the sciences is not science but humanities. (E) The history of science as the deployment of the intellectual drama involved in the discovery of new problems and answers, the study of the dominant paradigms in different periods, and of the intellectual or political influences that explain that dominance, are also humanistic aspects of science.

Most importantly, as Hume said, science is both from and for man. To what extent does man live from science? To what extent has science shaped modern European life since approximately 1600? In order to emphasize the negative aspects of science, the nuclear threat is usually brought to the fore. But, while we should never underestimate this risk, there are also possible constructive uses of nuclear energy, and of course, science and technology cannot be reduced to nuclear physics. Science has also produced the revolution in communications that facilitates exchanges between humans. If we talk on the phone with loved ones in a distant country; if the fax and e-mail reproduce a letter in an instant over thousands of miles, science is an important phenomenon in any inquiry about the humanities. In other respects, the lengthening of life expectancy and the improvement of the quality of life in affluent societies are due to progress in agriculture, nutrition, hygiene, and medicine—and development in less privileged societies can only come from the fair distribution of those advances.

It would be myopic to overlook the human and humanistic dimension of medicine, present before birth when the doctor watches over the mother's psychosomatic condition, and man's companion in the time of illness, perhaps the most critical situation of one's life. For Laín Entralgo illness is first and foremost a human experience. As anatomical, physiological or psychosomatic dysfunction, it is a problem of science. But illness is also pain, acceptance of one's own weakness, of our neighbor's need for help, and the cause of economic anxiety. Both in the scientific and in the existential sense, illness is a subject of the humanities. The aspects of the sciences that have been highlighted as humanistic are those in which the inherent link of scientific research with the whole of human reality is clear. This link is the interdisciplinary moment of all the disciplines, regardless of their specific subject, discourse, and goal.

However, though the natural sciences and technology exhibit a humanistic dimension, they are not humanities in a strict sense, because scientific discourse differs from humanistic discourse, and because the direct object of research for the scientist is not the human being as human.

The social sciences are psychology, anthropology, sociology, economics, ethnology, political science, and law with their ramifications. If we look at the catalogue of courses of a contemporary university, this is a poor listing. Human ecology, Women's Studies, and what around 1970 began to be called "Black Studies" are not mere sections of sociology but authentic new sciences that combine chapters of traditional biology, history, anthropology, sociology, and law, literature, music, etc. It is not worthwhile to waste time in determining the number of branches on the tree of knowledge, always fertile in new buds; the important thing is to decide in what way the humanities differ from these "sciences of man" (the current name of the social sciences in French books).

The difference between the humanities and the social sciences does not lie in the initial subject of study (man's being and behavior in its individual and social aspects) but in the type of discourse, or approach to that subject. We shall try to make this point clear with two examples in which the same reality is looked at within the social-scientific and the humanistic discourse respectively: scientific psychology versus the humanistic view of the human being, and the humanistic approach to society versus scientific sociology.

Human psychology is the empirical study of consciousness, and of the development and operation of the different faculties in relation to their biological background and social environment.[16] With regard to knowledge, psychology studies the relationship between the development and condition of the brain, the processes of perception, and the mysterious conversion of perceived data into a notion that may then become a concept or idea. When the psychologist faces the fact of knowledge, he classifies different types, builds concept maps which try to insert specific, detailed concepts into more universal ones, and constructs models, which may be clear but are always vulnerable to an excess of rigidity and therefore to over-simplification. What these models lack is that which the humanist contributes: analysis of the human ego as an individual who, in situations of relation, dialogue, dependence, dominance, friendship, distance or fear, develops with others, with the world as his circumstance (context), and is open to ideals. Psychological experiments on learning emphasize meaningful learning over memorization, and propose the construction of conceptual maps, which help learning by organizing knowledge according to reflective criteria. But the maps, admirable classifications and stimuli for better learning, presuppose a definition of knowledge, which after all is a form of memory. A human-

16. Psychology is so complex that professor Sigmund Koch proposed to replace its name with "Psychological Studies" (*Psychology in Human Context*, pp. 115–143). This warns us against simplistic generalizations, but after studying books of different trends, and perusing the last fifteen years of the *American Journal of Psychology* I think the summary given is based on competent information. Besides, my intention is to illustrate the humanistic type of discourse; if the term of comparison—psychology—were not competently described, it is of secondary importance.

istic approach to the idea of learning, as I see it (we must always reckon with the limits of our perspective), would explore the following avenues: (a) the conditions of learning: social means, family, school, curriculum, relationship in the classroom; (b) the learner: age, the interplay of ability and enthusiasm for learning; (c) learning from the point of view of the subject learned: from a poem learned by heart to the disciplines of medicine; (d) the process of learning as the transition from ignorance to knowledge; (e) the nature of knowledge: punctual and habitual knowledge or competency; general culture as preparation for listening, etc. The humanistic approach will profit from the scientific experiments, but will incorporate them into rigorous analysis of the different aspects of learning, thereby highlighting the value of those experiments.

With regard to man's basic attitudes in life, such as happiness or bitterness, it is also easy to see the difference between the scientific method and the humanistic background. By studying the lives of identical twins and checking the similarity of their reactions in different situations, psychologists may look for "genes of happiness." The method in these studies is statistical. If a considerable majority of twins raised in different environments have similar reactions toward certain stimuli, while other siblings show greater diversity, then it is demonstrated that the genetic condition has greater influence than the environment with regard to those stimuli. The humanist is also familiar with the results of these studies, but he will first try to disentangle the meaning and meanings of the word around which the experiment revolves: "happiness." For this definition one needs to look at man as an ego whose most intimate self-consciousness consists in being open to the world, and look at him in his creative contributions and in his attitude of loyalty or deceit. Man as projection or hope, or as paranoid illusion; the religious dimension, evil, resentment, crime, that is to say, the well-tempered and balanced life versus the unbalanced and frustrated one. In fact, in a book of psychiatry for nurses (scientific psychology), I find as an introduction a box with the title: "Philosophical beliefs of psychiatric nursing practice." The box contains thirteen propositions; first: "The individual has intrinsic worth and dignity. Each person is worthy of respect solely because of each person's nature and presence." Second: "The goal of the individual is one of growth, health, autonomy and self-actualization," etc.[17] Scientific psychiatry tries to locate the physiological or psychosomatic cause of illness; the humanities try to define the individual in the ideal, reasonable, generous and open family and society. The humanities are preventive psychiatry.

The second example is taken from sociology. Ortega y Gasset's *The Revolt of the Masses* was published in 1930. One cannot deny that it is a classic book on the society of its epoch, and of ours. In fact, aspects of mass society have developed with the passage of time, which in 1930 were only symptoms. But is Ortega's book sociology in a scientific sense? What would a sociologist have done when faced with the notion of the masses and the impression of their rebellion? To begin with, a scientist would have begun with a look at existing bibliography. Based on that information he probably would have tried to define the concept of mass in contrast to "people" and "crowd," the terms used by Gabriel de Tarde and Gustave Le Bon in the 1890s. Since the concept of mass hints at big groups and carries a negative connotation, the scientist would have contrasted his definition of mass with the common use of the word and its spontaneous association with "the working masses," or blue collar workers. The masses became conspicuous in the 1920s with newspaper pictures of Communist, Fascist, and Nazi crowds. In this case it was necessary to reflect on how a crowd (a concept that in itself is not negative) becomes almost automatically a mass with its pejorative connotations. Then the scientific sociologist would have defined the idea of rebellion and would have pointed out events in which that attitude was conspicuous.

In contrast to the scientific approach, Ortega in *The Revolt of the Masses*[18] observes from his *personal* perspective "the fact of overcrowd-

17. G. Stuart and S. Sundeen, *Principles and Practice of Psychiatric Nursing.* 5th ed. (St. Louis: Mosby Year Book, 1995), p. 9.

18. The book was considered so important that a reviewer of the English translation (New York, 1932) wrote in *Atlantic Monthly:* "What Rousseau's *Contrat Social* was for the

ing" in the decade of the twenties and contrasts it with the situation prevailing at the beginning of the twentieth century. Then, based on his philosophy of life, he offers his *personal* interpretation of the quantitative phenomenon that he has observed. In one century the standard of living had risen in Europe, not just economically but in the sense of creative energy or "vitality." A sociologist would have supported those statements with statistics and would probably have compared graphs for different periods of the century and for different countries. Ortega simply quotes the data on population growth. Then in chapter IV of his work, he jumps abruptly from the quantitative consideration of the crowd to judging the mass-man and mass-society in a qualitative sense. The mass-man is characterized by his enjoyment, as heir, of the commodities attained in the nineteenth century by scientific research and liberal democracy. But, as is normal with heirs, the mass-man cannot repeat the effort that led to those accomplishments and is, therefore, incapable of gratitude toward the achievers. The book ends with a verdict on the spiritual condition of Europe: "Europe is now without morals." This general statement may be accurate, but it is a *personal* impression, which in order to be scientific would require definition of its terms and quantification of its range.

The Revolt of the Masses is a perfect example of humanistic discourse. Looking at what Ortega y Gasset does, and remembering what has been said on scientific psychology as opposed to the holistic view (ontology) of man, I believe that the features of humanistic discourse can be summarized as follows: on the part of the mind, a holistic approach; with regard to the subject of study, an effort to encompass it as a whole; and in this attitude, knowledge and respect for the subject in its entirety imply an ethical dimension.

Holistic approach. The reality of a thing is revealed to us only when we do not separate it into its components. If it is necessary to look at

---

eighteenth century, and Karl Marx's *Das Kapital* for the nineteenth, Senor [sic] Ortega's *Revolt of the Masses* should be for the twentieth century." "The reader will find no more stimulating fare in a dozen publishing seasons" (J. D. Adams, *N.Y. Times Book Review*). These assessments appeared on the dust jacket of subsequent editions.

the components separately, at the end one must return to the whole. This holistic approach is intuition. In contrast to the models, classifications, maps, and statistics of the sciences, the humanistic method is intuitive. Intuition does not mean a hunch or a guess; it may entail many years of scientific study; but in the final instance, scientific research is preparatory work whose aim is a *personal* vision of the whole (for that reason I have repeated and highlighted the term *personal* when speaking of Ortega). The personal vision is not subjective, and much less subjectivist. In these considerations, for example, I am saying what I see on the topic of the humanities, but I say what I feel forced to say by the reality that imposes itself on me. Thus my personal ideas are presented as *ideas,* not as *personal.* And what I am saying does not intend to impose my ideas on the reader but invites him to look for himself and see if he can agree with my vision. In this case, even if he completely agrees with me, it will be his own vision. Intuition can reflect reality in the most objective way, but it does not demonstrate. Instead, it presents and invites the reader to think about or to discover the facts pointed to by the author. There might be many documents with facts about the life of Vicente Aleixandre, his manuscripts, and the publication of his works. But as soon as we begin to read his poems there are no more proofs; reading is a set of proposals and invitations. Intuition may be rigorous knowledge, but it proves only to the extent that it invites us to create.

The subject as a whole. Scientific discourse delimits different aspects of a field and is satisfied with partial results, according to the area of research laid out in advance. Humanistic discourse will try to see the articulation of the same field, but will aspire to the global vantage point. It seeks to unfold reality in all its tentacles, and in that sense it is pre-disciplinary, inter-disciplinary, and post-disciplinary. Pre-disciplinary, because the global visions of the moralists and of Montaigne's *Essays* preceded what was later dissected into the different sciences of man. Inter-disciplinary, because humanistic discourse, at least by reference or by allusion, will pursue all possible ramifications of the topics addressed; and post-disciplinary, because after the scientific discourse we need to locate its conclusions in the human whole in which they acquire their full meaning.

Ethical dimension. This insertion into the human whole suggests the third aspect of humanistic discourse: in a more or less conscious way the discussion of the humanities ends always in the sphere of ethics. Scientific research seeks to discover laws of fact; but it cannot forget the link between those laws and human life. Hence, in great measure, the interdisciplinary dimension of the humanities is the ethical dimension or is intimately related to it.

Man in his being, expression, and meaning is the subject of the humanities. Global vision, the global being or global reality of things, and the fusion of the intellectual dimension with the ethical, or with the level of values, constitute the features of their discourse. The humanistic aspects pointed out in the social and natural sciences show the same characteristics: physics becomes humanities when questioning its type of knowledge, its role in society, and when it recaptures man's trials and errors in its history. The humanistic aspects of science are the return from their linear methods to the nucleus from which they arise.

The humanistic disciplines also have aspects that are not humanities in a strict sense. These include: simple erudition, formalist analyses of a poem or attention to fragments and not to the complete text. But, if our classifications are valid as a means to achieve clarity, these classifications are no more than means, roads that pull us back to the complex reality. For that reason, it is necessary to avoid all rigid and mechanistic distinctions. If the humanistic nucleus with regard to a text lies in understanding it well, everything that helps us toward that end is humanities—the more or less would be defined by the relationship of a particular occupation with a text to the final goal, which is the understanding of that text. The important thing in the humanistic disciplines is that, in them, the discourse (global outlook) is fused with its object: man as man, in his expression (language and literature), being (philosophy and history), and meaning (theology).

II The Humanistic Disciplines

> ❧ *Whoever engages in a research without having first stated his problems is like a person who does not know where he is going.*

> (Aristotle, *Metaphysics*, bk. III, 1)

6. Language, culture, linguistics

We shall now describe the humanistic disciplines, beginning with language. "If language is the essential thing that makes us human beings, linguistics ought to be considered, to an eminent degree, as a science of man, and, therefore, as a humanistic discipline, perhaps the most genuine of them all."[1] These words by the Swedish linguist Bertil Malmberg present a thesis, but his defensive tone ("ought to be considered") indicates that the idea is not universally shared. Linguistics is indeed a humanistic discipline, but not all branches of linguistics use the humanistic discourse. On the basis of the distinction between the nucleus and the lines of discourse advanced in section 5, one may affirm that language constitutes man's essence in his reflective and potentially conscious dimension; therefore, the study of language in this primordial dimension belongs to the humanities. By contrast, the study of the formal structure of any specific language is part of the humanities only in a derivative way.

In spite of his conditional formulation, Malmberg takes for granted the definition of man as the speaking animal. The essence of something is what makes it what it is. If language is what makes us human, it conditions us from the moment of conception until death, in our state of

---

1. Bertil Malmberg, *La lengua y el hombre*, p. 25 (my translation).

wakefulness, of sleep, and of coma. This language-essence has to be something common to all mankind and is, therefore, a mental articulation that precedes any of the numerous tongues we speak, which are the "languages" in the common perception, i.e., modes of expression proper to different human groups.[2] But is the traditional definition of man acceptable? What is that language-essence which precedes any specific language? To answer these questions, I propose what I see as the main chapters of a systematic exploration of language from a humanistic perspective: expression, speaking, saying, grammar, linguistics, and metalinguistics or philosophy of language.

Expression: Two human beings who have not a single word of any language in common, meet; the mutual discovery as human individuals already implies a dialogue based on shared codes: mutual recognition, joy or fear, friendly or hostile gestures, etc. Our expressions, smiles, cries, and frowns are already language. The recognition of the other as a person who shares with us the same essence, is a system of natural signs on which the systems of arbitrary signs that constitute the different languages are founded.

Speaking: To speak is to express ourselves by saying something to a listener, who may be ourselves. Even if this book had nothing to say, I would still be conveying my enthusiasm for the humanities, and my intention to clarify all the questions that I consider worthy of attention. Thus even if I do not express things, I express myself. Before revealing reality, speech exhibits an emotional dimension that reveals the person who is speaking. One aspect of the emotional dimension is intentionality: he who speaks wants to say something, even though he may fail to convey what he wishes. That is why a text never quite manages to convey the author's intention completely. From the point of view of the

2. Sapir describes this distinction with the following words: "Literature moves in language as a medium, but that medium comprises two layers, the latent content of language—our intuitive record of experience—and the particular conformation of a given language—the specific how of our record of experience" (*Language*, p. 233). Medieval philosophers designated Sapir's latent content with the term *species impressa*, which can be translated as the primordial articulation that precedes the actual articulation in a particular language. The latter was called *species expressa*.

speaker, language manifests itself primarily as expression and intention.

Saying. It is possible to speak for hours and say nothing. Saying implies a listener and something that is said. This sentence contains four elements: the speaker, what is said, the person(s) to whom it is said, and the saying itself. To say something is the attempt to make a reality manifest, to convey a truth. In saying, though the speaker cannot avoid expressing himself to some extent, he tries to disappear as much as possible, so the subject being discussed—reality—reveals itself. The speaker submits to and depends on the subject. Unamuno understood well the difference between speaking and saying. In *Saint Immanuel the Good, Martyr* (1930) the narrator says: "What things he used to say to us! For they were things, not words." In saying things, it is reality that pierces through the words. When something is said in clear terms, the listener, instead of depending on the speaker, sees reality. On the contrary, when a statement is unclear, the listener hangs on the speaker and his words; to say things clearly is to liberate the listener (receptor) in such a way that he and the speaker (emissor) can find themselves on common ground: the reality seen by both.

Language as the essence of man. If we meet a human being with whom we do not have a single word in common, we still share a world of meaning in our mutual recognition, in expression, reactions, and even some cognition through gestures—not forgetting that expression and reactions are also varieties of cognition. But if we can imagine Adam complaining of loneliness before Eve was created, language as his essence was for him the meeting point of his search for meaning and the objective matrix of meaning which elicited his speech. Language as man's essence is the articulation of reality that originates with man himself. The objective structure of sense and man's immersion in it are inseparable, yet man is a receiver not a creator of the structure. And since the human being is inherently social, this linguistic condition applies to all individuals regardless of their level of development. The unborn fetus about which we talk and the deceased beloved whose memory we honor are the two extremes of human communication. Language as expression, as speaking, and as saying (at least of some things), is a universal structure that precedes any particular tongue.

This language-essence that precedes the specific languages becomes manifest in irony. If we say to a young girl, "Hello, granny," the listener knows that the perceived reality precludes a literal understanding of the words. The language-reality speaks by itself, to the point that it modifies or denies the meaning of the words uttered. Similar examples can be given in the case of connotations, implications, humor, figurative or double meanings, slang, euphemisms and every type of communication in which one needs to pre-understand one thing in order to understand the concrete questions at hand.

From that matrix of meaning which constitutes our essence as the linguistic animal, we look around, motivated by our intentions (interests and needs), and discover things that are either helpful or dangerous tools, or merely something to contemplate. To distinguish things is to participate and work with them in actions expressed by verbs, and to objectify them as different from ourselves by giving them a name. The awareness of the ego as opposed to the things in front of it brings about the dichotomy between subject and object, and verbs and nouns give birth to concrete languages, systems of arbitrary signs with which a certain community recognizes the same realities. These systems are the languages, as we commonly understand them.

The relationship between different languages and the language-essence is similar to that of the surface versus the core, or the particular versus the universal. Any concrete language, taken in the comprehensive sense just outlined, musters four functions or possibilities of signification: (1) the emotional function or self-expression; (2) intellectual function or pointing to realities; (3) sensorial function, or the manifestation of pictorial and musical aspects, which are specific to each language; and (4) the structural function or the repetition of patterns of sound or signs, which allows for associations, also specific to each language. A book invites one to see reality (the intellectual function), but if the book is wrong, it merely reflects the enthusiasm of the author (emotional function), it has a style that may be brilliant or dull (sensorial radiance), and an order that converts it into a systematic artifact or into a hodgepodge (structure).

Grammar is the study of the consistent patterns of a specific language. It describes recurring patterns, and converts them into rules.

Linguistics is more general than grammar. The study of the similarities and differences of the various tongues, the history of the differentiation of languages that derive from a single one, the universal components of all languages, and the definition of all pertinent terms, constitute the subject of linguistics. This science began in the nineteenth century as a study of the common traits of the Indo-European languages. The exploration of cultures all over the world raised new comparative questions. In line with intellectual currents of the time, language came to be associated with the "soul" of specific races or countries, and so linguistics became contaminated with sociology and nationalism.

Faced with this situation, Ferdinand de Saussure (1857–1913), professor in Geneva, Switzerland, created the science of linguistics by distinguishing between *langue* (language) and *parole* (speech). Speech includes all the elements of personal and collective life—from tone and melody to idioms and coded meanings—that affect communication. The subject of linguistics as science is not speech but language, the abstract system of elements that constitutes a particular tongue regardless of how those elements come out in speech. While speech and its varieties lend themselves to description, originating branches such as dialectology, psycholoinguistics and sociolinguistics, the science of linguistics analyzes the underlying structure of each language, and the "latent content" (Sapir) underlying all different tongues. A key concept in Saussure is "sign." He focused on individual words as signs, but he himself saw that communication is not conveyed in isolated words but in sentences, or rather in combinations of sentences: in texts. By analyzing a text, one can discern its various components *a posteriori*: propositions, words, syllables, and phonemes. This order implies that linguistics, if it starts with the study of phonemes, should ultimately lead to the text, which constitutes language in its reality, or communication as the conveyance of sense. Consequently, linguistics, still based on Saussure, has surpassed him by becoming text-linguistics.

Our reflections, while centered on linguistics, also go beyond it: they investigate the relationship between *language* and *speech,* between the act of speaking and the framework of meaning on which all speaking is based. This level of reflection, already philosophical, is metalinguistics. In my opinion, the most original and valuable analysis of language on this level of the humanities is found in Heidegger. His lecture on "Language" (1950) can be summarized in the following theses:

1. Language is the dwelling place of man. In its essence, language is neither an abstract construct nor an instrument of expression in the service of any subject, but rather the structure of meaning in which man finds himself and from which he establishes distances between things, applies concrete names to them, and acts with them.

2. Language speaks. And not man? Language speaks insofar as the speaker intends to reflect as faithfully as possible the articulation of reality. For this reason, to speak is to listen, and the decision to say what must be said, what is pertinent or appropriate. Hence, the next sentence:

3. Language calls. Language brings us closer to things, allows us to go to them and understand them in their proper place. Reality calls us, and to speak properly is to respond to this call.

4. Language speaks by articulating the crossroads in which the specific object and its underlying universal background both converge and diverge. The various languages and dialects are a legacy that we accept, while in actual speech we produce minor but constant changes in them. Speaking is the encounter of structure and the concretion given to the structure by the speaker. But prior to this encounter in every concrete language lies the structure of language as human essence, the articulation of the difference between the world (universal and taken for granted—*a priori*) and things (designated specific objects). In this point Heidegger is only rereading the old and persistent controversy about "the

universals," but recognizing in the difference the objective structure of reality, not something created by the mind. All concrete things manifest themselves to us in a wider background, and the last, all-encompassing, background is "the world," the very structure of meaning. Language is that articulation which lets every discrete thing be what it is, insofar as it appears integrated with all the other things in the world. Hence:

5. Language is "the peal of stillness" *(Das Geläut der Stille),* in other words, the articulation of reality in its being. The German term *Stille* means both repose and silence. Letting reality be in its objective articulation is letting it repose in itself, and since it is articulated in a meaningful way, that articulation breaks the silence, which would be the state of reality if we could imagine it without an intelligence that discovers its structure. The articulation does not exist without man, but man does not create it, as the different types of subjectivism would have it, man finds it as the objective structure of the real, and dwells in it.

The analyzed features become concrete in the language of each society, or in one's native tongue. The native language takes root in us with our cultivation of it (and with the devotion to it by the emigrant who cherishes his mother-tongue as the most profound symbol of his identity) and in this way it becomes the mirror of our own existence. Everything we tell ourselves at each moment and all that we are capable of remembering of the past constitutes our personality. The native tongue provides the objects and associations that originate in the sounds of the language itself (general connotations) or in personal attachments and phobias.

Although we call the language of our childhood our native tongue, and are molded within it in every sense of the word, we develop within it, grow within it, and we master it as much it masters us. But we are not born with it; the proof is that one can grow up bilingual or even replace a childhood language with one learned later in life. In the United States one can find many Hispanic or Italian couples who chose to burn their bridges and speak only English at home to completely assimilate into North American culture. The language of immigrants, the *Spang-*

lish—which can serve as emblem for any fusion of languages—shows that what shapes our reflective identity is not the abstract system of signs (English or Spanish), but rather the speech we create for ourselves in our personal development.

Learning a language is the process of associating meanings with certain noises (in speaking) or traits (in writing) that previously made no sense to us. Knowing a foreign language implies the quick association of meaning to words (signifiers), and knowing it well means associating the same connotations and the pictorial and musical sensations that these words arouse in native speakers. The English word "wood," for example, is translated into four different words in Spanish, depending on the context: *madera* (lumber), or *leña* (firewood). The plural "woods" would require *maderas,* or *bosque* (forest). And the English sentence "we're not out of the woods yet" would require a completely different idiom in Spanish.[3]

Experience with foreign languages makes it clear that a language is not a series of grammatical formulas, but rather the expression of the culture of a society. The words used in Spanish-speaking America that are unknown in Spain indicate that, although in general terms we speak the same language, there are cultural differences within the community of speakers of Spanish. Sometimes these differences are visible not in the words themselves, but in the meanings that a certain community associates with those words; an Argentine immediately associates the verb *"coger"* with coitus. In Spain, it has retained that meaning in animal breeding, but it is not the reference that comes immediately to mind upon hearing the word. Language becomes a native tongue in each concrete cultural system and in personal speech.

Unamuno, in his zeal to emphasize the identity of Spaniards and

3. Here we encounter Ortega y Gasset's difficulties in translating the English phrase "challenge and response": "The double category which he (Toynbee) entitles 'challenge' and 'responses.' In reality, the first of those two words is not good, because it is one of those words than one finds in every tongue in such an intimate way that it cannot be translated into another language. It is the word *challenge* which means at once 'obstacle,' 'threat,' 'provocation,' 'peril,' etc." (*An Interpretation of Universal History,* p. 222).

Latin Americans, said that language is the blood of the race. But the diverse historical paths taken by the Hispano-American nations have produced different cultures. Spaniards, Mexicans, and Paraguayans share to a large extent the same language as an abstract system of signs (Saussure's *langue*), but not as historical reality *(parole)*.

The coincidence and the distinction cannot be understood in rigid terms, but rather as a difference. The structure of Spanish unites in a way all speakers of the language, because it conditions their thinking along a specific pattern of associations that do not exist in other languages. In this way, the objective structure imposes a certain similarity of style between a Spanish and a Latin American writer and sets them apart from those who write in other languages. The power of the structure of a language in shaping the thinking of its speakers has led some authors to affirm that a language is a specific mode of thought. To a certain extent the claim is correct: some thoughts are possible in a given language because they are suggested by the sound of its words. When King Claudius calls his nephew Hamlet "my son," the prince replies with the phrase "A little more than kin and less than kind," that is, something more than a relative (because he called him *son*), and "less than kind." This expression has a double meaning; the more obvious one is "less than amiable"; but *kind* also means "species." Guided by the expressions of contempt with which Hamlet refers to his uncle throughout the drama, we can read the phrase as meaning: "somewhat more than a relative, yet not even of the same species." This play of words, based on the alliteration *kin-kind,* is impossible in Spanish, and so a Spanish writer could never have made the ingenious association made by Shakespeare. Spanish, on the other hand, expresses the fusion of constancy and change of the human being with the sentence "soy *el* mismo, pero no *lo* mismo" ("I am the same one but not in the same way"), which in English needs a paraphrase. In terms of an objective structure, therefore, language molds our expression and creates a special community among those who speak it. Nevertheless, the fact that we can translate the associations of one language into another proves that, beneath the differences of the languages, we are united in the common framework, the language-essence that makes understanding possible.[4] This language-essence allows for the changes that each individual makes in the structure of his language. For this reason the reality of a language is not its formal structure but the structure in the culture that it expresses and shapes.

In summary, language is central to the humanities: as the essence of man, who finds himself inserted in a world of meaning; as practical knowledge of languages; as grammar, linguistics, philosophy of language and, to the extent that all of this work is done in the concrete language of one society, as culture.

7. *Literature and literatures*

Literature is a phenomenon of verbal communication in which the word becomes substantive through its symbolic character. This definition is very abstract because it intends to capture a core that has unfolded in a myriad of variants. I am following Aristotle's idea, according to which a definition consists of two elements: genre, and specific difference. "A phenomenon of verbal communication" is the genre. In line with what has been said about language as call, communication should not be understood as the articulation of preexisting knowledge, but as a shared inquiry. Communication, as we shall see below, does not mechanically follow the acquisition of knowledge; both the acquisition and communication may take place simultaneously.

In daily conversation words are used as instruments to describe things, and to express to others personal affection, orders, or petitions. In all these cases, the word is basically a vehicle destined to vanish once it conveys the message. In the literary text, on the other hand, the means of expression becomes the message, or the vehicle becomes the

---

4. Sapir, after mentioning the two layers of language quoted in n. 2, affirms: "Literature that draws its sustenance mainly—never entirely—from the lower level, say a play of Shakespeare's, is translatable without too great a loss of character. If it moves in the upper rather than in the lower level—a fair example is a lyric of Swinburne's—it is as good as untranslatable" (*Language*, p. 223).

substance. The reason is that in the literary work, there is no content behind the form that constitutes the text itself. The experience of his father's death (content, message) inspired Jorge Manrique's *Coplas* (1479):

> Recuerde el alma dormida,
> avive el seso y despierte,
> contemplando
> cómo se pasa la vida,
> cómo se viene la muerte,
> tan callando.
>
> O, let the soul her slumbers break!
> Let thought be quickened and awake-
> Awake to see
> How soon this life is past and gone,
> And death comes softly stealing on-
> How silently![5]

Manrique wrote a masterpiece of poetry, but the same experience of death can lead to mediocre or even ridiculous verse. Love, religion, silence, and death are not in themselves great themes to put into rhyme; rather, the "greatness" or importance of these themes has been revealed in the great poems. Content and form are not separable; the literary work is a nucleus of meaning that resides in and results from a successful form.

We have mentioned the four functions of language: emotional, intellectual, sensorial, and structural. In the emotional function, the author exposes his intention and himself as a subject, his affirmative or negative attitude toward existence, and reflects his degree of affection or coldness toward the world around him. The intellectual aspect transmits ideas, information, orders, or petitions. The sensorial function manifests itself in rhyme and rhythm; this function is obvious in verse,

---

5. Trans. by Henry W. Longfellow. In E. Turnbull, *Ten Centuries of Spanish Poetry* (Baltimore: The Johns Hopkins University Press, 1955), p. 49.

but is also visible in a vibrant or dull prose. The structural function is reflected in the associations and dissociations that the sounds and meanings allow.

A literary text is the reverberation of language in its four functions, that is, in the plenitude of its signifying potential. This plenitude of meaning constitutes the symbolic character of language, from Greek *sym-boleuein,* co-incidence or convergence of the functions I have distinguished. In the purely intellectual aspect, the same idea can be expressed in different ways; in the full four-dimensional language, on the other hand, the change of just one word disrupts the sensorial and structural functions. From this point of view, the literary text is immutable.

It is commonly said that literature expresses beauty. But the concept of beauty has many facets; the literary text is not always pretty (there is also bad literature), and a literary work can be magnificent for its truth, grace, creativity, and other qualities that are not necessarily beauty. Our definition describes literature in purely formal terms without offering any criterion about the "value" of the text.

The remarks on the symbolic use of language that makes the literary text immutable seem more appropriate for poetry than for literature in general, but the definition is valid, in an analogous way, for the theater and the novel. In these two genres, dialogue and the interaction of the characters incorporate the emotional function; the distribution of the different motives and themes in the text constitute the structural function, and the style of the author and of the characters according to their gender, class, or level of education, represents the sensorial function.

Literature is a humanistic discipline: first and foremost as an act of creation, which embodies in language an effort to unravel truth. Second, the study of literature is humanistic as literary theory, which should deal with four topics: (a) What is literature, and how it arises; (b) How is the literary text produced, or what is writing; (c) What is reading; (d) Literature and culture in society. There are as many literatures as there are societies that recognize themselves in them. At the same time, as we previously noted when speaking of languages, beneath the concrete texts there is literature as a universal form of communication; therein lies the similarity of motives that are found in different literatures, and the justification for comparative literature.

Literature exists in both written and unwritten texts. All existing or future titles make up the first group: Cervantes' *La Gitanilla* or García Márquez's *One Hundred Years of Solitude*. But perhaps the first thing that occurs to us in speaking about these texts is that they are novels. This means: in literature, we occupy ourselves with general concepts that are not texts; in this case with literary genres. There are novels, plays, and poems; these universal concepts must be defined if we want to understand the texts. Each concrete text is just the tip of an iceberg, whose hidden mass draws us to deeper and more universal layers:

Specific Text,	which is part of the
Complete works of the author,	who is grouped with others in a
Generation (of '98, of '36)	or, in older literary history, in a
School (Salamanca, Seville),	or associated with others in a
Style (Baroque, neoclassical)	and may represent a
Cultural tendency,	i.e., Modern, postmodern.

The categories mentioned: generation, school, style, etc.—which are not the only possible ones—allow us to organize the history of literature. Every layer of the outline can be applied to a different national literature and to supranational entities such as "The European novel," "Neoclassical drama," etc. As we probe the hidden strata of the iceberg, we find points that intersect with other art forms and even with the entire culture of an age. For example, the categories of Baroque, Classicism, Romanticism, etc. can be applied to various art forms and even to the worldview of a historical epoch.

8. History

Few words are more ambiguous than "history." The basic questions concerning the humanistic features of this discipline are: (a) the subject of history; (b) historical knowledge; (c) ideology and evaluation; (d) history as human essence; and (e) historiology, or global reflection on the questions raised by history.

A. The *subject* of history ranges from the most private incident to "world history." A divorce, in most cases, does not have major social repercussions. But the divorce of Henry VIII from Catherine of Aragón is still affecting life—with death—in Northern Ireland and indirectly in the whole world. Local history, national history, universal history: in view of the tension between nationalistic demands by Basque terrorists, Basque democratic nationalists, and Catalans on the one hand, and European unification on the other, what is the meaning of a "national" history of Spain today?

Once we identify the subject of study, what do we look for in that subject: war and peace, conquests and diplomacy? Following the French school of *Annales,* historians since ca. 1930 have increasingly paid attention to the population of the country in different censuses, the distribution of the work force by sector, the price of goods and the standard of living of the members of society. History, in this case, is the description of social life in its different classes and the relationship between them.

In addition to political history there is also the history of the various human activities: philosophy, science and technology, etc. It is said that scientists rarely have to consult a periodical in their field that is more than ten or fifteen years old. When a paradigm loses its scientific relevance, it passes into the realm of the humanities because it remains solely as a testimony to man's effort and search. As we said before, strictly speaking, science and technology are not humanities, but their history is.

The abstract criterion for deciding about a subject of possible research in history is what German philosophers called "the historical threshold," that is, what deserves to be recorded because it has social impact. But the criterion is only abstract, since nobody can dictate to another what he considers relevant. On the point of relevance the extremes range from the exemplaristic history written by some Renais-

sance humanists, which concealed the weaknesses of its subjects as unworthy of study, to the resentful history of those who interpret every
heroic sacrifice as a strategy to acquire power and wealth. The decision
on what is or is not relevant must be left to the good sense of every historian. But the question of what is worth knowing and recording in history brings us to the second section: historical knowledge.

B. *Knowledge.* Here, the gamut extends from publishing an exhaustive
collection of documents to the construction of a grandiose synthesis.
Theodor Mommsen (1817–1903), for example, was a giant in both areas.
One basic problem of historical knowledge is the relationship between
the documents and "things as they actually happened" (Ranke). The actions of the past are narrated in chronicles; those of the present are
recorded in reports, magazines, newspapers, radio and television. Assuming that the informers were committed to nothing but the truth,
how much do they cover? Events take place in large amounts and in succession: are there patterns or constants in history? In his magnificent
book *The Science of Culture,* Eugenio D'Ors discovers behind the variety
of forms the alternation of two trends that he calls "eons": Classicism
and Baroque. Do these constructs or any historical generalization have
any meaning, since, as we know, they entail a lot of simplification?

Another fundamental problem in the construction of history is its
classification in different periods, and the criteria for such classification.
If in literature a text is the tip of an iceberg, in history the events are also
founded on universal categories that act as a sort of background without which the events supposedly cannot be properly understood. Karl
Jaspers posited the axis-time of human history between 600 and 400 B.C.
Spengler's "cultures" and Toynbee's "civilizations" were efforts in the
same direction, and according to Ortega y Gasset, the "generation" is
the basic concept in history and therefore in its study. History has been
classified in segments that range from fifteen years—the period of predominance of a generation, according to Ortega y Gasset—to the two
and a half millennia of Jaspers' axis-time.

Ortega also discovers some constants that condition and are in turn conditioned by the multitude of events that historical erudition can document. To begin with, the protagonist of history is the generation, not the individual or the facts. A generation, which embraces all individuals of a certain age in a given society, is characterized by certain goals and possibilities that are embraced by the majority of its individuals, and is articulated into a minority of leaders and the masses. The quality of life will depend on how faithfully the minorities fulfill their mission of leadership. In addition, according to Ortega, history presents rhythmic changes of age and gender. There are masculine ages as well as feminine ones, and ages of youth and of the old. How valid are these criteria in the effort to organize mankind's actions into a metahistory? "The dilemma for the modern historiographer is to do either sociology or psychology. To combine both tendencies and to unite reason and intuition, to reconstruct time as future and to stop writing 'purely critical constructs' or pure fantasies."[6]

C. *Evaluation.* History is concerned with human actions and the discourses that narrate those actions. The historian moves about in a world of crime, heroism, and daily routine. Is there room for an objective framework? To what degree is objectivity possible in narrating the Spanish Civil War or World War II? Is condemnation detrimental to objectivity in the face of crime?

D. *Human essence.* All the themes we have referred to are based on one: the condition of man as a historical entity. A mechanistic idea of time leads us to see human history as a procession of individuals and societies through a screen of days and years. In this way, we conceive of history as essentially identical to, but somewhat different from, natural history. In fact, our common image of human history is naturalistic: civilizations are born, grow and die just as animals or individual human beings do.

Heidegger introduced a new conception of the historical condition of man, which constitutes his essence. Man's nature lies in fulfilling a

6. J. Caro Baroja, "La investigación histórica," in *Razas, pueblos y linajes*, p. 25.

unique mission within the structure of sense (language) in which he finds himself. This structure of conditions and possibilities that allows us to project and embrace goals, Heidegger calls "the world." Human life is the effort to appropriate the mission that our society has made possible for us.[7] The act of appropriating this mission or vocation is called *Ereignis* in German. This word is translated in the dictionaries as "event"; but Heidegger plays with the etymological sense of *Ereignis,* which is "appropriation," and the conventional meaning, which is "event." The event *par excellence* that constitutes man's historical character is the obligation to appropriate our own ineluctable mission.

For man, time is not the abstract screen or path that our actions fill with content, but rather the set of possibilities and impossibilities that condition our vocation and contribution to society. We as humans are never in a neutral space such as that occupied by a book or a dog. On the contrary, we are in a garden, in a library, in the U.S., in the territory of the old Iroquois; that is, we are embedded in a historical framework. The human space is names, meaning, and tradition, that is, time. Even when we are in pure nature, we already demarcate it as "pure nature" that is, as the "other" to history. The historical character of man coincides with his linguistic character: an articulated awareness of his being in a world of meaning.

E. *Reflection.* Finally, the fifth section of an ideal philosophy of history would be the analysis of the four points we have sketched in this outline plus the fifth, or metahistory. The classical philosophy of history studied the laws of development of the object itself: civilizations and their logic (St. Augustine or Hegel). Others, such as Marrou and the analytical philosophers, paid attention to the objective validity of historical texts. I believe that a holistic reflection on history as a branch of the humanities would have to encompass at least the five points indicated in this section.

---

7. "Mission" is the translation of Heidegger's word *Geschick,* which is usually translated as "destiny." But the term is derived from the verb *schicken* (to send), Latin *mittere,* whence "mission," which preserves the connotation of freedom better than the word "destiny."

History tells of events whose meaning has vanished with time, but it also displays works and values of perennial relevance: the classics. When we speak of language, literature, and history, we cannot forget that the humanities *par excellence* have been the classical humanities, whose role in education has been in dispute since the eighteenth century, as we have seen in the works of Goethe and Jovellanos. It is apposite to ask how Renaissance humanism pertains to our definition of the humanities.

9. *Classicism*

From Petrarch to Erasmus, the *belles lettres* were Latin and Greek. These humanists (and here we may also remember Nebrija) limited their study of the Bible to the New Testament, that is, the original Greek and the Latin translation. But Cardinal Cisneros, in the *Polyglot Bible* of Alcalá (published in 1517), could not ignore the Old Testament and consequently the Semitic languages. *The Complutensis Polyglot* enriched the traditional humanism of Valla and Erasmus, who were not interested in Hebrew. In 1517, when the Trilingual College of Louvain was founded, Erasmus tells us that in all of Europe, where there were so many "ebrieists" (drunkards), it was impossible to find a Hebraist (a person competent in Hebrew), and the first chair in Hebrew at the College of Louvain was given to a Spanish convert from Judaism, Matthaeus Adrian.

In the modern tradition, Latin and Greek continued to be the pre-eminent languages of education. Even at the beginning of the twentieth century, French doctoral candidates still had to write two theses, one of which had to be in Latin. The indisputable conviction among Europeans that Western culture was superior to all others was based on the a-temporal value placed upon the classics: Latin as a vehicle of expression of high European culture up until the end of the seventeenth century, and Greek as the cradle and model of Western culture. Egyptian and Mesopotamian civilizations were integrated into the Greek as its precursors and background, and non-European civilizations were considered stunted, not having reached their full development.[8]

In Catholic countries, the mass and the sacraments were celebrated in Latin until 1965; this kept alive the attention paid to this language by a broad public. In Spain, the 1939 plan for the *bachillerato* (junior and high school), which was in force until 1953, contained an ample component of classical studies. It was intended to mold the Spanish student's education in the two pillars of national identity: the Spanish language and Catholicism.[9]

In other countries such as Germany and England, religion was not the reason for the study of classical humanities, since the services were conducted in the vernacular, but those countries preserved a powerful humanistic tradition and, if not the religious rites, the study of the Bible was still a stimulus for learning Greek and Latin, since classical philology in the eighteenth century was indispensable for theology. Ortega y Gasset points out that England's political hegemony since the eighteenth century can be in part explained by the fact that the students at Oxford were immersed in Latin and Greek, thereby becoming flexible and creative enough to respond to any emerging situation.[10] It appears, then, that among other useful functions, the humanities provide a broad background and a historical perspective that enable us to respond to the most diverse challenges.

Latin was also useful for being the *koiné (lingua franca)* of Europe until the end of the seventeenth century. From Krakow to Lisbon travelers were able to understand each other in Latin. In the eighteenth century, French assumed that role, and today the universal *koiné* is English. Since

8. For an example of a vision of history as a function of different levels of development in civilizations and cultures, see Kurt Breysig's *Der Stufenbau und die Gesetze der Weltgeschichte* (Berlin: Georg Bondi, 1905).

9. A few years later, the author of the plan recalled: "The spectacle of a renaissance of classic studies in Spain due to legislation proposed by me has been the crowning glory of all my interests in the area of cultural politics" (P. Sainz Rodríguez, *Testimonio y recuerdos* [Barcelona: Planeta, 1978], p. 257b).

10. Ortega y Gasset: "Within that unreal Greece, England's young men are educated in the essential forms of living; that is, they are trained in pure abilities which allow them to adapt to the most diverse concrete situations; by the same token, they are not prepared especially for any single occasion" (*An Interpretation of Universal History*, p. 25).

Latin was the cultural language of Europe until about 1700, without reading Latin any research on Western culture prior to the eighteenth century will be necessarily derivative or very narrow. Even the intellectual background and context of the vernacular classics (Shakespeare is a good example) is written in Latin.

Today, on the other hand, the *uni*-versity has become the *"multi*-versity,"[11] pluralistic to the point of being a mere juxtaposition of disciplines and schools with no visible organic connection. Consequently, it is difficult to justify Latin (and more so Greek) as a course requirement for all high school students. Also, the spontaneous association of Greek and Latin in referring to the classical languages makes us forget their different roles in our culture. The paradigm of Western civilization in which and from which we still live, took shape in Greek—philosophy, science, and The New Testament. But this paradigm was created and integrated into European culture to the degree in which it was translated into Latin. Great Christian thinkers, such as Saint Augustine and Saint Thomas Aquinas, who codified the language of Western theology, did not read, or at least did not master, Greek. With this I do not want to insinuate that we should dare to discuss Plato or Euripides without reading them in the original language, but the majority of us will never study these writers with the aim of advancing classical philology; we need to be familiar with them as the ones who first formulated the pattern and the categories of our culture. Between the "all" of reading Plato and Sophocles in the original Greek, and the "nothing" of not reading them at all, we should guarantee knowledge of the Greek culture—which is ours—through translations.

With respect to Latin, the situation differs. Latin is a dead language, but it is the "mother" of the Romance languages and to a great extent of English. As I have said, one cannot do primary and rigorous research on Western civilization without reading this language. If we believe that every educated citizen ought to know the history of his nation and how it is integrated into Europe as a whole, the study of Latin becomes nec-

11. I adopt the term "multiversity" from Clark Kerr, former president of the University of California system. *The Uses of the University,* pp. 1–45.

essary in proportion to the degree of competency we wish to have in twenty centuries of European culture (from the expansion of Rome beyond the Italian borders in the third century B.C. to the end of the seventeenth century). Nevertheless, one must avoid simplistic panaceas; genealogy is not the only acceptable criterion for studying a culture. Knowledge of the past is obviously important in order to understand the present, but where do we cut off the list of ancestors?

It can also be argued that to understand the present it may be more instructive to study other cultures and languages of the present in a comparative approach. The history of Spain has largely been built on the basis of a radial image in which the country appears as the expansion of a homogeneous nucleus: "Castile has made Spain." In contrast to this thesis, Catalan sociologists and anthropologists point to the original differences among the peoples who settled in the various regions, and the persistence of those differences up to our time. This vision of the formation of the country through the incorporation and mutual bonds of different peoples appears more true to history than the radial and genealogical image. But in both versions, Tarraconians, Carpetans, Lusitanians, Gallaecians, and Baeticans encounter Latin everywhere. The Basque people have a completely different language, but their conversion to Christianity and their participation in Western civilization made them Latin as well. The destiny of the Christian Basque is that of Íñigo de Loyola, the Basque soldier converted into the Roman Ignatius, founder of the Jesuits, a company of indefatigable missionaries throughout the entire world. Is Ignatius less Basque for being more universal?

I do not think that a study of classical languages can be justified as a means of learning to write well. In fact, the opposite may be true: the imitation of the classics led to farfetched extremes on the model of Cicero's long-winded paragraphs, or on the model of concision found in Seneca or Tacitus. The two tendencies affected Spanish writers of the seventeenth century, and were called respectively *culteranismo* and *conceptismo*. Regarding the usefulness of Latin for good writing in the vernacular, I find the following idea of Azorín quite apt: "Reading the classics will impart a perfume of good taste, elegance, and distinction, to the style and words of their readers. But the nuance that these classics put on such speech and writing should be almost imperceptible; good sense and tact on the part of the speaker or writer will allow him to walk the fine line that separates elegance from affectation."[12] Good writing requires a clear idea about the subject we are studying, and success in communicating that idea in the most simple and clear style. The goal is to clarify reality, not to imitate the classics. As the Latin poet Horace said: "He who truly knows the topic about which he is speaking will not be at a loss for words or for a lucid order."[13]

In this matter of ancestors of a given culture, Spaniards are faced with the possible importance of Arabic and Hebrew, given the Muslim and Jewish dimension of Spanish history. Indeed the history of Spain until 1492 is basically the struggle against the Muslims, and is conditioned by the presence of a significant number of Jews some of whom occupied high social positions, especially in finances and medicine. Muslims and Jews became in Spain the intermediaries in the transmission of Greek culture to medieval Europe. Architecture, water works, and flamenco music bear witness to the enduring influence of Arabic culture in Christian Spain. But, in spite of all this, Spanish culture, as written discourse, is embodied in Latin and in the vernacular languages derived from Latin. The religious barrier made effective cultural communication between Christians and Muslims impossible, in spite of living so close to each other. I fully agree with the great historian Claudio Sánchez Albornoz: "The fundamental Hispanic fiber did not become Arabic in character."[14] As for the Jewish influence, if one can identify a specifically Judaic element in Spanish culture, it was never recognized as such. The "Jewish Bible" is for the Christian his own "Old Testament," and if a Jewish thinker such as Maimonides was an authority for Chris-

---

12. Azorin, "El político," in *Obras completas*. Edited by Angel Cruz Rueda (Madrid: Aguilar, 1975), p. 855a.

13. "Cui lecta potenter erit res, nec facundia deseret hunc nec lucidus ordo" (Horace, *Ars poetica*, vv. 40–41).

14. Claudio Sánchez Albornoz, *España. Un enigma histórico* [1956], cap. IV. 3rd ed. (Barcelona: Edhasa, 1991) I, 189–240. Cf. Julián Marías, *España inteligible. Razón histórica de las Españas* (Madrid: Alianza, 1985), pp. 114–16.

tian theologians, it was as a scholastic philosopher, not as a Jew. My purpose with these observations is not to deny off-hand Muslim and Jewish influence in Spanish culture, but to lay bare the complexity of the problem and the precision that is necessary when dealing with this subject.

10. Philosophy

Another discipline—better, a number of humanistic disciplines—is philosophy. Our vacillation on whether we are speaking about a singular or a plural concept already poses a paradox. In principle, philosophy is a set of disciplines that are very different from one another: logic, cosmology, philosophical anthropology, theory of knowledge, metaphysics, theodicy or natural theology, ethics, natural law, aesthetics, and history of philosophy. The dividing line between some of these disciplines is not always clear. Logic, for example, is related to aesthetics only to the degree to which all discourse ought to be based on coherent reasoning. Cosmology, the image of the physical universe that surrounds us, does not appear to have much in common with ethics. Nevertheless, the persistence of the term "philosophy" in the singular upholds the fact that all its different disciplines are concerned with finding ultimate explanations. A serious study of ethics, for example, cannot ignore the power of the environment and of biology as factors that condition our freedom. Here ethics shows its connection with cosmology. In fact, this connection has never been ignored. Today we ask about the relationship between DNA and freedom; but the same question is posed by Calderón in *La vida es sueño* (*Life is a Dream*, 1636) in the terms allowed by the science of his time: freedom vs. the position of the stars at the moment of one's birth. Throughout history, lineage has been the most persistent criterion for discrimination between individuals and groups. Racism, after all, is based on the relationship between freedom and biological heritage.

As we have seen, Callicles in Plato's *Gorgias* already questioned the value of philosophy. From ca. 1890 to 1933, philosophy was the center of intellectual life in German universities. Towering figures such as Dilthey, Hermann Cohen, Husserl, Max Scheler, and the young Heidegger not only won respect for philosophy in Germany but contributed to the spread of that prestige all over the world, from Buenos Aires to Tokyo. In any discussion on education the philosophers were the experts to be consulted. Before that period it is impossible to find such concentration of talent and, as a result, of public acceptance of philosophy. Kant did not receive in his time a competent review of his books, and he begins his *Critique of Pure Reason* stating for metaphysics what in fact applied to philosophy in general: "Time was when metaphysics was entitled the Queen of all the sciences; and if the will be taken for the deed, the preeminent importance of her accepted tasks gives her every right to this title of honor. Now, however, the changed fashion of the time brings her only scorn."[15]

In our time philosophy has lost prestige and intellectual relevance even where it once occupied the center, such as the questions on the nature of knowledge, hermeneutics, and education. One reason may be the ever narrower role of the humanities in the corporate university, but the other is the inadequacy of the two most popular tendencies of philosophy today: analytical philosophy, and the metaphysics of nonsense—deconstruction. I have nothing to say against the former, since I am trying to be analytical myself, and recognize that its rigor has cured us modest professors of the vague speculation to which we were destined in the wake of existentialism. But I would like to concern myself with reality, not with mere analysis of propositions, and would like to apply the analysis to the subjects, in this case the humanities, in their entire scope, as far as I am able to glimpse. Wittgenstein's *Tractatus logico-philosophicus*, for example, operates with concepts such as language, ego, and world, which he never defines. The entire book, with its apparent clarity, is marred by the failure to define its basic concepts. When the most renowned philosophers of America today publish a systematic

---

15. *Critique of Pure Reason*, Preface, p. 7.

approach to a real object, they practice phenomenology, even if unwittingly. But the mass of articles we read in analytical philosophy suffers from esoterism, fragmentariness, and horrible English.

For about twenty-five years (1970–1995) "deconstruction" was the catchword in American academia, and its nebulous application to literary texts by people without preparation in philosophy has brought it into ridicule and in fact instigated the present backlash against theory. Philosophically, deconstruction makes sense, even if we disagree with it. The word derives from the German *Ab-bauen,* used by Heidegger in order to un-cover the groundlessness of European metaphysics. Deconstruction, often identified with "post-modernity," is in fact the climax of the most visible feature of modernity: secularization. From Descartes to Sartre, philosophy was a methodically secular construction, but one that respected the hierarchies and values inherited from the theological tradition. Sartre denounced as inconsistent a culture that, pretending to be rational and secular, upheld the values established in the Middle Ages under the aegis of religion. "The existentialist, Sartre wrote, is strongly opposed to a certain type of secular moralism which seeks to suppress God at the least possible expense. In other words—and this is, I believe, the purport of all that we in France call radicalism—nothing will be changed if God does not exist; we shall re-discover the same norms of honesty, progress and humanity, and we shall have disposed of God as an out-of-date hypothesis which will die away quietly of itself."[16] "Postmodern" philosophy has carried Sartre's proposal to its logical conclusion. Descartes was the first who, purporting to found philosophy on new ground, held on "provisionally" to inherited morals (*Discourse on Method,* 1637, section III) until he would build the new rational ethics. Sartre accuses the French radicals of the same inconsistency, and Derrida points out that, once we have killed the father, his voice, the *logos,* no longer holds the world together in any structure of sense. Deconstruction is at least one, if not the only logical consequence of atheism. For us it is a call for better justification of our convictions on the basis of reason.

16. *Existentialism and Humanism,* p. 33.

This need to be open to the real and to the other solely on the basis of reason is a very positive thing for the present world. In the past, simple tolerance of other religions was a sign of generosity. Today, reason requires that we move beyond tolerance to positive respect and to recognize in each individual the right to his or her own religion. This is not because we advocate relativism but rather because we consider ourselves limited creatures, and whether we worship in the temple or in the mosque, an infinite God accepts everyone who lives in spirit and in truth. And, as the scholastic philosophers already pointed out in the Middle Ages, human reason is but a radiation of divine intelligence, and is therefore the ultimate criterion available to man for distinguishing between good and evil. In our global and pluralistic village we must develop a purely rational system of ethics not based on any concrete religious tradition. I consider this the supreme challenge to the humanities in our time.

All the disciplines of philosophy are humanities because they study the workings of the mind or the meaning of reality. But some disciplines, like logic and cosmology, may be too dependent on the scientific method or discourse. Ethics, on the other hand, is a humanistic discipline in the strictest sense; its subject is to define man as he is, and that implies also what he can and ought to be. The humanistic discourse in ethics consists of approaching the subject, observing its different aspects in a global way (factors such as heredity, psychology, biography, projects, ideals, and aspirations) and ordering them in a systematic manner. Human ontology is ethics, and vice-versa, as stated by Heidegger in his *Letter on Humanism* (1946).

Ontology is another fundamental discipline in the humanities. Aristotle called it "the first philosophy," and it continues to deserve that title since it is the branch of knowledge that deals with knowledge itself, with the idea of meaning, and with the ultimate structure of reality and the mind. Ontology is the study of the first assumptions of human reasoning and the knowledge we can acquire with this reasoning. An inquiry into the meaning and value of the humanities such as the one we are undertaking here can be considered a chapter of ontology.

Aesthetics is currently discredited for two reasons: the negative connotation of aestheticism as an escape from social responsibility, and the traditional association of aesthetics with subjectivism and sentimentalism. But in the mind of its pioneers, Baumgarten, Kant, and Schiller, aesthetics is the science of the perfect equilibrium of the powers of the soul. Together with the traditional faculties of memory, understanding, and will, Baumgarten elaborated on sensitivity (calling it a faculty "analogous to reason"), the faculty that discerns what is beautiful and correct, not by following preexisting rules but by a leap of good taste. For us, aesthetics is the study of the primary images of the mind. The efforts of the mind culminate in: (a) a series of universal categories or principles from which philosophy and the sciences arise; (b) primary images or archetypes, which originate artistic expression; and (c) a primordial yearning for meaning in everything, which is expressed in religion. Aesthetics is the study of the imaginative nature of the human mind.

11. *Religion and theology*

Another humanistic discipline is theology, a paradox, for, as we already mentioned, the "good letters" of humanism arose as "profane letters" in contrast to "sacred" ones. But in the Renaissance and even in Kant's time theology was what we call today a "vocational" or useful field, since it prepared its students for positions in the church and in the royal courts. Today it must be considered a humanistic discipline, as the exploration of the existence of God, creation, providence, and the meaning of human life in relation to these questions. For, as Unamuno said to God: "If you existed, I too would really exist." As we shall see in section 23, the crisis of values in our time is intimately related to the absence of God in our society.

Theology is a reflection on God and on the revelation given by God to human beings. In Spain, our primary reference point is Catholic theology but the definition is valid for other confessions. As a reflection on a concrete divine revelation, theology can be born in sectarianism and foment it. In this case, far from being a branch of the humanities, it becomes a dangerous weapon, as has been seen in religious wars and as we still see today with all forms of fundamentalism. For this reason, the first and most general issue of theology as a humanistic pursuit is the universal fact of religion in all its forms of expression. Respect for another and a consensus in maintaining the theological discussion at the honorable level of ideas ought to be the conviction of human decency that precedes any dissent in creed. Given the large number of religions and the difficulties of dialogue between them, in our pluralistic world ethics is more basic and universal than religion. Ethics is apt to unite, while religion may unfortunately divide.

The second issue is how the different religions perceive the nature of God, his presence in human history, and the fate of the individual after death. Is there a basic consensus on these primary convictions? The basis of that consensus must be sought in the fact that belief is a primordial characteristic of the human mind. In this regard it is important to ask if the framework of substructure and superstructure proposed by Marx and Freud, and Ortega y Gasset's doctrine in his essay, "Ideas and Beliefs," define the structure of belief on which a religious faith is reasonably based. From these questions of principle, one would engage in the historical study of the diversity of religions and the influence religion has had in creating bonds or resentment between different societies.

In the Christian sphere, one of the fundamental issues of the twentieth century has been the very status of theology as science and its dependence on the ecclesiastical *magisterium,* whether from the Pope (among Catholics) or from the respective synods among the Protestant confessions.[17] The fundamental theme in Christianity is the figure of Jesus Christ as God and man. Another key question is the role of Christianity as a fulcrum of Western civilization. A confusion of nationalism and pseudo-religion has solidified the association of particular religious positions with national boundaries: the majority of people in the Latin nations are Catholic, while Germans and the Anglo-Saxons are predominantly Protestant.

17. See Melquíades Andrés, *Pensamiento teológico y cultura,* p. 211.

If the study of classical humanities is justified by their presence in our culture, it is scandalous not to include the Bible in the education of every individual in the Western world. The Bible has been *the book par excellence;* its presence is palpable in our most important writers, and it has been a source of national glories and disgraces in European history. The Psalms, the Prophets, and the Books of Wisdom are poetry and literature of perennial value. The Gospel, even for those who do not believe in its divine origin, is a testimony to the most sublime example of humanism ever proposed on this planet.

Protestantism and Catholicism, in whose names so much Christian blood has been spilled, owe their origins to a philological dispute: different readings of the Bible. The professors of literature who have discovered literary theory in the last thirty years can learn a rich spectrum of methods and theoretical discussions about the interpretation of texts from the biblical exegesis of past centuries.

12. *Signposts without boundaries*

We have enumerated the humanistic disciplines in a strict sense, based on their specific object and on their types of discourse. I consider this reductive approach necessary, because we need clarity about the value of these disciplines in the education of students and of society at large. But as we have already stated, the humanities are not just the disciplines we have mentioned, for the natural and the social sciences also have their humanistic components. What is more, we have limited ourselves to the disciplines of a traditional curriculum, purposely leaving aside the creative fields of music, art, dance, and literature. Who is the humanist in a more fundamental sense, Cervantes or a critic of *Don Quijote?* Are Luis de León and Saint John of the Cross great humanists for their poetry or for their philology? And like Luis de León and Saint John, in the twentieth century the Machado brothers, Vicente Aleixandre, José Angel Valente, and many others have blended the most original creation with the most lucid commentaries. The literature of creation, the lyric poetry and music of entertainment, film, art, and dance: they are all humanities.

In fact, one fundamental aspect of a literary work is the awareness it tends to reflect about the writer's effort in creating it. In Spain, from *Razon feita de amor* and Berceo (thirteenth century) to the contemporary poets and novelists, many writers incorporate in their work the effort of composing it. *Don Quijote* is the pre-eminent example in literature, and in painting Velázquez's *Las Meninas*. These observations make clear that, despite the validity of the demarcations of humanistic disciplines given in this chapter, the dividing lines are not walls that separate, but rather lookout points from which one can always contemplate two sides. The borders help us to distinguish different areas, but they also unite those areas. The common roots, the overlapping, and the coincidence in both subject and type of discourse of the humanistic disciplines constitute their inherent interdisciplinary character.

III *The Interdisciplinary*

> *Though our ideal of perfection may dwell on a height that is hard to gain,*
> *it is our duty to teach all we know, that achievement may at least come*
> *somewhat nearer the goal.*

> (Quintilian, *Institutio oratoria*, I. x. 8)

13. *Interdisciplinary disciplines*

"Interdisciplinary" is an ambiguous notion that designates an intellectual style open to serious risks, the first one being excessive or premature generalization. Knowledge advances for the most part in short steps that bring new precision to old questions. And secondly, if interdisciplinary research digs at the borders of various disciplines, chances are the practitioner will not be sufficiently competent in all of them.

On the other hand, when a researcher broaches ideas that are more universal in scope than the work of the specialist, he is praised for the light he sheds on different fields of inquiry. Generalization is the result of specialized research, which forces one to define the concepts involved and to discover the patterns and laws that underlie the particular phenomena. Thus, though the reflections of the previous chapter may not have contributed to progress in any of the humanistic disciplines, they have articulated in a concise manner the scope of those disciplines. Progress in the interdisciplinary fields does not follow a linear but rather a spiral or spherical pattern. Instead of advancing, interdisciplinary research returns to its premises and progresses in the sense that it deepens. And as for the risk of incompetence, it accompanies every human endeavor; all we have in our power is the commitment to work, not the success.

The humanistic disciplines are interdisciplinary by their very constitution regardless of the practitioner's wishes, most often against those wishes. The analysis of language has presented us with an index of themes, the study of which requires expertise in other disciplines. Language as the expressive nature of man is a problem for linguistics and philosophy; as a structure of signifiers, it overlaps with logic and mathematics; as the discourse of a culture, it is related to sociology and history; and finally, as concrete speech and as grammar, it crosses into psychology and all the branches of general linguistics mentioned above. Furthermore, all human activity is reflexive or susceptible to conscious reflection—even the subconscious, since we are conscious of its existence. Thus language permeates all knowledge and all relationships between human beings.

In the connection of language and culture one perceives that all human knowledge, especially the humanities, is inserted in and cloaked by language, even though the specific formulation of each theme justifies the distinction of the other humanistic disciplines from linguistics. The culture expressed in our "native" language allows us a particular pleasure derived from the vivid perception of its nuances and from a sense of belonging to a particular community. The reading of ancient or modern books that open a dimension of depth into the past and of breadth into the present, endows us with a permanent habit. And the more languages we know, the broader is our world. In addition to literature, whether classical or popular, music and art of all types and styles are a common cultural patrimony, which shapes our identity. Different sectors of society may enjoy one style over another, but culture is not the private domain of any single profession or class. The majority of people can read, and although their reading may not reach the ideal level of rigor that we propose in Chapter VI, it is nonetheless legitimate and educational.

Rhetoric condenses the psychology of the ego and of communication into tropes and figures of speech. What we call means of persuasion and entertainment are in fact psychology embodied in language.

History is interdisciplinary on its very surface. If we open a book on any national history, we will usually find a series of juxtaposed chapters on the state and its institutions, the economy, art and culture, and popular life. In Spain, a heading such as "The Generation of '98," refers to the war of independence of Cuba, to the political situation, social life, the education and international prestige of Spain at the end of the nineteenth century, to the Spanish-American War, and to the writers who are conventionally grouped as members of that generation.

Philosophy is interdisciplinary because it poses the questions that precede and follow all other disciplines, the very nature of knowledge and understanding. Philosophy also deals with the relationship between the mind and the surrounding world, with the possibility of establishing theories, of wresting truth, and with the definitions of all those concepts.

Theology asks the ultimate "human question," that is, "the desire to know what will become of you and of me and all of us, once you and I and all of us die" (Unamuno). To be sure, theology is not limited to the inquiry about immortality, but this question is at the root of all the others. For the existence of God as creator and the immortality of the soul are the ultimate guarantees of sense for human existence.[1]

The humanities center on man as a complex whole (hence the different disciplines): man as he finds himself projected and projecting, dependent on a family, on groups, and on society, and open to a present that condenses in itself both past and future, memory and hope. The social sciences study man and his conduct, but these are specific discourses whose final meaning becomes clear only when they are integrated in the whole. In section 5 we saw how the scientific and humanistic methods differ in their approach to psychological and sociological questions.

Another example taken from Ortega y Gasset explains the normative power of humanistic discourse to incorporate and clarify the facts of the social sciences. In his first course at the Institute for the Humanities

1. On this question see Robert Nozick, *Philosophical Explanations,* chapter VI: "Philosophy and the meaning of life" (pp. 571ff.). Further discussion on this point would distract us from our project.

in Madrid (1948) Ortega confronted Arnold Toynbee's thesis according to which, after many hundreds of thousands of years, the first real civilizations of Mesopotamia and Egypt suddenly sprang forth about 5000 years ago. Egyptian culture began when a climatic change forced some villages of the high plains to seek the waters of the Nile. Ortega cannot accept this sudden leap for which obviously there are not solid proofs. But if Toynbee draws conclusions on probable evidence, how can the Spanish philosopher deny them? Simply put, from a philosophical premise: human life is the response to the challenge of the moment. Man has always been in some form of civilization because being human already entails it. When the inhabitants of the high plains of Egypt were forced by drought in their territory to descend into the valley of the Nile, they did so to save an agriculture they were already practicing when the drought caused them to migrate. Based on his conception of human existence, Ortega concludes that a leap of civilization is not necessarily a radical change in the lifestyle of a particular society, but rather an acceleration of its rhythm of progress.[2] This example shows how not only Toynbee's conjectural history, but any history based on documents may be misleading, because the historian fails to define the concepts underlying the developments he describes. As Américo Castro said, one cannot understand the "factual history" of Spain without pausing to describe what is meant by the subjects "Spain" and "the Spaniards." This idea is even more valid today, when one of the most vexing issues in our society—in Spain—is the recognition of "differential nationalities" within the traditional nation.

The humanistic approach (global and interdisciplinary) is the beacon from which the social and natural sciences must take direction. In the case of economics—taken here as an example of the social sciences—the human aspect may be summarized in the common phrase, "Man is not made for economics, but economics for man." The economists posit their variables and determine the number of inhabitants the planet can sustain, or which benefits workers can receive in order to make a

---

2. "Una vision de la historia universal" [1948], ch. X, in *Obras Completas*, IX, p. 174.

company competitive. In this calculation, the worker is but a function in the productive process. On the other hand, for a humanistic, ethical economics, the worker is a person with a family and with legitimate needs, feelings, and ambitions. Ideally, his work situation would provide him with the resources necessary to fulfill those needs, except when they become unrealistic dreams. Those economists who favor raising the level of wealth and letting the economic process operate under its internal laws clash with humanist ideologues, both moderate and radical, who cannot neglect the variable of the human being in the spectrum of economic parameters.

In the natural sciences, the conception of the universe has most gravely contributed to social discrimination and to the restriction of freedoms. The clearest proof is found in biology: the physical type and the plebeian or noble inheritance have practically determined (with all respect for exceptions) an individual's development throughout history. Today, biology continues to be the science in which it is most necessary to remember the human dimension. From a theoretical point of view, biology makes us face the dilemma of genetic determinism and freedom.

On February 23, 1997, the birth of Dolly, a sheep cloned in Scotland, was announced to the world. Science now knows how to manipulate genes and create—as the television commentators said—either a Mother Teresa or a Hitler, though there is still a distance from Dolly to the two specimens of man's versatility just mentioned. It is utopian to think that the experiment will not be practiced on humans even if some countries do declare it illegal. Racism and ethnic hate, still so profound and prevalent today, show the wellsprings and poisons of Nazism that apparently corrupt us all. In this case, only an ethical position that recognizes "the sanctity of all human life," as Pope John Paul II says, can save us from the white-gloved genocide that sanctions abortion today. Abortion is legal because that is what a majority of voters decided through the political process. Because no power can or should suppress the democratic system, any pressure against an institutionalized crime or against the manipulation of a person can only come from that same society through the influence of religion or of a rigorous philosophy. The enemies of abortion, instead of resorting to crime or fantasizing about a benevolent dictator, should fight with determination and honor so that society will accept their message democratically.

The clearest discrimination derived from biological theories in Western civilization was the discrimination against woman. It was believed that her physical constitution made her "the weak sex," and that her brain was not suited for intellectual work due to an excessive degree of humidity. This "scientific" conviction seemed corroborated by women's scarce contributions to high culture. When women excelled, as in the case of Saint Teresa of Avila and Sor Juana Inés de la Cruz, they were appreciated as "monstrosities," aberrations from the general law, and therefore served to perpetuate the conviction corroborated by "science" or philosophy. In this case, the *anti-scientific* rebellion of some women (Saint Teresa and Sor Juana among them) in the name of equality, revealed the shallowness of that so-called science. What has been said about women can also be applied to the native abilities of all races. Today, once we unequivocally reject all pseudoscientific criteria of discrimination, it will be possible to account for the obvious differences between man and woman, not in terms of hierarchy, but in terms of otherness; in the case of women, in what Julián Marías called in 1970 the "gendered reality" of the human species.[3]

The analysis of the interdisciplinary character of the humanities and the examples of their relationship to the natural and social sciences, point to two different meanings of the term "interdisciplinary": the horizontal, or search for the common border of different disciplines, and the vertical, or the search for the nucleus where the differences originate and converge. The humanistic disciplines constitute both the foundation and the culmination of all the other disciplines: they are pre- and post-disciplinary.

3. "Sexual activity is a small province of our lives, very important but limited, one that doesn't begin with our birth and tends to end before we die, founded in the gendered condition of human life in general, that affects the integrity of that life at all times and in all its dimensions" (Julián Marías, *Antropología metafísica* [1970], chap. XVII. In *Obras*, X [Madrid: Revista de Occidente, 1982], pp. 113–14).

14. A specialist in general ideas

The interdisciplinary character of the humanities illustrates in the most vivid manner how we the generalists, are also condemned to specialization. To begin with, who can claim competency in "Spanish literature"? How many original texts and how much scholarship on those texts do we really know? And how many do we know well? Specialization is forced upon us, due to human limitation and to the complexity of many particular questions, which require exclusive dedication to them. Galdós and Unamuno mock in their novels the "bookworm" who unearths the glories of his small village or catalogues insignificant writers of the past while turning a blind eye to his own time. Indeed, there exists the erudite eccentric who can take a stone found in a stable and from it recreate the plans of an imagined cathedral, or has "proof" that Christopher Columbus and Cervantes were both born in his town. But to criticize an essential dimension of the mind such as factual learning with picturesque examples is frivolous and misleading; it tends to reveal envy of the serious scholar, and it unmasks the petty tyrant inside many of us who pose as liberals. For no one has the right to dictate to others what should interest them. Excessive specialization, empty erudition, concentration on detail without a sense of the whole (fragmentariness), and pure formalism, are anti-humanistic attitudes within the humanities. But the only response is to try to avoid those pitfalls, if we know how, and to take advantage of what the factualists and formalists can contribute to the whole picture. To know if Góngora sold an olive grove on a certain date doesn't help much in reading his poem *Polyphemus* (1613), but there comes a time when the reader of the poem wants to know its context down to the smallest detail, and in that case any document could contain clues. For that purpose, a collection of documents on Góngora should be as exhaustive as possible, and it therefore should not discard the deed to the olive grove.

The interdisciplinary character lies in the subjects themselves, which have a density and background, not in the individuals who cultivate them. *Don Quijote* is a text that is part of the *work* of Cervantes, about which there is debate over whether it represents the peak of Erasmism, of the Baroque, or of both cultural trends. Obviously, if Cervantes' work reveals the influence of Erasmus, the work must contain some theological elements that are rarely associated with Cervantes. At the same time, many studies read into *Don Quijote* theological and political messages that cannot be based on the straightforward meaning of its words. If one prefers to associate Cervantes with the Baroque, it is necessary to clarify how the literary Baroque relates to the Baroque in the plastic arts, in architecture, and in music. All these layers of the density and background of *Don Quijote* demand specialized research, indispensable for understanding the text. And since comprehensive understanding is the prerogative of God, we must be satisfied with a reading that aspires to learn and appreciate the greatest possible number of aspects. Hence the meaning of Ortega y Gasset's sentence regarding the interdisciplinary: "The scholar is destined to be a specialist, but reality is not."

Ortega's words enunciate a paradox: it is assumed that the interdisciplinary is the opposite to the specialized, while all serious study is based on specialization—prolonged effort, rigorous method, and well-founded conclusions. This paradox explains the suspicion of superficiality raised by interdisciplinary approaches to problems. On the one hand, one proclaims the greatest appreciation for the "Renaissance man," who enlightens us about the single and common root of many branches of knowledge. The thinker, whom we credit with a higher degree of wisdom, is usually not the professor who teaches in a specific area, but rather the one who reveals the links and the borders between his field and others. And yet, at the same time, the reservations toward the generalist or the "essayist" are pervasive in the name of rigor, that is, of specialization.

Specialization is unavoidable, but it should not be confused it with narrow-mindedness, which is the concentration on an excessively limited subject. If a professor of philosophy devotes his life to collating Kant's manuscripts, one must acknowledge his intellectual contribution, but he probably will not contribute an enlightening reading of Kant. The same can be said of purely formal or erudite studies in literature, despite the fact that both the formal and the erudite work are necessary if readers are to have authentic texts, pertinent collateral information, and clarity regarding difficult passages of the text.

Specialization in a positive sense is synonymous with serious intellectual work. The reader may think that this book is blind and completely erroneous. But if I have corrected it five times before sending it for publication, it is because in the first four versions I was even more critical with it than any of its readers. Specialization is the study of, and search for, the best ideas on a given topic, expressed in the best possible way. This book intends to be the work of a specialist, though in "general ideas," as it investigates the common background of several disciplines.

The paradox "specialist in general ideas" is based on a rule of Greek and medieval logic: the more general a concept is, the fewer concrete features it encompasses, and vice versa (extension is in inverse proportion to comprehension). The reason for this is yet another paradox: everything we know and do is particular, including the universal. Little is offered here in any of the humanistic disciplines. However, if this interdisciplinary experiment is successful, it can illuminate the foundation where all those disciplines converge and originate. The interdisciplinary does not span so much as it provides a foundation (pre-disciplinary), it floats on the borders (interdisciplinary) and hovers above the specific research (post-disciplinary). But the foundation is different from the object founded upon it, as meta-literature or meta-history are not literature or history. We are not God: everything in us is particular, and most of all, the universal.

The mutual implication of the universal and the particular justifies once again the remark that in this field there is no room for rigid distinctions, because there are no linear boundaries but rather a nucleus or sphere in which all the lines converge and differ while being intertwined. This definition of the interdisciplinary differs from the common perception, in which the interdisciplinary is conceived as a mere juxtaposition of perspectives on a given topic. Because of this, it becomes necessary to define the concept more precisely in order to eliminate any mechanistic idea.

15. *Juxtaposition*

As an example of interdisciplinary studies, I will mention some books in which two notions appear united by an "and," the copulative conjunction being a symbol of the border where two fields or disciplines meet. Looking at random to the left of my library I read the titles: *Arte y anarquía (Art and Anarchy)* as well as *Literature and Technology.* The two titles have the copulative *and,* which indicates the intention of relating two fields presumably to determine the similarities and differences among them.

The title *Art and Anarchy*[4] leads me to expect an analysis of creative activity and of art as rebellion against the ideology and the prevailing artistic forms in a certain society and period. To the extent that art is original, the work of art is generally a rebellion against the established styles. Nevertheless, this rebellion can unfold in various degrees. Gonzalo de Berceo's poems (thirteenth century) are unique and original, but they rework a traditional material taken from other written texts; they are creative translation. The artist of the Middle Ages was original, but his conception of art implied the reformulation of stylistic, structural, and thematic clusters handed down to him: cycles and *topoi.*[5] Histories of art and literature pursue this alternation between classicism, which conceives of art as an inquiry into perennial aspirations of mankind, and experimental texts and works of art in which the rebellious expression of an individual asserts itself.

The title *Art and Anarchy* prompted me to look for the aspects of the inherent connection between the two concepts. In its standard meaning, anarchy is the complete affirmation of the individual above the social forces that limit one's freedom, and art is the creation by an individual of a unique work that transforms the preceding history. From these ideas about the compared terms, the *and* in the title seems to promise the analysis of individual creativity as the meeting point of the two con-

4. Edgar Wind, *Arte y anarquía* [1963]. Trans. Salustiano Maso (Madrid: Taurus, 1967).

5. This is the meaning of *topoi* and of the constants noted by Ernst Robert Curtius in his classic work *European Literature and the Latin Middle Ages,* pp. 79–105.

cepts. If I were to develop that title, I would write, more or less, the following chapters: Art and freedom; the limits of freedom—artistic creation as the response to a need, namely to a personal calling and a collective need; creative freedom and the impact of the structure of language and of the literary genre; art and ideology; anarchist art throughout history (some examples of libertarian art in specific societies and periods); European avant-garde and anarchy. In each of these cases, the conjunction *and* or the preposition *in* represents a point in which the two terms necessarily meet, so we relate them not out of subjective interests but obliged by the nature and history of art.

Now, after devising my own outline based on the title *Art and Anarchy,* I open the book and find the following contents: Prologue; I, Art and anarchy; II, Aesthetic participation; III, A critique of being "well versed in the arts"; IV, The fear of awareness; V, The mechanization of art; VI. Art and will. Instead of a systematic unfolding of the topic promised in the title, the book is a compilation of loose lectures not organized according to the objective aspects offered by the subject. Even the first essay, which gives the book its title, makes references to Plato, Baudelaire, Goethe and Hegel, to the imagination, and to the "interesting" within experimental tendencies in art, but it fails to define "art" and "anarchy," and the point where they necessarily converge and diverge.

The title *Literature and Technology* raises—not just in me but objectively by the very meaning of its words—these expectations: First, a definition of the literary and the technological discourses. In general, literature as the reflexive discourse of a society probably musters some parallelisms with the technology of that society. Needless to say, technology is not just an application of science but an inspiration for science as well. In a more concrete sense, that is, taking literature as a set of specific texts, the word "literature" is very rich in meanings; to begin with, it takes form in different literary genres, and the relationship to technology is different with each genre. In poetry, for example, we tend to highlight imaginative freedom and its opposition to technology, which we often associate with alienation and oppression. However, the tendency called "futurism" and some modernist currents have praised technology as one of the major wonders ever to spring from the human imagination. For Marinetti (1876–1944), the author of the Futurist Manifesto, "A roaring car that seems to ride on grapeshot is more beautiful than the *Victory of Samothrace*."[6]

Technology has a particular quirk in that it quickly becomes antiquated. An antiquated artifact becomes an antique, a pretty object. Today we collect candelabras and farmhouse tools from past centuries. And the first personal computers are museum artifacts. An obsolete device is a poetic object because, once divested of its function, it becomes a link to the life of a certain person or group. From history as well as from technology, all we are left with are the flashes of the human effort and creativity that were displayed in them.

The novel may have as the subject of its plot technology and its impact on human existence. It can also present the individual as a mere tool and number in his environment, or as the actor who manages to create his own life by assimilating anything external into and from an inalienable interior core. In theater, the connection between literature and technology is even more intimate. As a phenomenon of total art, the potential images, movements, and changes of scene afforded by technical resources permit artistic possibilities that would have been unimaginable in times of more primitive technology. Film is the best example of the collaboration of literature and technology in a unique type of discourse. The simple focus on the different literary genres immediately suggests the wide range of expectations raised by the conjunction *and* in the title *Literature and Technology*.

In the book *Literature and Technology: The Alien Vision*, by Wylie Sypher,[7] we find six chapters subdivided into various sections. The six chapters are: I. Conquest by Method; II. Romantics and Aesthetes; III.

---

6. Filippo T. Marinetti, *Let's Murder the Moonshine: Selected Writings*. Trans. by R. W. Flint, and A. A. Cappotelli (Los Angeles: Sun and Moon Classics, 1991), p. 49. The Futurist Manifest was first published in *Le Figaro*, Paris, Saturday, February 20, 1909. See also Juan Cano Ballesta, *Literatura y tecnología. Las letras españolas ante la revolución industrial (1900–1933)* (Madrid: Orígenes, 1981).

7. New York: Random House, 1968.

Mimesis, the Visual; IV. Alien Worlds; V. Participation; VI. Proximity. The chapter headings do not reveal anything about their content and ostensibly have no direct relation to what the title of the book suggests. It begins by describing Mallarmé's goal of eliminating the poet's feelings from poetry, as stated in the famous sentence, "the poem consists of words, not feelings." In fact, the book continues with references to different authors and scholars without addressing the topic of literature and technology in a theoretical and systematic way.

Conferences tend to produce books that are considered interdisciplinary but are the mere juxtaposition of disparate papers linked by the general topic of the conference. Titles such as *The Book of Good Love and Its Literary and Historical Milieu* and *Spain at the Dawn of the Twenty-first Century* exemplify my point. In the first, all the textual and contextual research focuses on a single book. At first glance it is difficult to understand how this can be interdisciplinary. Nonetheless, even if there were no reference to its social and cultural milieu, the *Book of Good Love,* simply as a fourteenth-century book, requires from the scholarly reader familiarity with the codices in which it has been preserved, the linguistic and poetic aspects, the references to theology, to law, and to the life of its audience; the notion of "good love" as compared to other ideas of love and their literary expressions in its time and others; the poetic quality of such a Protean book, etc. Despite the variety of possible perspectives, since the collected essays deal with a single text, the range of questions that can be asked is narrower than that of the second title: *Spain at the Dawn of the Twenty-first Century.* In this case the topic attracts specialists in sociology, economics, science, philosophy, literature, art, history, religious expressions, and popular culture(s), and each one speaks from within his or her own specialty. The result is a juxtaposition of views on the various aspects of a subject as broad as "Spain." The term "Spain" here stands only for the space or stage on which the activities studied by the specific disciplines occur. If this type of study intends to go beyond mere juxtaposition, the concept "Spain" should be analyzed as the pre-disciplinary reality wherein the various disciplinary considerations find their common root and center of fusion. Specialized work on demographics, the life of different sectors of production and consumption, scientific activity and popular entertainment, all should be integrated on the basis of the subject of study: Spain.

Unfortunately, at those so-called interdisciplinary conferences, the basic question, which suggests the title of the gathering *(Spain at the Dawn of the Twenty-first Century),* is usually skipped out of fear of grandiose visions and generalizations. When this happens, studies about concrete authors and texts may be excellent and useful, but they float without an anchor. The title of the conference implies that the participants sought clarity, not only on the terms that are related, but also on the "and" that holds the term together and apart. The interdisciplinary is not the juxtaposition of different approaches to a subject, but to the "and," that is, to the point in which the two related terms unite and separate from each other.

16. *The And*

Here are two titles: "Science *and* Poetry," "Literature *and* Philosophy." Science: we imagine a researcher trying to isolate the AIDS virus and immunize cells against its attack. Is it possible to find an inherent relationship between this activity and poetry? At first, it is difficult to see what the *and* could mean when dealing with two such different discourses. But, if in this example the relationship between science and poetry may be far-fetched, not all science is viral and genetic research. Plants, animals, and the landscape have aroused the admiration of both scientists and poets since the most ancient literatures. Azorín puts these words in the mouth of his character Yuste: "What determines the measure of an artist is his awareness of nature, of landscape."[8] If both literature and science are concerned with nature, they are separated not by the object but by the respective type of discourse. Therefore, the first question when considering the relation between "Science and poetry" is how the mind functions in each of these activities, and whether there

8. *La voluntad* (The will) (1902), chap. XIV. In *Obras Completas,* ed. A. Cruz Rueda (Madrid: Aguilar, 1975), I, p. 471b.

are several foci or one where they intersect. The point where science and poetry meet is imagination or creativity. Scientific advancement implies an imaginative leap much akin to poetic creation. In addition to the common origin, both science and poetry attempt to discover the truth, and complex molecules are as beautiful as a poem, though in different respects. Still a third point of interaction of science and poetry evolves around structure. Literary creation is guided by the structure of the language and of each genre. These structures shape the creative process by giving it a mathematical configuration. In the end, the comparison between science and poetry will bring forth more differences than commonalities, but in the course of comparing them, we will have discovered points of contact and above all, it will have served to refine our knowledge of both the poetic and the scientific discourse. The *and* is a crossroads where similarities and differences intersect.

In the case of "Philosophy *and* Literature" there are more points in common, and the question becomes more complex. In the first place, literature unfolds in different genres, and philosophy comprises different disciplines. The essay occupies a space on the borders of literature and philosophy. Poetry penetrates the deepest secrets of language on the border between the expressible and the ineffable. Novels and theater often contain philosophical discourse, as can be seen in some of Pio Baroja's novels, or in Umberto Eco's *The Name of the Rose*. Literature is always related to, and mostly depends upon the predominant cosmology, psychology, and worldview of each epoch. In the final analysis, the literary work is an immersion into the deepest aspects of the mind, just as philosophy is. It is in this search for the ultimate meaning of life that literature and philosophy coincide. Again, they are not distinguished by the questions they ask, but by the way of asking; therefore the *and* means both the similarities and differences between the literary and the philosophical discourses. The comparison ought to highlight the differences, but also the points where they converge, affording a better understanding of the two fields.

Similar observations can be made about the relationship between theology and the scientific image of the world at a given time in history.

As we know, in the second half of the nineteenth century many biologists brandished Darwinism against the doctrine of creation, and in response, the Catholic Church condemned evolution or suspected the "evolutionary hypothesis" and "theory" until Pope Pius XII considered it admissible in 1944, and Pope John Paul II reaffirmed it in 1996. But beyond the conflicts and truces recorded in history, are there objective facets that link religion with biology? The first question would address the problem of life as an organic process, and the essence of the spirit. What possibility is there of surviving the disintegration of organic life? Another important problem: man's conduct is conditioned by divine predestination, the genetic code, and his position in society, with the possibilities of achievement allowed by that position. Under these conditions, is man really free to choose good over evil? From a theological perspective, what does the incarnation of God and his life and death on earth mean? Great theologians such as Teilhard de Chardin and Karl Rahner already included serious biological knowledge in their studies of theology. Today, I do not believe that one can speak seriously of creation, of monogenism and the redemption of all men through Christ, without being aware of the search for the possibility of life (for now just life, not human life) on other planets. In all the cases we have mentioned, the *and* is the crossroads or meeting point, not of topics that are being united by the personal interest of the scholar, but of realities that were united before being separated by specialized interests.

The scholastic theologians distinguished between two ways of acquiring knowledge *(modi sciendi):* definition and division. The examples of interdisciplinary study mentioned here around the *and* belong to what was called division. Comparing and contrasting is the best method of defining different types of discourse, and thus the different sciences. The problem with the *and* is whether the individual, given man's limitations, can attain competency in the two fields being contrasted in order to say something meaningful about both. Let us take another title: "Biology and biography," with its distinct possible sections: human existence as the intersection of freedom and determinism; behavior and genetic code; genetic and social conditioning of violence; hereditary ability, and social productivity, etc. Is it possible for an individual to be competent both in biology and in the philosophy of human biography?

Even if no single individual can offer a valid response to these questions, they do not lose their meaning, for, once again, according to Ortega, it is reality that is interdisciplinary, not man. Maybe the collaboration of specialists is the only way to approach complex questions. But the level of specialization and understanding is always relative. Recognizing the spectrum of degrees of competence (the more the better), it is not necessary to be equally versed in the two fields compared. A specialist in ethics is not expected to contribute original research in biology, but he is competent for his work if he is honestly and honorably informed of current research in genetics and its implications.

We never master two fields of knowledge with equal competency; we never master even a single one. Besides, what is a field? But this fact should not paralyze our desire to clearly formulate the knowledge we have attained and its limits. To do so, one must shun naïve arrogance and recognize that knowledge is first and foremost search, not possession; research, not mastery. Writing is the best way to learn, and if, admittedly, many things that are written in order to learn should not be published, even publishing intends not only to teach, but also to ask. The association of speaking and writing with teaching is an unconscious atavism. In societies consisting of educated minorities and illiterate masses, to speak and, above all, to write was a sign of authority. The revolt of the masses brought about a new, more accurate, awareness. Today, all intellectual communication is a question, and even though it may take on the appearance of dogma because we utter it with enthusiasm, it should always be open to correction.

There is one reality, and the division of knowledge in disciplines stems from human limitation. But the disciplines can be transcended because, after all they are produced by man and for his sake. "Man is the measure of all things," said Protagoras of Abdera (490–421 B.C.). The dictum should not be interpreted as if man would conform reality as he pleases, but in the sense than man is the crossroads where reality and knowledge meet.

17. The Renaissance man

The person who is capable of seeing things from a broader perspective than those defined by the individual disciplines is given the familiar name of "Renaissance Man." Actually, only a few men of the Renaissance were known for the universality of their learning: Leone Battista Alberti (1404–72), architect, painter, educator, musician, and author of theoretical works on several arts; Leonardo da Vinci 1452–1519, painter, architect, engineer; and Pico della Mirandola (1463–94), who tried to condense in his philosophy all the sciences known in his time. But the number of luminaries who straddled several fields was always small, and even the three mentioned were only human. As much as we may admire the breadth of their learning, we admire some minds even more for their audacity in introducing new ideals of life, new political ideas, and for exposing the dubious mixture of pagan ideas within the Christian faith. Petrarch and Boccaccio launched ironic and bitter critiques against many false ideas and postures of their time. Lorenzo Valla systematically attacked and demolished the medieval system of thinking with his new method of reading the Bible. Erasmus and Luther displayed the same audacity along the path initiated by Valla. In politics, Machiavelli's *The Prince* (1513) turns upside down the political doctrine inherited from Aristotle, for whom politics was a corollary of ethics. Even though the ethical ideals might never be implemented in political praxis, the idealist theory was upheld as the truth. Machiavelli exposed the inconsistency between doctrine and praxis, described politics as it was actually practiced, and from that description he extracted the "general rules" that govern political behavior. In this way, he demolishes medieval political theory, and thereby initiates the methodology of the modern social sciences: to observe the facts, and infer *"le regole generali,"* that is, derive general laws by way of induction.

In Spain, Nebrija, the Valdés brothers, Miguel Servet, and Luis de León possessed similar intellectual strength and courage. Nebrija's critique of incompetent Latinists, which at times sounds presumptuous; the youthful audacity of Alfonso de Valdés in criticizing the Papal court and the French and English kings as traitors to Emperor Charles V; Juan de Valdés in his religious ideas, and Servet and Luis de León in their respective readings of the Bible: all of them demonstrate an independence that is quite simply subversive. The Renaissance man is universal because his intelligence is not mere knowledge or imagination, but an intelligence-power, strong in questioning tradition and in opening new directions.

This audacity spurs a zest for geographic and intellectual exploration. In this sense, what distinguishes the Renaissance man is not the breadth of his knowledge so much as the thirst for knowledge; not the possession so much as the attitude. Universal man is not one who can discourse on any subject but rather the individual who has an interest and a receptive attitude to listen to everything or at least many different subjects. The ability to listen presupposes two conditions: (a) the ethical attitude of humility by which we acknowledge our ignorance; and (b) the possession of a background which allows the listener to understand the message of the experts on a certain subject. The universality of the Renaissance man is his enthusiasm for knowing; that which the enthusiastic and dedicated teacher conserves into the autumn of his career, and keeps him young, curious, appreciative, and receptive to what is new even if he finds it unacceptable.

That universal curiosity, mental audacity, and the attention to detail produce another quality in the Renaissance man: grace-discretion. The ideal man in the Renaissance is "the courtier" whose central feature was good taste or discretion: the person who knew what to do and how to behave. The term that summarizes the attitude of the Renaissance man is *vertù*, a fusion of mental lucidity and resolve dressed in an elegant form: courtliness. The courtier is a man of the world, one who combines the art of learning with the art of living, and knows how to mix spontaneity with the perfection acquired by dedicated effort. Even the ability to tell a joke at the appropriate time rounds out the beautiful soul. In Spain this combination of qualities was given theoretical expression in Baltasar Gracián's *El Discreto* (1646). Discreet is the man of taste who creates the rule of perfection with his own conduct. Discretion was translated into German as *Urteilskraft,* that is, the power of discernment, which lies between reason and will. The "classical man" and neoclassical art are defined in the eighteenth century by the perfect equilibrium of reason, will, and sensitivity, the three powers unraveled by Kant in his three critiques.[9]

The Renaissance man became in the eighteenth century the "intellectual." Ortega y Gasset, a man with the best credentials for the title, defines "the intellectual" as follows:

> I do not refer to the poet or the technician, types of mankind that have existed throughout humanity since earliest times, and who have a very definite profile. Nor do I refer to the men in special sciences . . . I refer now to certain strange men whose condition has never been defined, equivocal men, without office or post, but never to be suborned, never submissive, who for the very reason of their incomprehensive condition have not found an adequate name *in any language* [italics in the original text].[10]

Ortega links the intellectual to the biblical prophets. In the Middle Ages and in modernity they would be the counselors who told kings the truth as opposed to the sycophants, and when societies defined themselves through their citizenry and not through the governing oligarchy, they were those capable of perceiving reality with lucidity, denouncing deviations, and proposing the correct paths to follow. The modern intellectual retains something of the prophet, but distilled through Machiavelli, Erasmus, Montaigne, and other "Renaissance men." The intellectual has broad interests, a capacity for synthesis, an ethical vocation, gracefulness of style, and original ideas on border-issues.

If the *and* pointed to a nucleus where distinct lines converge and diverge, the deepest pre-, inter-, and post-disciplinary root, from which all types of discourse radiate, is the nature of man.

9. For Gracián's influence on European aesthetics see H. G. Gadamer, *Truth and Method,* pp. 35ff. The book *Del cortesano al discreto* by Bernardo Blanco González (Madrid: Gredos, 1962) establishes a contrast between Humanism and the Baroque. For the history of aesthetics the continuity of the two styles is more faithful to history than the contrast, which refers to existential attitudes such as expectation (Renaissance) versus disillusion (Baroque).

10. *An Interpretation of Universal History,* p. 184.

IV Man: Values

Human Nature is the only Science of man, and yet has been hitherto the most neglected.

(Hume, *A Treatise*, p. 273)

18. The root

All disciplines are founded on a basic one, the theory of knowledge, which is in turn founded on a primordial root: the human being who lives and dies, and investigates how to live and what he can expect after death. Man is an abbreviated world, a physical body like the stone, vegetative like the pine tree, sensitive like the animals, and on top of all this, endowed with reason. Man can be studied from all of these perspectives: his biochemistry, heritage, genome, and behavior. When the natural sciences, especially biology, study man, they approach him as another natural being, not in his specifically human character. In the social sciences, one chooses fields of human behavior: institutions (sociology), economics, the development of individual consciousness and reaction to the environment (psychology), and the scientist designs experiments whose initial orientation conditions the results.

All these approaches are correct, but ultimately they all are based on, get their meaning from, and revert to a center that precedes them all: man seen in his specific and original character, as a nucleus or core from which all paths of research, which are the individual disciplines, arise. For this reason, all the usual concepts of our everyday language need to be redefined when they are applied to man. Nothing is more obvious, for example, than the contrast between the interior and the exterior.

Well, man happens to be an open or external interiority, and an intimate or internal openness. The distinction between interior and exterior as mutually exclusive opposites does not suit the human being. Internal and external are two diverging lines that originate and converge in a nucleus or core. The different aspects of that core, which will constitute the subjects of the different humanistic disciplines, can be called the articulation of the nucleus. Articulation is synonymous with arrangement, and conscious arrangement is language as human essence. The humanities are the rigorous study—and in that sense scientific, as we said in the introduction—of this articulated or linguistic nucleus.

The preceding consideration on the external and internal applies also to time, which is commonly understood as divided into three segments: past, present, and future. Yet, human time is also a nucleus in which the three segments originate as vectors arising from, and combined in a common matrix. The human being lives as human in a present that is constituted by the awareness of the surrounding world, and also by memory (past) and hope or projection (future). Of course, man also passes from the past to the future as segments that are cut off from the present, but this way of living in time is not specifically human; we share it with other beings. The human past is mechanically different from the present to the extent that what has been done cannot be undone. As long as the individual is consciously or unconsciously affected by the past, the past maintains its presence, but it also maintains that aspect as pure other, of something severed from the present.

Man is an articulated nucleus. As a nucleus, we always come back to it. And as articulated, we speak in linear terms, as science does, because our mind proceeds step by step and establishes "outlines," classifications. But, as we have seen with the examples of space and time, a linear analysis only makes sense when it is reinserted back into the nucleus.

In positing this nucleus as prior to all methods, we are not implying that the humanities should be learned before the other sciences, or on the side. General concepts without empirical knowledge are mostly empty generalities. For this reason, the general concepts must be studied as a prerequisite or background to understand the disciplines, but prerequisite does not imply precedence in a linear sense. Of course, the investigation of a subject presupposes a general view of it (thesis, ideology); then we enrich and transform the general notions through particular analytical research (antithesis), and finally we return to the initial general concept, now as "concrete universal," that is, illustrated by the research (synthesis).

This sounds like Hegel's dialectics in its most popular version. But in contrast to Hegel, who portrayed this process as progress—or so it has been read—the dialectics we are proposing does not take progress for granted in the process of acquiring knowledge. In misguided research, in spite of hard and meritorious work on the part of the researcher, the result will be worse than the point of departure. All human activity is dialectical in two ways: nothing is given to us without effort or mediation, and the different concepts are welded in the nucleus, or the center, which is the total human experience. But effort does not guarantee progress, and the dialectics of the nucleus is not successive but rather simultaneous: the opposing terms are not subsumed into a more advanced synthesis; on the contrary, they sustain each other in their mutual convergence and divergence. The true dialectics is the difference (Heidegger), which can be called a simultaneous, not a linear, dialectics.

There have been many definitions of man: from "little less than God" in a Psalm of David (8.6), to Pascal's "thinking reed" (*Pensées,* p. 59). The philosophical definitions are condensed in two paradigms: the rational animal (a definition inherited from the Middle Ages as translated from the Greek, "animal endowed with language"), and "Being-in-the-world" (Heidegger). In these two definitions the particular character of the humanistic discourse shines through in contrast to the discourses of the natural and the social sciences.

19. Rational animal

The classical definition of man is "rational animal." The term "animal" denotes the vegetative and sensitive faculties, habits, and activities we share with other sensitive beings, and "rational" is the "specific difference" or that element which makes us human. But even though the two words, rational and animal, appear to simply juxtapose two distinctive components, in fact they express a fusion. Reason gives to the biological component of man its specifically human dimension, while reason (or the spirit) is permeated by the material, vegetative, and sensitive components, in spite of the fact that through the spirit man can communicate with God and receive his revelations.[1]

The definition of man as a rational animal has been criticized from many corners. Ortega y Gasset considers it too optimistic and says that reason is achieved by only a few civilizations and only on rare occasions in the lives of individuals. Ortega referred, of course, to the ideal level on which reason works. He knew perfectly well that the term "rational" in the traditional definition did not refer to the way in which individuals and societies use reason, but rather to the distinctive feature of human nature, which admits of many concrete levels. He himself went to great lengths to distinguish some of these levels: pure, vital, and historical reason. In fact, "rational" in the Romance languages implies all the possible modes of human conduct, under which are also found the "irrational." In the individual human being, rationality extends from the zygote to death, dreaming, wakefulness, and to our normal state of uncertainty regarding the forces of nature and society. This state of uncertainty is a type of sleeping-wakefulness in which the nature of reason is revealed to us: a crossroads between consciousness and unconsciousness with regard to the forces that surround us.

The biographical spectrum from cell to adult consciousness, and the levels of both clarity and darkness as an adult, make up reason in the sense of a nucleus as described at the beginning of this chapter. But in science, or when we write a book about the humanities, we surpass that nucleus and embark on a rigorous and objective discourse, which is also called rational. Rigor demands that we immerse ourselves in the subject

---

1. Caro Baroja quotes J. von Uexküll's universals of human conduct from the biological perspective: response to the environment, to spoils, to the enemy, and to sexual appetites (J. Caro Baroja, "La investigación histórica," in *Razas, pueblos y linajes*, p. 23).

of study so that it is the subject that shines, and objectivity obliges us to reveal the truth even if the conclusions run contrary to our interests and desires. Reason, or rational discourse is the name we give in our everyday language to this search, which is ideally immune to personal influences. Is this ideal objectivity possible? We try to answer this question below, in section 39. For the moment we shall analyze reason in its meaning as the definition of man, prior to its application as rationality in the different types of discourse.

As human essence the word "rational" includes human consciousness in all its forms and levels. Rational or scientific discourse is a derivation of the original meaning, but not in a mechanistic sense, since scientific discourse educates and thus influences the very reason that practices that discourse. Scientific reason stands in opposition to spontaneity, sensitivity, choice, and faith. Reason as human essence, on the other hand, includes these seemingly opposed functions. If reason is surreptitiously identified with the specific rationalist approach required by the scientific or rigorous study, then distinctions emerge in which reason seems opposed to other human experiences. This misconception leads to polar opposites such as reason and faith, reason and sensitivity, where the *and* has an adversative rather than a copulative meaning. Antonio Machado dramatized the opposition between reason and feeling in the following verses:

Reason Says:	Let's find the Truth.
The Heart:	A vain effort.
Reason:	Ha, who can achieve truth!
The Heart:	Vanity; truth is hope.
Reason answers:	You are lying.
The Heart replies:	You, reason, are the liar,
	For you say what you don't feel.
Reason:	We will never understand each other, Heart.
The Heart:	We shall see.[2]

2. A. Machado, *Poesías completas*, Poem CXXXVII, section vii. In *Poesía y prosa*. Edited by Oreste Macrì (Madrid: Espasa-Calpe, 1989), II, pp. 585–86.

The final response of the heart: "We shall see," upholds the original unity of reason that feels and the heart that sees, a unity already highlighted by Pascal in his famous aphorism: "The heart has reasons of which reason knows nothing."[3] Clearly the battle between reason and the perceptive lucidity of the heart is a brotherly strife of twins in the womb of reason as human nature. Again, the vectors are articulated and made possible in the nucleus of the sphere.

As human nature, reason is a constant reality, habitual, prior to all other states of being and concrete actions. The states of reason include the period of gestation and childhood until we reach self-conscious maturity, the moments of most lucid consciousness, and consciousness shrouded by periods of illness or sleep. And because "life is a dream"— which is to say that we reach a high state of lucidity only in exceptional moments—reason is the daily situation in which we allow ourselves to be carried along by what others do or say, or by obligations that, resulting from free commitments, have become routine. Reason usually lives within the "routine" of daily life, in a state of "sleeping-waking."[4] Only the first act of accepting a commitment is reflective or completely conscious, and even then, not always. The proof is how often we distance ourselves from our own decisions and promises.

Reason as human essence, when fully developed, is self-reflection, a dialogue with ourselves. The mind is at any given moment open to two objects: to the one we are studying in our conversation or research, and to itself. Reflection converts us into the object of our own analysis, "to become the issue of our questioning" as St. Augustine said. Self-reflection is the basis of irony and of human biography. Irony is the reflective moment of consciousness that allows for self-criticism. When we are in a state of enthusiasm, be it out of love, admiration or hate, we do not keep the distance that makes it possible to criticize or accept an object lucidly. For this reason, the individual who is totally satisfied with himself does not accept irony, and religion does not admit of irony at all.

3. Pascal, *Pensées*, n. 423, p. 154.
4. These ideas are based on Heidegger's philosophical paradigm. See *Being and Time*, chap. IV.

The believer only prays before God, asks for something, and tries to understand His mysterious ways, but does not criticize. God is always right.

Through the experience of our own development we learn that human reason is not an abstract faculty but one conditioned by man's biography. Because we develop over time, we devote a few years of our lives specifically to education, and the rest to practicing a profession, although education never ends. Given this biographical condition of reason, a theory of the humanities must weigh the importance of a discipline or field of knowledge in abstract terms, the diffusion it merits in view of its relevance for the educational of the students, and the moment at which it should be included in the curriculum.

Reason as consciousness performs its acts in a context of assumptions and consequences. This awareness of the context climaxes in the awareness of our ignorance; reason is always conscious of its unconsciousness. Freud, as is well known, identifies human "truth" with a spontaneous "subconscious," which always influences and occasionally determines rational decisions. In contrast to Freud, a comprehensive view of reason sees it as the crossroads in which the subconscious is revealed to us in its fleeing and in its opacity. We know how much we do not know. That is why reason finds itself limited, searching, in the presence of the absence.[5]

Individual reason is conscious of its social dimension. To live, even in a purely biological world, means to depend. We are conceived and raised, two forms of dependency. Self-consciousness is that which is distinctly human and, therefore, solitude within society. This will appear paradoxical only to someone who conceives of the distinction between solitude and society in a mechanistic manner. In our idea of the articulated nucleus, it is just another example of how the linear concepts turn on themselves and return to the human core or point. This apparent paradoxical core is the locus of freedom, which in its philosophical di-

---

5. "Reason's last step is the recognition that there are an infinite number of things which are beyond it" (Pascal, *Pensées*, n. 188, p. 85).

mension is not the ability to make decisions, but rather the consciousness with which we accept, tolerate, or reject an inevitable or evitable reality. We make decisions based on this primordial dimension. Freedom, as reflective consciousness, or reason, is the original nucleus on which acceptance, rejection, and decision or choice, are founded.

Memory is not just a faculty of reason, it is reason itself in its self-perception as biography, that is, as a point that is the condensation of a line or horizon. By simply looking at houses, land, and forests, we find something that existed prior to ourselves: we find the past. The human being is always anchored in a society with a certain degree of historical development, a patrimony that conforms the individual even if he rejects it. Appropriating the opportunities afforded by that society, the individual engages in his rational pursuits, including pure science. Thus reason is historical in its essence, and pure rationality is founded on the historical dimension of reason.

The difference between our cold attitude in research and our emotion in the presence of a beloved person has made popular the rigid distinction between reason and feelings, as we have seen in Antonio Machado's verses. But reason is sensitive in its very constitution. If reason is stripped of its affective moment it gets confused with rational discourse, not realizing that the supposed coldness of rational discourse or science is just another form of feeling: enthusiasm for truth. Emotion and affection are not attachments to an aseptic reason, but constitutive moments of reason. Of course, emotions may become completely irrational, but that irrationality is yet another variant of reason: when man is "beside himself."

Another popular distinction, which once again converts the human pomegranate into rigid conceptual categories, is that of reason as opposed to choice. This dichotomy was codified in the scholastic distinction between intellect and will. A mechanistic distinction sometimes leads us to consider irrational certain decisions or attitudes, such as love. But experience proves that the strongest feeling of love is the one based on the reflective appreciation of the beloved person. One may feel temporary infatuation toward an individual whom we do not appreciate, but it is difficult to persevere in love toward that individual. Thus, Spinoza's expression "intellectual love," far from being a paradox, defines the kind of love corresponding to human reason. It is not the colorless coexistence with a self-sacrificing spouse, but rather, the conscious acceptance and enjoyment of another presence in total openness and trust, which Unamuno expressed in his verse "You, Concha, are my habit." Nothing is more intense in man than that which he accepts in all lucidity, including love. Any other enthusiasm is fickle and, as a result, weak.

The last polarity within reason, whose two elements have been generally regarded as opposed to one another, is reason vs. faith. Unamuno highlighted this contrast to the point of making the two incompatible. That is why, for him, man's existence is "the tragic sense of life," in which faith wants to believe in God and immortality, while reason undermines faith. On the other hand, Ortega y Gasset in his essay "Ideas and Beliefs" (1934) affirmed that the ideas—scientific or popular—with which we react to things are in turn founded on convictions that are prior to them and taken for granted. Ortega calls these underlying convictions beliefs. Rational discourse is founded, therefore, on human reason, as a sphere that includes faith.[6] Faith is not rational in the sense of admitting logical proof, but it is reasonable. For example, we all walk down the street pretty sure that we will not be shot; acts of terrorism are possible because of that assumption or belief. Relationships with family and friends are based on trust, which is why we are vulnerable to deception and betrayal. These examples display the nature of reason in its global sense as a nucleus of trust on which the acceptance of rational propositions is founded.

One specific form of belief is the religious: faith in the existence of God, in the immortality of the soul, and in the dogmas of a particular

---

6. "It is better to leave this term—ideas—to designate everything in our lives which appears to be the result of our intellectual activity. But beliefs come to us with the opposite features. We do not arrive at them after a labor of understanding, rather, they already operate in our background when we start thinking about something" (*Obras completas*, V, 385).

creed. This is not the primordial belief of which Ortega speaks; religious faith is the discourse of reason that consciously commits and captures the whole person. This discourse is an idea, but so well rooted that it comes to be the pedestal upon which, and the atmosphere within which, man finds himself settled (faith). There is no true opposition between reason and faith, but rather conflicts between the faith that affirms the existence of God, and the faith that rejects Him; or possible conflicts between scientific and theological theses that might appear mutually incompatible at a given time in history. In many cases the conflict does not arise from the theses themselves, but from the conclusions that some individuals draw for ideological motives. Darwin did not deny the guiding hand of Providence behind the evolution of species, but materialist biologists have used the doctrine of evolution as proof against the existence of God. This corollary was not in Darwin's work.

The preceding analysis lets reason appear as a sphere and nucleus from which subsequent distinctions emerge whose terms seem mutually incompatible but are not. The *and* in phrases such as reason and feeling, reason and love, reason and choice, reason and faith, has a binding function; it is a meeting point, not one of contrast, and certainly not one of contradiction. In fact, the opposition between reason and feeling does not contrast two different attitudes of man but two different reactions of reason in reference to time. If we decide something based on emotion, "without thinking," it is still reason that makes the decision, but on the spur of the moment, instead of pondering the pros and cons of the decision. The contrast between reason and emotion in this case is a contrast between an unmediated act and one performed in the context of projects and values in our life. But the temporal condition of man's mind is better understood from the definition of man as existence or "Being-in-the-world." The discussion of man as a rational animal leads to the idea of reason as an articulated nucleus, where all the oppositions that have been mentioned—and others that may have escaped my attention—gather in their common cradle.

20. *Being-in-the-world*

Heidegger wrote his book *Being and Time* (1927), following Husserl's idea of phenomenology, which in Husserl's words, aimed at the intuition of the essence of things. Taking this motto as his point of departure, Heidegger affirms: "The essence of man lies in his existence."[7] This sentence means: man's nature lies in finding himself surrounded by other human beings and by the many things of the world, having to grow ("make himself") in response to the opportunities and limitations offered by his society. According to Heidegger, the traditional definition of man as the rational animal places the accent on his animal character, even if the adjective "rational" added to the noun "animal" purports to highlight man's specific nature. Once the animal character is placed at the center of reference, says Heidegger, the possibility of defining man in terms of his humanity is jeopardized. In fact, Heidegger eliminates the words "man" and "life," and substitutes for them *Dasein* ("Being-there," open being) and "existence," respectively. The substitution intends to relegate to their proper place the biological connotations of the terms "man" and "life." For Heidegger, human life is essentially biography; the biological dimension must be understood as a means that facilitates or hinders man's growth as human being.

Heidegger defines existence as "being-in-the-world." The hyphens are necessary because we have to use linear concepts to express a nuclear reality (a point in space and time) in which all elements converge and originate. "World" in Heidegger is not the totality of external things that we perceive through our senses, imagine, or yearn for in our feelings; it is the framework of origin, reference, and purpose in which we find ourselves inserted; the reality that makes its presence felt and at the same time withdraws as the background of all the things that we use and know in our existence. The insertion in the world, as defined by Heidegger, provides the possibility for the discovery of concrete things in their respective usefulness as tools for our goals. Being-in-the-world,

7. *Being and Time*, section 9.

therefore, means that man is inherently open, not a closed ego who eventually opens up to an external milieu. Man does not first discover things as objects of contemplation, and then act upon them; instead, he finds himself in a pragmatic world of activity and relationships, and pure contemplation is but one way to implement this pragmatic constitution. Once things are isolated as subjects of pure perception, they can be studied in scientific discourse, but we can understand them only if we do not forget their original roots within the human world as a whole. This is the philosophical background of what we said in the introduction about science and legitimate alternative forms of knowledge.

Any effort to close ourselves off from the world will always fail, because to close ourselves presupposes the essential openness that constitutes us.[8] For this reason, one cannot apply to man the rigid categories of the external as opposed to the internal, or the subjective versus the objective. In the words of Ortega y Gasset, man is self-absorption in his aperture *(ensimismamiento en la alteración)* and vice-versa. The subjective would be the purely arbitrary. My personal ideas, insofar as they are an effort to capture and share reality, are objective. I (subject) am saying what I believe must be said, what imposes itself (object) upon me. This idea of Heidegger's undermines some rigid distinctions and dichotomies that have a specious clarity in philosophical texts. I see the following:

(a) Person versus relationship. Since Aristotle, the category of relationship has been considered an accident; but it so happens that the human being is a person to the extent that he or she is related.

(b) Formal versus final cause. After Aristotle, the form of a thing was called its internal cause, and its purpose (final cause) external. Man's existence is the purpose of self-realization, thus the goal is an integral moment of man's form.

(c) Being versus duty. Our life as biography is primarily the obligation to grow and fulfill ourselves, and thus, to search. Therefore, the el-

8. "Human life is a reality in which everything is internal, even that which we call external" (Ortega, *An Interpretation of Universal History*, p. 12).

ement of obligation is inscribed in our being. Only because we have this structure can our life be a failure.

Similar considerations apply, as we have indicated, to (d) subject versus object, (e) interiority versus exteriority, and (f) substance versus time, or permanence versus historical change.

Our essential openness is being with others. Again, the ego is not a monad that opens up, but rather somebody who needs others, counts on them, and takes care of or neglects them. This social dimension of man becomes concrete in three different forms: institutions, the group, and private life. Beginning at his birth man finds himself in institutions, from the tribe to the state, from the church to the economic structure, and most importantly, in the language-culture he inherits. These institutions constitute what is the predominantly social, in the sense of most impersonal. Society imposes itself on the individual, but not completely, for it is in turn influenced and transformed by individuals.

On a more immediate plane, man belongs to a group: family, friends, colleagues at work—in general, the sum of the individuals who enter his life and whom he recognizes by name. In the face of institutions and groups the individual asserts his freedom, which is always shaped and bound by his dependency on them. Freedom is freedom insofar as it is limited by this dependency.

Man's world, which we have defined as the framework of origin, reference, and purpose in which he finds himself, is primordially constituted by time. As physical and animated entities, we are in space; but as human beings, we are in a house, a city, a state, in front of a computer, that is to say, in structures of meaning created by man and referred to man. We are in a historical space: time. Even nature, as the milieu of life and as landscape, object of our use, abuse, admiration or fear, is not for us humans what it is for the animals, but rather a challenge or a resource for our existence. The space belonging to man as man is history.

History means to exist in a society that offers us some limited opportunities within which we have to determine the unique, unrepeatable, and irreplaceable mission that constitutes us, according to what is offered. In order to be aware of that mission we look to the past and we try to open up a future for ourselves. But past and future are condensed in an open present that is projected to the most remote past by our memory and into the future by our more or less concrete aspirations.

For being inherently open to society, to history and to the concrete things that surround him, man is the center in which society, history, and nature become condensed and articulated. The language we speak, the mission we assume, and our place in the face of natural forces constitute a meeting point of two magnitudes: one, the ego, and the other, those forces—language, society-history, and nature—that both conform and condition it. The truth lies neither in the "whole" that eliminates the ego, nor in the ego in opposition to the whole, but rather at the meeting point of these two magnitudes. Man is the center that deploys centrifugal lines. These lines are the discourses of the disciplines, while the analysis of the meeting point of the linear discourses—of the difference— constitutes the humanistic discourse.

When speaking of reason and sensitivity I have said that, at bottom, the issue revolves around two ways in which reason relates to time. The vision of human life as biography allows us better to understand this point with a brief analysis of the experiences of spontaneity, sincerity, and mediation. In man, spontaneity generally does not exist. Our spontaneous reactions to an event are mediated by our education and by the values that continually shape our life. If I am convinced that the death penalty is barbaric, when I contemplate the body of a victim of terrorism my immediate reaction is no longer to demand the death of the terrorists. The spontaneity of any given moment in our lives is the result of the training undergone in life itself. But is not that training a repression of sincerity? This is Freud's idea in his *Civilization and Its Discontents.*[9] Yet, we are not sincere when we simply follow our first impulses; we are sincere when we behave as we believe we should. My true ego is not the one that surrenders to a momentary impulse, but the one that I want it to be. This is proven by the fact that if I do something spontaneously for

9. Freud, S. *Civilization and Its Discontents*, VII, p. 70.

which I should be embarrassed the rest of my life, my sincere ego is the embarrassed one, not the one who performed the shameful act.

I think that what I have just said is true, but not the whole truth. The one who did the shameful act was also me, and if it caused damage to another person, I am responsible for it. The whole truth would seem to be this: the pairing of spontaneity-mediation cannot be understood in a mechanistic way; in man's life everything is both mediated and spontaneous at the same time. Human existence is shaped by three elements that are relatively constant: ability, circumstance, and ideals. Ability includes our inherited way of being, our intelligence and creativity, and everything that heredity, education, and the environment in which we grew allow us to contribute at any given moment. If "ability" epitomizes everything that is achieved and accumulated from the past up to a certain moment, "circumstance" implies everything that surrounds and influences us in the present; and the ideals are our aspirations for the future, which range from concrete goals to vague yearnings. On the basis of these three elements we perform concrete acts that are leaps, conditioned but never determined by the constant elements or coordinates. Hence the fact that sometimes the most dignified individual commits a shameful act, and that we are disappointed by best friends or someone close to us. When we are ashamed of our own acts or disappointed by a person we admire, it is because one of us has done something that could not be expected from our ability, circumstance, and ideals. The imbalance between the coordinates and the spontaneous leap of each action defines man's life as a difference—crossroads, meeting point, struggle—of steady convictions and spontaneous leaps, and vice versa.

The definitions of man as a rational animal and as "being-in-the-world" are founded on the two fundamental paradigms of Western philosophy. The first, extending from Plato to Nietzsche, began with the dualism of subject and object and tried to find the connecting links between the two. After the first dichotomy (subject-object), several more were discovered, putting reason on one side, and sensitivity, memory, will, and belief on the other. We have tried to both explain and deconstruct these polarities. In some obscure way, the philosophers always took for granted that those dichotomies were founded on an underlying unity, but that unity was forgotten as soon as the philosopher took the duality subject-object as the point of departure for his thought. Ortega y Gasset, for example, wrote in 1914: "I am I and my circumstance." After Heidegger's definition of man as "Being-in-the-world" (1927), Ortega claimed that he had anticipated Heidegger by thirteen years. But since he never defined the "and," he showed a sort of dissatisfaction with the traditional paradigm, but never surpassed it. Heidegger's analysis of "being-in" as *Befindlichkeit* (finding oneself; existentially affected consciousness), understanding, being fallen, and articulation in language[10] is the analysis of that *and* in which subject and object are fused before they separate as opposites. In this way, the traditional definition of man retains its validity as long as it is inserted in Heidegger's existential definition or model.

In the two models man is a nucleus which, being aware of itself, creates a discourse appropriate to his nature: a spiral discourse that delves into man as a discursive subject, and into the nature of the discourse itself. The obscure perception that all linear or scientific discourse is founded on a unifying root (the traditional *a priori* of the philosophers) explains a constant feature of Western thought that has been reflected in several fields: the prestige of the "golden mean." In ethics, Aristotle defined "virtue" as the search for the mean between extremes. In aesthetics, the "discreet" incarnates intelligence, will, and sensitivity in an ideal equilibrium. Perfection in art was associated for centuries with balanced structure ("proportion"). And in great measure the operation of our mind throughout history, from the most banal disagreement to the deepest philosophy, usually begins by describing two extremes, between which one hopes to find the middle ground. The appropriate description of this nucleus in which opposites are reconciled in an *and* that is at the same time a copulative and an adversative conjunction, constitutes the humanistic discourse.

10. *Being and Time.* Ch. V.

21. Humanistic discourse

The discourse about the human being is generally clad in a series of polarities, the most pervasive of which are: subject-object; reason and conscious attitudes seemingly opposed to it, as analyzed in section 19; external-internal; action-passion; emission-reception; eternity-time; mastery of a subject versus searching and research; truth-perspective; consciousness-opacity; universality-concrete situation. The dashes or the *and* in these cases are the locus of encounter, of the "difference."[11] In the pair time-eternity, human time is a present instant in which are condensed the memory of the past, the awareness of our circumstances, and goals for the future. Unamuno called this condensation of time in every present "the eternal tradition."

Now it is possible to justify and clarify the statements on humanistic discourse made in the first chapter. From man as a nucleus and a point in contrast to linear discourses, the first feature of the humanities is that, instead of progressing linearly, they stay in place assimilating and enriching a traditional legacy. Progress in the humanities is a spiral that starts from a center, rising or diving to higher degrees of reflection, but always revolving around that nucleus. In humanistic knowledge there is no progress but difference, a sort of Moses' bush perennially burning without being consumed. Unamuno correctly perceived this condition of the humanities; for that reason he contrasted the concepts not in dialectical but in "polemical" form (Unamuno's term). Instead of resolving the opposite concepts in an ensuing synthesis, he sustained the polarity by highlighting the mutual imbrication of the opposites.

For Dilthey the discourse of the *Geisteswissenschaften* is characterized by the effort at understanding, while the natural sciences aim at explanation. I have used the German term *Geisteswissenschaften* (not human sciences) because, although they do not correspond strictly to humanistic disciplines, the intent to understand as the defining feature of their

---

11. There are also, however, pairs in which the *and* has a disjunctive function, such as in "good and evil." Man is capable of only a limited good, but the limitation cannot be equated with evil.

discourse does apply to the humanities as I have defined them. It is possible to find fault with the distinction between understanding and explanation, since there cannot be any other purpose to explanation but understanding, as is the case in the natural sciences. But the terms must be understood in accordance with Dilthey's intention and context. To understand literature or history is to display some concepts or events, and to discover their similarities and differences, and their mutual implication so that they explain each other. In the humanities understanding means the reconstruction of what Dilthey calls the *Zusammenhang*, that is the mutual interplay of related concepts and events so that each concept or event acquires its specific meaning in that interplay. The Baroque style, for example, manifests itself differently in the different arts, but with some common parameters and within a common tendency. It is not that literature explains painting or vice versa, but rather, that features of one art are analogous to features of the other, so that each art contributes to justify the general rubric we call Baroque. Explanation, on the other hand, typical of the sciences, is the discovery of a previous cause that explains the theme studied as its effect. The idea can be exemplified with Freud's explanation of the different types of love.

Love is an experience of enjoyment in the life of the beloved, a perpetual dialogue with her, a generous attitude to the point of giving up life for her, pleasure in her pleasure. If the beloved is not a relative and meets certain requirements of health and age, the happiness of mutual enjoyment may express itself in sexual embrace. From this human point of view, love is a form of language (one expresses love) and depends on our psychic equilibrium, since it is a pleasure that excludes all selfishness and vanity; therefore, it sometimes may call for sacrifice. The sexual magnitude in love is either secondary, or it doesn't exist at all, as in the case of love for one's children or for a sick wife. Even in moments of health, the sexual is nothing more than the culmination of a sincere dialogue. This description of the varieties of love is phenomenology. Freud, on the other hand, explains all those varieties as a "scientist," by postulating a primary libido that develops into different manifestations, from rape to mystical contemplation. In this case scientific discourse flees from the complex phenomenon in order to give a unitary explanation. And even if the science were correct, we still must at least describe the different types of love. The humanistic vision tries to disentangle love in all its complexity, while the explanation steps out of the phenomenon to locate its presumed origin.

The name given by Edmund Husserl to this effort of describing a reality from all possible angles is phenomenology. Husserl defined this word as "intuition of the essence of things." In the Germanic and Romance languages the term "intuition" connotes immediate impression or spontaneous hunch. For that reason Heidegger replaced the term intuition with "hermeneutics," which means mediated intuition, a result of all the effort we put into knowing something. My method in this book is mediated intuition: a personal vision willing to correct and to open itself to more precise analysis of the very theses it proposes. I show and display, and my proof is the invitation to the reader to see for himself if he can agree. A well-developed phenomenology will discover that even the theses that look most objective include personal vision as an ingredient of their objectivity. Hence the three characteristics of humanistic discourse that we announced before: holistic approach, the subject in all its aspects, and the ethical character imbedded in the epistemological analysis.

22. *The essay*

Art and creative literature display truth by focusing on man as the nucleus or core that precedes the partial aspects studied by the sciences. In one way or another, literature and art, from sculpture to film, interest us because in their works and texts we perceive truth in a broad sense. Hence we should not dismiss as totally unfounded the popular saying that one can learn more psychology in Shakespeare and Cervantes than in a textbook of that discipline. The implication of this saying is that in literary works we perceive man in a search for identity and awareness before that search breaks up into disparate fields of research or into particular discourses. However, it is equally clear that the literary work cannot provide the articulation or systematic picture of man in his different facets. Except for one genre: the essay.

The essay is the genre that explores the difference. It is analytical, rigorous, systematic, and objective, like a philosophical or scientific work, but it passes its objective visions through the filter of the author, and in this sense, it is intuitive. Intuition, that is, hermeneutics, must be the result of thorough study. "The essay," said Ortega y Gasset, "is rigorous knowledge without explicit proofs."[12] The essay does not follow a linear discourse; instead, it aspires to the global vision, to encompass the sphere that can in turn become the source of new scientific or linear discourses. In fact, the essay was the original expression of the modern social sciences. Montaigne gave the title *Essais* (1580) to the book in which he introduced the genre, but did not use the name to designate the particular essays, which he called "chapters." Montaigne ostensibly did not realize that he was inventing a new literary genre, he was simply presenting *"les essais de ma vie,"* the "experiences" of his own existence. "Essay" referred to the author's "fortunes and trials," not to the genre as such. In the prologue Montaigne advises his readers not to waste their time with a book that only contains personal opinions. But those opinions were not subjective; instead, they looked at human behavior and described it in a new, lucid manner. When the personal vision invites the reader to see things as they are in themselves, it is objective study.

Since the subjects to which Montaigne turned his attention were not part of the disciplines studied at the university, this type of knowledge had no prestige or recognizable place in a school curriculum. In this vein Feijoo (1676–1764) said that many of the issues broached in his *Teatro Crítico* "are not studied in any department, either because they do not belong to one, or because they are equally the purview of several of them."[13] And yet, those analyses of human behavior that were not disciplines of any curriculum gave birth to political science from Machiavelli onward; to sociology, economics, esthetics, and psychology. Essays be-

---

12. *Meditaciones del Quijote,* in *Obras completas,* I, p. 318.
13. *Teatro crítico universal* (1726). Ed. by F. de Onís (Madrid: Espasa-Calpe, 1968), I, p. 80.

came sciences when the personal visions of those human phenomena were subjected to analysis and to objective methods of research.

The essay is usually defined as "a short literary composition dealing with a single subject, usually from a personal point of view and without attempting completeness" (Webster). "Short": Many books in the eighteenth century were called "essays" (e.g. Locke), and Montaigne's essay 12 in book II can also be published as an independent book. "Dealing with a single subject": Kant's *Critique of Pure Reason* and Hegel's *Aesthetics* deal with a single subject, too. "Usually from a personal point of view": I think this is the cornerstone of the definition, provided "personal" is not confused with "subjective." The essayist is a person in search of objectivity. "Without attempting completeness": this note presents the essay as a provisional exploration without serious commitment to the explanation of a subject—the common perception of the genre.

Against this common perception history proves that the essay was the genre that explored psychological, ethical, and social subjects before these subjects were approached with scientific method. The essay should therefore be defined, not by the ingenuity or intention of its authors, and much less by its extension, but as the type of discourse imposed by certain themes. And after psychology, ethics, economics, and social life became subjects of scientific research, the essay remains alive as the pre-, inter-, and post-disciplinary genre, the one that brings all knowledge back to the source from which it arises: man.

23. Values

The vision of man proposed in this chapter helps us to see the extent to which the humanities are concerned with the study of values. Even though scientists are obliged to pursue truth and veracity, the analysis of truth itself and the implications of veracity are not their subject. It may be argued that in many cases the humanities do not examine or promote values; we may point to many literary texts that evoke an enervating pessimism, injustice, or bourgeois complacency. But even the drift toward negative values demonstrates that literature dwells in their realm and cannot ignore them.

We tend to conceive of values as a column of duties or desirable ideals that runs parallel to the column of rational discourse about reality. In a study of my desk, for example, science would concentrate on the components of the desk. Moving beyond science, one may note that the desk has been made by carpenters and its wood logged by other workers. This awareness adds a social dimension to the concept of desk, and if it matches the decoration of a well-organized room, it exhibits an aesthetic dimension in addition to the scientific and social ones. Science, ethics, and aesthetics were the three branches of modern culture, according to the Neo-Kantian Hermann Cohen.

Nevertheless, from the point of view of man as the center, the ethical and aesthetic elements cannot be abstracted from the reality *desk,* if we want to know it as it is. Man exists in a world of meaning (in the sense described in section 20) which comprises the scientific, the ethical, and the aesthetic dimensions, and it is this primordial nucleus that subsequently breaks up in to the rational, the ethical, or the aesthetic discourse. The decision to focus on the rational activity relegates values to a secondary level, but the rational discourse continues to rest on them. This is why values serve as the foundation of science, although they are not its primary focus of attention. At the same time, when the humanist turns to the consideration of values, he is not adding a pillar of good will to aseptic rationality, but merely highlighting the ethical and aesthetic dimensions contained in the very effort to understand.

In popular language, we have three words that express the original fusion of rationality and values: attention, consideration, and understanding. The social prestige of the courtier, the nobleman, and the magnanimous individual is evident because they muster: a generous intelligence that anticipates the needs of their fellow men (attention); an open mind that puts what is said and done in the most positive light, and appreciates the other, not as superior or inferior, but just as another (consideration); and a maturity that recognizes and accepts human limitation and error (understanding). Adjectives such as "reasonable," "attentive," "considerate," and "understanding" connote the same fusion of the epistemological and the ethical dimensions of knowledge before the distinction between reality and duty becomes entrenched. A reasonable person is not the one who happens to be a genius in mathematics, but rather the one who is capable of attention, consideration, and understanding.

It is commonly accepted that values change in time and that in our age, given the fast pace of life and technology, they are changing still faster. Another common view is that, with regard to values, our society is in a state of anarchy, or perhaps of complete amorality. But these attitudes do not sustain scrutiny. In the individual, the primary value is personal balance: to know what we can aspire to and realistically expect, and to have the means to develop our potential in full. Has this ideal died out, when both society and state today offer more means than ever to develop the creative abilities of their citizens? Ideally the individual reaches a stage in which he becomes conscious of his accomplishments and limits, accepting himself with both. This is the stage that may safely be called maturity, in which we take definitive positions toward certain values. With regard to some of them, such as the right to life, the personal position is the free acceptance of a rule that we consider binding for all human beings, whereas values linked to the cultural traditions and personal education of the individual cannot be imposed on others. "The old man, said the Latin poet Horace, is querulous, nostalgic of the past, and critical and censorious of the young."[14] At this stage maturity turns into fixed ideas, an unmistakable symptom of decrepitude.

On the social level there are basic values that have not changed, nor can they change: loyalty or truthfulness, solidarity or charity, and other values derived from them, such as attention, sensitivity, good manners, and kind words. No amount of wealth or power can bring or replace the pleasure of feeling at ease among family and friends or in a conversation in which one does not have to come out smarter than our partner. The secret to maturity and social success lies in seeing and appreci-

14. *Ars poetica*, vv. 173–74.

ating the other as another, and immaturity is to worry about whether he is inferior or superior to us. Vain pride and servility are probably the worst obstacles to human communication.

The pretense that our society has lost its sense of values is frivolous. The awareness of basic human rights and our striving toward them; the fact that educational opportunities are available to individuals at every level of society; and the respect for different races, religions and cultures place our time far above any previous era. To be sure, there is still a great deal of racism, but only in the private forum that cannot be reached by legislation. In public, what remains of discrimination and racism is what remains of the past. And what is still immoral in our time is what we fail to do to advance freedom, equality, and fraternity for our own society and the rest of the world.

It is not values that have changed but ways of behavior that in an un-reflective way were once considered immutable. The Catholic Church has not changed its doctrine on divorce, and for those who believe in matrimony as a sacrament, divorce is not licit. What has changed is the respect for personal choice, and therefore, even those of us who think that divorce should not happen still spend time with divorced friends. The partnership of gays and lesbians may be legalized for the purposes of inheritance or social benefits; they may even be considered civil marriages; the only word that is not appropriate for them is "matrimony," if it means a Catholic sacrament.

In any case, with the state no longer regulating many aspects of conduct in which it previously intervened, we have been left with a freedom that is unsettling, because it calls for responsible decisions on our part. The stress of having to be on the front line in order to prosper professionally, the loss of the social impact of religion, and the healthy pluralism that shatters the familiarity of the old homogenous and predictable society, arouse the impression that everything is in flux and crisis. But nostalgia does not make sense. The good old days, with all sorts of discrimination entrenched in both legislation and philosophy, were worse than the present. And even if they were better, they are not ours. The crisis of our time must make a difference as the crossroads in our search for greater veracity and solidarity.

V *The Crisis*

❧ *No young scientist of any talent would feel that he isn't wanted or that his work is ridiculous, as did the hero of* Lucky Jim, *and in fact, some of the disgruntlement of Amis and his associates is the disgruntlement of the under-employed arts graduate.*

(C. P. Snow, *The Two Cultures*, p. 18)

24. *Symptoms*

The crisis of the humanities has two basic aspects, one that is specific to the humanistic disciplines, and a second one that extends to a general crisis of values, culture, and education. In the specific area, the humanities were never the most important branch in the European university. Until the eighteenth century they were grouped together with the sciences in the Faculty of Arts, which was the equivalent of modern high school, where the student obtained the basic preparation for the lucrative schools: theology, law, and medicine. In all of Europe schools of engineering and of technical studies were founded during the eighteenth century as independent institutions, sometimes attached to, but not as an integral part of the universities.

In the nineteenth century there arose a new conception of the university that created the field of political and economic sciences and transformed the technical schools into university fields. It became increasingly problematic for modern minds to consider theology as a "science," and the new social sciences introduced new subjects and methods of research that shattered the traditional university. The new fields certainly did not relegate to the back burner law and medicine, which were also traditional fields but conferred social prestige and economic power. It was then that the humanities—linguistics, literature, and history, since philosophy and theology came from the old curriculum—were introduced as independent fields of research and teaching.

The common background of the "moral and political sciences," including the humanities, was the positivistic method. Positivism is a general notion whose many variables share the principle that all knowledge must be based on experience. Even thinkers like Dilthey, who attempted to surpass positivism, did so, not by shunning experience but in the name of a more accurate experience than the one posited by hard-core positivists. Thus the age of positivism and of the spread of modern science was also the golden age of the humanities. Linguistics, classical philology, and the vernacular literatures, in both their learned and popular manifestations, became the focus of rigorous study. As the natural sciences progressively severed their traditional amalgamation with philosophy, the latter recognized itself fundamentally as theory of knowledge, ethics, aesthetics, and "natural theology"—the effort to answer with pure reason the question about the existence of God and the sense of human life.

While the monumental works of philologists and historians all over Europe raised the humanities from the ancillary role they had played in the old faculties of arts, discussions immediately ensued about the two questions we are analysing here: criteria of knowledge, and usefulness of such study. Today, as we have seen (chapters I and II), the idea of the humanities can be outlined with relative clarity, delineating a field of rigorous research, and using phenomenology as the ideal method. Rephrasing what was said in section 21, phenomenology intends to be, not a particular method, but the attitude and art of looking at things so that they present themselves as they are, allowing reality to manifest itself, and keeping in check as far as possible the subjective wishes of the scholar and the limited perspectives imposed by the specialized methods. While the specialist who looks from his own perspective or interest selects particular aspects of reality, the phenomenological position intends to embrace that reality in its fullness. This approach, far from invalidating the findings of research on specific questions, learns from them and appreciates their real value by integrating them into the whole. For this reason, the scientific approach cannot be in and of itself a rival of humanistic research. To the extent that the latter is a form of discourse, it is also a method (the universal is also particular); but to the extent that it reverts to the nucleus while taking advantage of the discoveries of science, it is the revelation of truth.[1]

Even when the theoretical question about humanistic knowledge is answered, there still lingers the question of usefulness. The introduction of the new sciences that responded to urgent—though perhaps not more important—human necessities displaced first the old liberal arts from the central position they occupied when there was practically no science, as then they displaced the modern humanities, in spite of their acclaimed contributions in history and philology. Also, since the scientific laboratories demand more money than the humanities, the resources applied to the sciences far outweigh the ones earmarked for the latter. In our time scientific research is done in cooperation with industry, thus the university becomes more tied to the demands of society and, even if the resources of the humanities increase in absolute terms, they decline in proportion to other departments of the university. Thus, the first symptom of crisis in the humanities is their decreasing visibility in the contemporary university vis-à-vis the broadening of the applied sciences (social studies, management studies, labor relations, and others) and technology (computer science, electrical engineering, biotechnology, etc.).

But, of course, no reasonable humanist will deplore the spread of these studies or the cooperation of industry and the university. Industry must be constantly innovating, so big companies are not only agents of production but also of education. Although it has always been necessary to keep abreast of innovations in order to remain competent in one's profession, today the changes are much faster and this fact forces all institutions involved in research to assess their educational function.

1. On this point I follow the appropriate title of the book by Hans-Georg Gadamer, *Truth and Method.*

In theory it seems easy to reserve for the university the education in general principles while leaving specific applications to the workplace. But, while this distinction is in some way valid, in practice it does not hold, since theory and praxis do not relate as knowledge and application in a linear manner, but in a circular one in which technical practice frequently leads to revisions of theory. The university must respond to the needs of society and should open itself up to them and take advantage of them for their possible contribution to technical progress, which is scientific progress.

The contemporary university, based on the coexistence of what are called educational and vocational studies, was largely inspired by the work of Andrew Dickson White, first president of Cornell University, founded in 1865. During the 1855–56 academic year, White had studied Egyptology, the history of Greece and Italy, modern general history, and physical geography at the University of Berlin. When the State of New York and Ezra Cornell's personal generosity put him in charge of Cornell University, he tried to imitate the Berlin model, but with an innovation which had far-reaching consequences. Berlin was founded on social premises that did not apply to America, and on the Aristotelian definition of science as the study of universal concepts. The mechanic arts and any activity that required work with matter had been traditionally practiced by the lower classes, as something that did not entail the use of the intellect. In 1719 Robinson Crusoe's father still reminds his son that he does not have to follow the life of "the mechanic."[2]

Andrew D. White reasoned that all human activity, when reflected upon, reveals patterns of behavior, and those patterns are legitimate subjects of science. With this idea he broke the old opposition between liberal and mechanic arts, and made the engineering and agricultural schools full members of the university like the fields of history and Latin. Not long after, Cambridge University in England followed the

---

2. Robinson's father says to his son "that mine was the middle state, or what might be called the upper station of the *Low Life,* which he had found by long Experience was the best State in the world, the most suited to human Happiness, not exposed to the Miseries and hardships, the Labour and Sufferings of the mechanic Part of Mankind" (D. Defoe, *Robinson Crusoe,* edited by M. Shinagel (New York: Norton, 1994), p. 5.

Cornell model.[3] The new idea of science and of the university has prevailed, and now it is the humanities that need justification in the mechanical and corporate institution.

Since the curricula of the university and high school have been enriched with so many new disciplines deemed necessary for all educated people, old trees will need pruning. The need to study new sciences, and global access to education with the justifiable predominance of the practical careers, lead the states and boards of education to cutbacks in the humanities in elementary and secondary schools. These cutbacks have a double effect: the general culture of society becomes poorer and poorer, and fewer students will have information and the adequate preparation for taking humanities at the university. The second and most visible symptom of the crisis of the humanities lies in the fact that they are losing their presence in the curricula due to the widespread conviction of their uselessness.

25. *The wound*

The symptoms described are only external signs of the true illness. The popular impression of the uselessness of the humanities would inspire strong and maybe even convincing responses, if the crisis were not deeper and more objective. A degree in math or biology may not offer more job opportunities than one in English or Spanish language and literature, yet few people will question the rigor of biological and mathematical knowledge. It is neither the state nor our colleagues in engineering that question the educational and social value of the humanities; it is

3. "An eminent and justly respected president of one of the oldest Eastern universities published a treatise, which was widely circulated, to prove that the main ideas on which the new university was based were utterly impracticable; and especially that the presentation of various courses of instruction suited to the young men of various aims and tastes, with liberty of choice between them, was preposterous. It is interesting to know that this same eminent gentleman was afterwards led to adopt this same 'impracticable' policy at his own university. Others of almost equal eminence insisted that to give advanced scientific and technical instruction in the same institution with classical instruction was folly; and these gentlemen were probably not converted until the plan was adopted at English Cambridge" (A. D. White, *Autobiography*, I, p. 318).

the humanists themselves, anxious about the intellectual seriousness of the knowledge we acquire and impart in these disciplines. Here is the reaction of the novelist-humanist Vargas Llosa to something said by the humanist George Steiner:

According to the statistical artillery that Steiner fires in support of his theses, the humanities now attract only mediocrities and university rubbish, since the talented youth go *en masse* to study the sciences. Proof is that admission requirements to the Arts at the best academic centers in England and the United States have steadily decreased to shameful levels.[4]

The theoretical question offers several aspects, but it can be poignantly formulated thus: what does it mean to know *Don Quijote*? No one will claim that he knows it if he only has heard of its existence. But do we know *Don Quijote* after the first reading? If we agree that rigorous knowledge of *Don Quijote* requires extensive research, then research of what, of the type of letter and the textual variants of the first editions, or the frequency of conditional conjunctions? These questions, on which valuable scholarly work is done, touch only the surface, because they do not engage in reading the text, which is to jump from the signifier to the signified and its significance. One should not reject any contribution, even grammatical and formalist ones; but in these cases a clear distinction must be made between the superficial and auxiliary contributions, and the truly humanistic approach to a text.[5]

The questions concerning the knowledge of *Don Quijote* lead to broader ones, such as what is reading, and what constitutes literary knowledge in a strict sense. And these examples taken from literature apply to history and to the other humanistic disciplines, in the distinctive way pertaining to each one, as defined in Chapter II.

Aside from the epistemological problem, visible in the simple ques-

---

4. Mario Vargas Llosa, "Las profecías de Casandra," in *El País* (Madrid), June 2, 1996, p. 13.

5. Georg Simmel already noted in 1911: "The philological effort frequently turns into micrology, pedantic efforts, and an elaboration of the unessential into a method that runs on for its own sake, an extension of substantive norms whose independent path no longer coincides with that of culture as a completion of life" ("On the concept and tragedy of culture," in *The Concept of Modern Culture*, p. 43).

tion of what it is to know *Don Quijote,* doubts emerge which motivate both the dismay of parents when their son studies humanities, and the budgetary reductions of the government. Let us assume that we reach a satisfactory answer about knowing *Don Quijote* and other more complex historical or philosophical realities, such as "Spain in 1492," "The philosophy of Ortega y Gasset," or "Post-modernity and its Educational Implications." A new challenge looms: what good is this knowledge? Of course, with a degree in the humanities we may have a job as teacher or professor. But man does not live by bread alone; in order to teach with enthusiasm and feel intimately satisfied with it, we must be convinced that our work contributes something useful to society.

Some people may find comfort in remembering that doubts about the value of the humanities are as old as philosophy, while others may find cause for greater anxiety. We have already mentioned Callicles rebuking Socrates for wasting time and energy in adolescent games. Plato himself tells us in the *Theaetetus* that Thales, the first Western philosopher, while walking on a road, followed by a young female Thracian slave, stepped in a hole and tripped. The maid told him: "By looking so much at the sky Your Grace does not see where you put your feet on earth." The divine Plato put up for sale in a slave market in Aegina on orders of his disenchanted student the tyrant Dionysius of Siracusa (Sicily), is perhaps the shrill symbol of the defeat of the humanist.

We tend to believe that in the European Middle Ages, a time of scarce science and technology, and supposedly dominated by the Catholic Church, the humanities were the triumphant branch of knowledge. But in medieval society the dominant culture in the secular world was also pragmatic and empirical. I find the most obvious proof in the higher social appreciation of the nobleman in comparison to the clergyman. Don Juan Manuel (1282–1348) cannot conceive that a clergyman, although he touches the very body of the Lord with his own hands, can be superior to him, the grandson of King Ferdinand III of Castile. This is why, for D. Juan Manuel, the nobleman who fulfils his duties in war will go to heaven just as the friar who takes the three religious vows.[6] Even St. Thomas Aquinas and St. Bonaventure, both theologians and mystics, maintain that the supreme level of intelligence does not correspond to the theoretical theologians, but to the prelates, because they combine theory with action.

One finds testimonies of the scorn for "the useless knowledge" in every century and Western nation. Sometimes we have consoled ourselves with the claim that, while scientists study nature, engineers build bridges and managers create the conditions of our prosperity, we are the guardians of human values. But, as I have recalled in the first and fourth chapters, the discontent increases because few people, including most humanists, take this claim seriously. Indeed, the reflection on values belongs to the humanities, but reflection is not praxis. Scientists are watchdogs of truth and veracity, while the humanists are more inclined to play with them, or even proclaim that "there isn't such a thing."

The crisis that worries the humanists comes from the humanistic discourse itself, because they are forced to move around the circle without progressing from one stage to another. For this reason, while the classics of science are venerable ruins, those of the humanities remain alive and fresh. Suffice it to remember Greek philosophy and art. A response to the sensation of crisis in the humanities must be based on a stance regarding tradition and progress, and the idea of truth.

26. *The crisis of truth*

Far from being unaware of the world of values, science and technology are the only fields in which truth and truthfulness can be neatly distinguished from the error and the lie. In the instruction manuals for the use of complicated tools we demand transparency, not ambiguity. The click in the computer that allows us to read Spanish newspapers from thousands of miles away is an aesthetic and creative marvel. In the hu-

---

6. *Libro de Patronio y el Conde Lucanor,* example III.

manities, on the other hand, there does not seem to be any stable value, as we notice in the crisis of the idea of truth, the crisis of culture, and its corollary, the crisis of education. But crisis means crossroads, just a problem that keeps us alert against complacency, and this is not an evil.

With regard to truth, the legitimate rejection of dogmatism leads many to the extreme of not looking for truth altogether and of shunning the very use of the word. Whoever seeks truth is easily ridiculed as naïve or fanatic. In philosophy, the basic thesis of the post-modernists is that we cannot build a valid world of meaning, but must let ourselves be guided by the furrows opened by writing, which eventually get lost without a thread and a trace in the forest of history. For St. Augustine, history was the unfolding of divine Providence in the world; for Hegel, the progressive development of a reality that secular reason called "spirit." In Ortega y Gasset's works history is a project conditioned by the ideas and beliefs of the past from which a society plans its future.

In spite of their differences, St. Augustine, Hegel, and Ortega coincide in seeing history as an evolution with meaning. Jacques Derrida, on the other hand, questions all the criteria of meaning, hierarchy, and value. According to Sartre, as we already mentioned, modernity claimed to base thought on pure reason, substituting secular culture for the theological universe of the medieval scholastics. Nonetheless, the same thinkers who put their religious faith in brackets in order to create a purely rational philosophy maintained the hierarchies of culture inherited from the theological age. Derrida's deconstruction is the logical conclusion of modern secularity. As he says in words borrowed from Freud, if we have killed the father and consequently silenced his voice, the Logos, there is no reason to accept the world that was organized by that voice.

Derrida's doctrine has not had important social consequences. The liberal thinkers of the eighteenth century had already broken the barriers between the nobility and the bourgeoisie; Marxism, the symbol of all the efforts made in Europe to elevate the quality of workers' lives, contributed to advance freedom by demanding equality of opportunities, guarantee of subsistence with dignity, and access to education. And the equality of women in our time is the last step to date in the liberation of half of humanity from many types of dependency.[7] We know all too well how much remains to be accomplished in the conquest of equality and freedom, but at least in Europe and in the United States we already have the theory, have progressed in its implementation and, in spite of punctual disruptions and deviations, a return to conditions of the past is not only unacceptable but unthinkable.

But if deconstruction has not had a direct social impact, it has had an indirect one, due to the radical crisis of values it has caused in the academic world. On the one hand, deconstruction has brought a healthy questioning of literary canons, of the supposed superiority of Western culture, and of the very idea of culture. Today, whoever considers the European culture as "superior" to the Chinese or who calls *Don Quijote* a masterpiece, must show his criteria for establishing hierarchies, and be ready to pinpoint the qualities that constitute a literary masterpiece. Works by women and excluded minorities are incorporated into national canons to the extent that they have been a component of their history. In this sense, deconstruction has been positive for the humanities.

However, besides the salutary effects described, deconstruction or post-modernity has become synonymous with relativism. Many professors and students are convinced that "the reader makes the text"—and there is no deep meaning behind the shallow sentence—they repeat that all knowledge is a game, that truth is inaccessible, and that values "depend"—with all the vagueness of the verb—on the biological and cultural heritage. Although similar attitudes can be found in texts from the ancient sceptics and cynics, deconstruction has served as the abyss on which the conviction is founded that there is no foundation.

Surprisingly, this doctrine, which was for years the most popular fad in the humanities, and is fond of playing with language, coexists with science, technology, and medicine, which are embarked on projects of ever-growing complexity and risk, and demand ever more exactness and

7. I traced the history of this development in my book, *El "alma de España": Cien años de inseguridad* (Oviedo: Eds. Nobel, 1996), pp. 280ff.

honesty. While scientists intensify their accuracy, humanists relish linguistic games and delight in looking for the moment when the text "subverts itself," or the author "undermines" his own position.[8] The practitioners of deconstruction have not been able to analyze complete texts but only fragments. It would be infantile to attempt a deconstruction of *Don Quijote,* when one of its main problems is to understand how it is constructed in comparison to modern novels, and how it fits its socio-cultural world and ours.

The contrast between the games of the humanists and the rigor of the scientists, the legitimate pluralism that forces us to question the validity of all criteria of hierarchy, and the illegitimate partiality governed by interested ideologies and not by the vocation of truth, have resulted in the discredit of the intellectual. The true revolt of the masses is this lack of respect, with its two faces: the positive one (the need to be vigilant) and the negative, i.e. relativism. The outcome of this situation of discontent is the crisis of education.

Our point of departure and firm position is that truth exists, and that it is reachable. But we need to define it, because many confuse the attainable truth with the absolute and ideal concept, and fall into dogmatic relativism out of resentment for not being gods. In other cases, truth is denied in the name of freedom, because only fanatics claim to possess it. These positions demand a brief reflection on the place of truth in human life.

The first aspect of language is that in expressing something we express ourselves. In the preceding chapter we spoke of the ethical dimension ingrained in all knowledge. As a logical conclusion of these premises, truth is first and foremost veracity: the desire to look for and to tell the truth. The relativist is the self-centered individual, closed off to further searching. That is why I have used the term "dogmatic relativism." Though we can never be sure of hitting the target in anything, research and inquiry are an enthusiastic affirmation that truth exists. As the out-

8. Harold Bloom calls these attitudes the "School of Resentment" (*The Western Canon,* p. 20). "Shakespeare's eminence is, I am certain, the rock upon which the School of Resentment must at last founder" (ibid., p. 24).

come of a search, truth is the revelation of what something is. For this reason, "truth" is often opposed to "appearance." This word has a double meaning: fool's gold is not true gold, but true gold also has its appearance, which in this case is the visible face of reality. Appearance and reality are not opposed; reality is a surface with a depth, and truth lies in uncovering or revealing reality in both its deep level and its surface. Applying this example to a reality such as "The foreign policy of President Carter," the superficial level is any type of information, more or less organized, on the subject. The deeper level would be the well-organized result of a study of the facts, motivations, setbacks, and the place of this question in the whole of American politics during the Carter presidency. In *Don Quijote* the surface would be the vague knowledge gained in a first reading, while the truth would be the clearer one attained after lengthy study. As a step from purely superficial impressions to serious knowledge of a thing, truth is dis-covery (*des-engaño*, as Calderón de la Barca called it).

From the perspective of these descriptions, both dogmatism and relativism are erroneous extremes. Truth is what no single individual can possess, because "truth is what it is, and continues to be true, even if the contrary is said" (A. Machado). To find and present a truth is to point out something in reality that can be shared by all who are prepared to reproduce the reasoning that led to its discovery. Truth is always collective.

Truth, as a human experience, is limited. Total truth is outside of man's reach, and this limitation makes all conquered truth a springboard for further research. But this experience of limitation, far from justifying relativism, shatters it, because the experience maintains us in a longing search for greater knowledge and clarity. Progress in the search for truth goes in two directions: along a horizontal line—new issues—and a vertical one—a more precise analysis of the concepts involved in the search. To the extent that truth is exploration and search rather than possession, truth is historical in the sense of Unamuno's "eternal tradition": a crossroads between permanence and change.

27. *The crisis of education*

At this turn of the new century and millennium there is a proliferation of books on the end of many things: of modernity, colonialism, post-modernity, and of history. These dirges to the death of something tend to proliferate in certain moments such as the turn of a century, more so of millennia, and comparable situations. In 1918 a book was published that was a bestseller during the twenties: *The Decline of the West,* by Oswald Spengler. In this philosophy of history, Western culture had arrived at its final stage. Of course, whenever one applies to a collective reality the biological attributes of an individual, as are life and death, illness or spinelessness (Ortega y Gasset wrote *Invertebrate Spain,* 1922), the historical discussion gets lost in metaphors that convey the author's mood, but lack intellectual precision. History does not end, it is in perennial crisis, because human existence is inherently crisis: confrontation with old and new problems. In fact, even if we imagined the impossible: that one generation would solve all its problems and "live off the liberal abundance of robust oak trees" (*Don Quijote,* I.12), the following generation would have to work in order to receive this enviable legacy. Man is an active passivity, and vice-versa. Even inheriting requires work.

This observation should lead to a search for balance between general principles and personal life in education. One can come up with valuable abstract reflections on the humanities; but the individual is a person who lives in a specific time and has certain years of education, productivity, and retirement. In the abstract, all languages and all branches of culture can present their credentials as magnificent instruments of education. But in our schools we must select and eliminate certain subjects to the extent that new knowledge is introduced. This is why it is so difficult to decide on the subjects in a concrete curriculum, even if we respect the importance of all of them. Without getting further into curricula, we should remember what was said earlier about the Renaissance man; to be educated is not to possess the ability—much less the audacity—to talk about many things, but the preparation for, and attitude of, being able to listen.

The defining trait of a well-educated person is that he does not dismiss any field, although it may not interest him. Antonio Machado expressed this experience in his famous lines: "Miserable Castile, yesterday's ruler, wrapped in her rags she rejects what she does not know." We reject what we do not know because it is not an ingredient of our world, and feel that we can dispense with it. This experience shows that even the best curriculum, ideal and complete, will still produce incomplete men. Man knows very little; consequently, we as individuals must be cautious in trying to project what has served us onto a social system of education. After speculating in the abstract on the very best in the humanities, we must return to the individual biography and to each concrete society in a given moment, and structure education according to a broad consensus that avoids the illusion of omniscience. Persistent dedication to study overcomes the limits of all plans, and the best plan fails with the detached student. One does not teach, one learns. In all learning the teacher has an immense responsibility, but the ultimate responsibility and merit for learning lies with the student.

However, something concrete can be said about education in high schools and universities. The disciplines that respond to urgent necessities are the professional ones and those that change most rapidly; they are the fields that require specialization. General education, on the other hand, should prepare us to assimilate in a conscious way the changes that affect us in our personal core. We all need to know how to express ourselves; language and writing are fundamental subjects that should be cultivated at all levels of schooling. The same applies to ethics and religion, which search for the meaning of life.

The history of one's own nation is necessary for everybody who wants to know where he really lives. Let us not forget that history is man's space as man. Yet, the history of one's own nation can be understood only in comparison with others, and from the background that is common to all, especially in the European nations. In turn, history in its diverse forms—political, artistic, or literary—provides a perspective, but it can become a hindrance to education when it is nostalgic or narrow-minded. History is what man does when going forward, and looking to the past can be an escape from present responsibility.[9] In post-Franco Spain and in the communist bloc after the collapse of the Soviet Union, the need to rewrite national history has become quite conspicuous. But all nations need to re-evaluate their past "glories": the notion and the value of war-related heroism, the way or ways of life in different regions and times, educational ideals, the role and power of oligarchies, etc. In general, humanistic education in high school and college should stimulate creativity, and educate in everything that empowers the human being in his world.

One branch of history that should be offered as an optional course to all university students is the history of each nation's thought. A national thought does not need to be nationalistic, but it is more than the study of national philosophy. It should be understood as the set of issues that have concerned society at a given time, and of the principles from which those issues have been discussed. In the case of World War II, it is fine to know the names and places of the main battles and the number of soldiers and aircraft involved, but it is more important to know the principles and reasoning which originated the struggle and sustained each camp in arms. This study can be carried out with a high degree of precision by listing the names that the contenders applied to themselves and to the enemy. Words are in this case ideas and values. This type of study provides the background that all learned persons should possess about the country in which they live.

The reconstruction of the principles or theoretical background from which one responded to those problems, allows an intelligent position vis-à-vis facts that are repugnant to us. We are far from the discourse of conquest, of empire, and of power. We feel sorry for the lives of the Aztecs and the Spaniards who fell in the conquest of Mexico. But of those sad days and nights there remains a value that does not expire: the

9. Nietzsche sharply confronted the paralyzing power that past history can have on societies. He envies the animal that confronts its milieu spontaneously, without the horizon provided by memories of the past or future projects. Even though he may be right in criticizing exaggerated reliance on history, those of us who cannot and are not interested in being animals must try to cope reasonably with our historical condition. See "On the uses and disadvantages of history for life," in *Untimely Meditations*, pp. 60–61.

heroism, sacrifice, and creativity of Cortés and of the Aztecs who defended themselves. Maybe this sounds like simple moralization, but it is a search for clarity, because those who still use the concept of decadence presuppose moments of greatness, which were those of the conquest and domination. Actually, there are still remnants of colonialism and other forms of imperialism, so that even in a world that feels more civilized, there is still a discourse of greatness, of military force as worthiness, and of empire. Therefore, we have to make history of history and sift out the condemnable (the conquest) from the exemplary (heroism and sacrifice).

28. The social structure as crisis

Education is an individual process conditioned by the stimuli offered by society. Society consists of the institutions and usages that offer us all the possibilities of growth and achievement, while they also direct and delimit us. Society pays attention to deviations from the daily norm, to both the saint and the pervert, but more to the pervert, because negative acts have a more visible immediate effect than positive ones. A gunman can destroy in seconds lives that spent many years perfecting themselves and their neighbors. For that reason, society always gives the impression that evil predominates over good, and the decadent over the creative. This explains a constant in cultural history: the alienation of the majority of people from their society. The present has usually been considered a period of decline with regard to the past. Hence the commonplace already formulated with suspicion by Jorge Manrique: "It is painful to see, how in our view it was always better in the past," which responds to the popular expression of "the good old days."

The individual is unique in society, and he survives or succumbs as an individual. In education we cannot be carried away by the pessimism of a society which is apparently without values, because, in fact, they do exist, and not only in the sciences, as I have pointed out several times. The problem does not lie in the lack of values but in the fact that each individual is forced to appropriate them, and this appropriation requires effort in two directions: the ethical attitude of wanting to receive, and the intellectual preparation to receive values and to assimilate them. Society lives in crisis, but within it the individual can create a comfortable home for himself. Freedom has brought good and evil: it allows the clever ones and the honest, with luck, to acquire the fortune of Midas, and it condemns others to sleep in cardboard boxes on the sidewalk. But man is there to regulate the flexible laws of supply and demand, and to redistribute the wealth so that each citizen has a roof. Housing the homeless is within our reach.

Freedom allows us to accept traditional religion or to rebel against it; but it stimulates all individuals to become conscious of their religious dimension. In any event, neither the Inquisition nor any type of fundamentalism is a reasonable means of getting people into the temples. Since neither the church nor the state should impose forms of conduct in a free, secular, and pluralistic society, our problem today is to find a basis for what is universally valid. Education provides awareness and with awareness comes freedom within social coordinates that guide us in a certain direction. Education is therefore the means by which the individual can save himself in this society.

Education is the interaction of different individuals: those who do not have solid charts of values but are searching; those who profess values in conflict with the ones held by the majority; and those who are guided mostly by interest. Again, one does not teach, one learns. That is why education ends up being the responsibility of the parents while the child depends on them, and of each individual when he reaches adulthood. After a certain age, nobody can blame others for the shortcomings in his education. We are what we make of ourselves.

Biography imposes one final observation: everything in its own time. We would love to know everything at all times, but our life is continuous learning. Consequently, we should respect this human condition and be willing to extend our learning for a lifetime. We do not learn only by reading or listening, but more through writing. And on the eve of death we all will be tempted to repeat what is attributed to St.

Anselm, the wise bishop of Canterbury: "Oh, to die now, with all that I have left to study!"

The social structure is one of permanent crisis because human life is freedom made possible and constrained by objective coordinates. In linguistics and literature it is possible to speak of the author's disappearance, imagining a codified language that imposes itself on the subject who speaks or writes; this was structuralism in its extreme form. At the opposite end, it is easy to accentuate the role of the subject and forget the objective structure that is acting on him. Truth lies in the dynamic point of encounter of the two poles. Parallel points of encounter can be found in other humanistic disciplines. In philosophy and in history, the biological and cultural determinants vs. individual freedom, and in theology, freedom vs. divine foreknowledge and predestination. The constitutive crisis of the human and of the humanities is that dynamic point of convergence and divergence, which precedes all extremes, and rejects all extremisms.

29. *In the United States*

The crisis of the humanities presents specific features in the United States, and given the American presence in the rest of the world, it is important to say a word on the two faces of the humanities in this country. In contrast to the European nations, which live from their triple tradition—Greco-Roman, biblical, and modern science—the United States is a melting pot of immigrants from all cultures. While a Spanish student may accept without objection that he must read *Don Quijote,* an American student of Polish or African ancestors may ask why he should spend his time reading a book published in Spanish in 1605–1615. Because of the plural and heterogeneous background of its population, schools in the United States are more universal than in Europe, where hardly anything foreign is read during high school.

Of course, there is also a North American tradition defined by Puritanism, Protestantism, and the Anglo-Saxon culture. But today only a small percentage of the population recognizes itself as heir to that culture. The descendants of former slaves cannot muster unconditional admiration for Shakespeare, who was as innocently racist as the immense majority of Europeans in his day.[10]

The lack of tradition in the United States produces a special attitude toward literature. In Europe classical philology and the study of modern languages and literatures—I take literature as the most conspicuous example, but the idea is equally valid for all humanistic disciplines—were in their origins a search for the roots of national identity. Although this focus changed in the course of time through new methods of analysis, the connection with the national tradition never disappeared completely, since that tradition is a historical fact. In America that sense of continuity between the classics and modern literature is difficult to establish, and with regard to modern literatures, not even the English—perhaps with the exception of Shakespeare—counts as a catalyst of cultural unity. Thus the study of the humanities in the United States cannot be justified as appropriation of a common tradition shared by the majority. The positive effect of this situation is that one does not start with aprioristic perspectives. There are no canons or critical authorities, and the university disciplines are not linked to national identity, mainly because we study those of many nations. But there are also negative effects: the tendency toward relativism, the search for the latest fads, and the prevalence of playful attitudes in the study of the humanities.

A very positive feature of teaching in the United States is that in all classes, instead of listening to a teacher's lessons, students directly read classic texts on the topic of the course. The teacher is a mentor who puts the student in direct contact with the masterpiece, and the student learns by reading the masterpieces. The negative side is the risk of losing the sense of order, if the professor does not give a final synthesis of each work, and of the course in general.

Another positive feature is the student's participation in his own edu-

10. "Shakespeare evidently shared the anti-Semitism of his time" (H. Bloom, *The Western Canon*, p. 48).

cation, choosing his courses, contributing in class, and writing two or three papers for each course. Instead of learning by rote, the students learn to think and to do things: laboratory experiments and textual analysis. The risk in this kind of active learning is that someone who still does not know enough may talk too much, resulting in a waste of time and a loss of order. In the United States one aspires to know things, not in order to show off in oral debate, but to create an attitude and an aptitude for lifelong learning, i.e. research. Emphasis is placed on writing and fluid expression, not on extemporaneous knowledge. The walking encyclopedia, the social chatterbox, and the sharp wit that makes every one else quiet down, are objects of scorn in the United States. In a conversation, the goal is not to come out on top, but to illuminate the topic of discussion in courteous dialogue.

The list of advantages and risks of teaching in the United States points to the dynamism of university life in this country. One lives in the tradition of innovation, because there is no common tradition and therefore no consecrated canon. Everything has to be justified, and one must be open to everything. One starts from a diversity of backgrounds, all converging in a society that resists any idea with universal claims because it considers it dogmatic and pretentious. Anglo-Saxon analytic philosophy has also contributed to the suspicion against general statements. And the experience of European totalitarianisms has reinforced those who eschew generalization, although, as mentioned in the introduction, that attitude may go too far. The caution against generalization explains the ambiguous situation of the essayist and the interdisciplinary. On the one hand, intellectuals, dissatisfied with fragmentariness, constantly propound the necessity of the interdisciplinary, and on the other, there is a visceral suspicion of the generalist.

Unlike most nations, whose sense of identity depends heavily on their past history, the symbol of unity in the United States is "the American dream," a factor that hangs in the future. The United States are today the barometer of what will and must happen in the rest of the world. The homogeneous societies based on religious, racial and cultural unity, patriotic pride (of village and nation), and the masterworks of the national literatures, are broken or breaking down. The future is that of the mestizo, the ecumenist, the citizen of the world, the coexistence of Cervantes with Yasunari Kabawata and Toni Morrison. This situation is uncomfortable compared with the security once provided by the cozy sense of belonging, but it is the new reality and, therefore, a challenge. The United States is today the anvil on which the humanities of the future are being hammered and shaped.

VI Reading

Between the unattainable intention of the author and the arguable intention of the reader there is the transparent intention of the text, which disproves an untenable interpretation.

(Umberto Eco, *Interpretation and Overinterpretation*, p. 78)

30. Concept versus image

The questions on the criteria of rigor in the humanities can be grouped around three words: reading, understanding, and knowing, and those that refer to their practical import, around two: usefulness and value. In the analysis of reading we shall take literary texts as examples, because the literary text is more complex than those in linguistics, history, philosophy, or theology. Reading Calderón's *La vida es sueño (Life is a Dream)* we discover nuances of the phenomenon of reading that would not shine through in reading Ortega y Gasset's essay *The Dehumanization of Art*. On the other hand, the conclusions about reading reached on the basis of a literary text can be easily applied to other texts.

At first glance reading is the act of passing our eyes through a book. But this is a superficial image, not a concept. Let us imagine a humanist who for lack of practice has forgotten the ancient Greek he learned as a student, but still recognizes the letters; in this case he may pass his eyes over the text and articulate its words without understanding them. Would he be reading? The same person may articulate the words of a modern newspaper to an illiterate native speaker, who does not recognize the writing but understands Greek. This person who understands the content is the true reader. If we read a text to a blind friend, we are both reading if we both understand the text, but if it is on subject on which the blind person is an expert and the one who lends his eyes understands nothing, then the blind friend is the actual reader.

Reading is the effort to understand a text. The definition has three elements: the reader, the text, and the understanding or the burst of meaning, a process in which the text becomes transparent, or through which we become more conscious of its obscurity.

Reading, seen from the angle of the reader, presents the aspects of all human activity described in chapter IV. It is both a series of punctual acts and a continuous activity. For this reason, I prefer to speak of the *phenomenon,* not of the *act* of reading. In *acts* we read isolated sentences whose ultimate meaning and value can be fathomed only after reading the complete work. The picaresque novel *Lazarillo de Tormes* (1554) begins with these words: "I think it good that such singular and, probably, unheard and unseen things come to be known by many." This beginning lets the reader expect a tale of brave feats. At the end of the book we learn that Lázaro has achieved the dream of all men: an advantageous marriage and a royal office. The only drawback is that he must share his wife with the archpriest of San Salvador, who gives her "his meat (flesh) for Easter," and the royal occupation is that of town crier. According to the legislation of the time, the jobs of town crier, swineherd, and executioner were dishonorable, so that the descendants of such officers were disqualified for many positions, including, among others, entering a college in the universities. The ending of *Lazarillo* contains the key that allows us to perceive the irony of the beginning. This example shows that we understand the first lines of the novel only when we know its ending. As the reader passes through the book he receives impressions that he then embraces, rejects, or reorganizes in view of the whole. In terms of literary theory this means that all particular signs must be judged on the basis of the complete text.

Reading is a biographical fact. Dámaso Alonso, a master of reading, was born in 1898. When he began to spell in primary school he was already preparing his authoritative reading of Góngora's *Soledades,* which he published in 1927. The child spelling his first words is reading, as is

Dámaso Alonso when he *translates* Góngora's poems into Spanish, thereby helping other readers to find meaning in the enigmatic words of the poet. Most texts—publicity, newspapers, certain letters—we read only once. But texts such as Hegel's *Phenomenology of Mind* [1807] or Góngora's *Polifemo,* are generally read not only once but several times, that is to say, they are studied. To read is to study. He who spends his life studying Cervantes seeks only to give us a reading of Cervantes' work: to read is to investigate, an effort at learning. Each reading brings about, if not a correction, at least an enrichment of previous readings. Even when we read new texts, we are prepared for them by the texts we have read before. After a long life dedicated to study, a spontaneous act of reading is no longer spontaneous, but the result of the many years of preparation.

Repeated and reflective reading is, actually, writing. The reading of a text is the work of interpretation that we write about that text.

As a human activity, reading is a social phenomenon. The illiterate and the blind man who are read to are also reading. A student who is being helped by a teacher to understand a text is reading, as is the teacher when he consults a dictionary to understand words whose precise meaning he does not know. We all read with the help of someone else. What about the first reader? The first reader was the first writer and, therefore, he knew his own vocabulary and that of his public. Usually, if we find a contemporary text difficult, it is because it refers to a specialized field for which we do not have the proper background. On the other hand, with regard to a text from other centuries, even if it refers to general human experiences or belongs to our field of specialization, we need help because its language is not ours; the meanings of the words have changed ("transformation" in Shakespeare as compared with its meaning in our time), certain associations of words have vanished ("For this effect defective is by cause"), and new associations and references have been formed.

From these premises we will now read an old classic text, Calderón de la Barca's *La vida es sueño* (<u>Life is a Dream</u>), and two contemporary ones: the sonnet "To the great nought" by Antonio Machado, and a poem from Pablo Neruda's *Las manos del día* (*The Hands of the Day,* 1968). They are chosen practically at random, not because they are suitable for proving any particular thesis.

31. "*Life is a Dream*"

Calderón's famous play begins with these lines:

Hipogrifo violento,
que corriste parejas con el viento.
¿Dónde, rayo sin llama,
pájaro sin matiz, pez sin escama,
y bruto sin instinto
natural, al confuso laberinto
desas desnudas peñas,
te desbocas, te arrastras y despeñas?[1]

(Oh violent hippogriff, you that ran alongside the wind. Where— Oh lightning without bolt, bird without shading, fish without scales, and beast without natural instinct—do you foul your mouth, drag and hurl yourself in this labyrinth of bare and tangled rocks?)

We probably need a dictionary or the editor's explanatory note to understand the term "hippogriff." Even for many native speakers of Spanish it will be useful to note that "shading" is synonymous with "color." But the key word with the most esoteric meaning is "violent." In contemporary Spanish and English it is synonymous with savage and wild, a

---

1. *La vida es sueño,* ll. 1–8. p. 85. Edwin Honig translates the first lines thus:

Where have you thrown me, mad horse, / half griffin? You rage like a storm, / then flicker like lightning / outspeeding light, off in a flash (*Life is a Dream* [New York: Hill and Wang, 1970], p. 3).
Gwynne Edwards translates:
This headstrong horse must think itself / An eagle or some fabulous beast / That can outdash the wind for speed; / Or lightning, perhaps, without / its flash of light (*Calderón, Plays: One* [London: Methuen, 1991], p. 103).

Both translations miss the key sign *violento;* whatever their merits for popular performance, they are too free for scholarly analysis. Obviously we cannot use them here, and have subtituted our own.

meaning that ties in well with the scene. But "violent" in the scholastic philosophy of Calderón has the precise meaning of "contradictory."[2] Something is "violent" when it contradicts the essence of a reality or its normal way of behaving. From this new meaning, the text can be understood with ideal precision. The hippogriff is "violent" because it is the contradictory fusion of two different species: the horse and the "griffin," which is in turn the impossible union of two others: "an imaginary animal with the body and hind legs of a lion and the head and wings of an eagle."[3] In all of Calderón's plays "violent" takes on the philosophical meaning of "contradiction"; as synonyms Calderón uses "monster," "prodigy," and "wonder," "confusing abyss" and "confusing labyrinth."

The monstrous horse condenses the four elements in contradictory states: bolt without flame (fire), bird without color (air), fish without scales (water) and beast without natural instinct (earth). The beginning lines of the play do not contain the slightest hint of irony, and yet, they are also ironical. This is made clear by a comparison of those lines with another passage in act III of the same play, and by knowing that Calderón describes the horse with the same motifs in all his plays, and that he himself makes fun of his own mannerism.

> En un veloz caballo
> (perdóname, que fuerza es el pintallo
> en viniéndome a cuento),
> en quien un mapa se dibuja atento,
> pues el cuerpo es la tierra,
> el fuego el alma que en el pecho encierra,
> la espuma el mar, el aire su suspiro,
> en cuya confusión un caos admiro,

---

2. "In violento motus non tantum ab extrinseco est, sed etiam contra inclinationem rei, cui violentia infertur" (Josephus Gredt, *Elementa philosophiae aristotelico-thomisticae.* Ns. 271, 912, 914 [Freiburg Br.: Herder Vlg., 1953], I, 226; II, 332). Cf. Aristotle, *Nicomachean Ethics*, III-1, 1110b15. The Webster's Dictionary of English records this meaning ("Forced; not voluntary; compulsory") as "obsolete," but it proves that it once was usual (*New Twentieth Century Dictionary.* 2d ed. [New York: Collins, 1979], p. 2040).

3. Webster's, ed. cit. p. 801.

pues en el alma, espuma, cuerpo, aliento,
monstruo es de fuego, tierra, mar y viento (ll. 2672-81).

(On a fast-running horse [excuse me, for as soon as I mention a horse I feel compelled to describe it] in which one can see a map of the world; for its body is the earth; the fire is the soul inside its chest, its froth the sea, its breath the wind, in whose confusion I admire a chaos, for in its soul, froth, body and breath, it is a monster of fire, earth, sea, and wind).

Another parallel and, in general, the many cases in which Calderón jokes about his own commonplaces, allow us to document the ironical twist of the first lines beyond reasonable doubt. In the comedy *Lances de amor y fortuna* (*Strokes of Love and Fortune,* ca. 1625), a character mentions a lady on a horse, and Aurora interrupts the speech:

> Tened,
> que vais muy apriesa; poco
> os han llegado a deber
> ese caballo, esa dama,
> pues la relación hacéis
> sin pintar uno ni otro,
> que es de relaciones ley.

(Hold, you go too fast; that horse and that lady apparently are not much worth your attention, for you are making the narrative without portraying any of them, which is the rule of all tales).[4]

Returning to *La vida es sueño,* from the "violent" horse another contradictory hippogriff has fallen: a woman dressed as a man (androgynous), who is also a noblewoman without honor (a contradiction of

---

4. Edited by Ángel Valbuena Briones (Madrid: Aguilar, 1973), II. 175a. I studied this topic in greater depth in my book *Calderón. Pensamiento y teatro* (Santander: Sociedad Menéndez Pelayo, 1982, 2d ed., 2001), and in "La ironía de la escritura en Calderón," in K. H. Körner and D. Briesemeister, eds., *Aureum Saeculum Hispanicum. Festschrift für Hans Flasche zum 70. Geburtstag* (Wiesbaden: F. Steiner Vlg., 1983), pp. 219–30.

death in life). In line 78, Rosaura and Clarín—a pair similar to Don Quijote and Sancho—who have arrived in Poland "in search of adventures"
(l. 26), find another violent being: "there's a man lying there in heavy
chains, wearing animal skins" (l. 96). When that man, a magnanimous
prince endowed with high natural intelligence, compares himself with
other natural beings, he finds himself equally monstrous, contradictory,
or violent: "Why should I, whose soul is greater than a bird's, enjoy less
liberty?" (l. 131).

Rosaura's dialogue with Segismundo is interrupted by Clotaldo, the
prince's mentor, a nobleman unfaithful to the woman who loved him,
and indulgent, capable of abandoning the offspring of a mature love
(Clotaldo is an old man). He recognizes in Rosaura (still dressed as a
man) his son, but according to the law, anyone crossing into the secret
abode of Segismundo had to die. Clotaldo is now caught in a "confusing labyrinth" between the love for his son and loyalty to the King. As a
nobleman he chooses loyalty over love, and decides to offer the King a
violent and monstrous solution: "That he is my son, and the King
should kill him" (l. 460).

The scene changes abruptly from the mountain to the court of King
Basilio, who is greeted by Astolfo and Estrella as, "Wise Thales, learned
Euclid" (l. 580). Thales was the father of Western philosophy, the con-
templative who tripped on the ground because he was looking up at the
sky (see section 25 above). A king was expected to have his feet firmly on
the ground, and to devote his time and energy to governing with strong
intelligence—to perceive with wisdom and act with fortitude on the
needs of his Kingdom. This combination of intelligence and strength
differs deeply from the idealistic and speculative one, typical of professors dedicated to intellectual life, but who are never original (originality
is strength).[5] A king like Basilio, devoted to mathematics and astrology,
was for Calderón and his readers a monster, as we see in Baltasar
Gracián, who compares Alfonso V, King of Aragón (1416–58) and con-

---

5. In my book *Nuevas meditaciones del Quijote* (Madrid: Gredos, 1976), pp. 24ff., I analyzed three levels of intelligence: memory-intelligence, fantasy-intelligence, and strength-
intelligence.

queror of Naples in 1442, with Alfonso X the Learned, King of Castile
(1252–84): "The Magnanimous of the Alfonsos had the virtues of office
among the primary ones in his concern. What does it matter that the
other be a great mathematician, if he is not even a mediocre politician?
He tried to correct the framework of the universe, and was on the verge
of losing his Kingdom."[6]

In his intellectual vanity, Basilio, Segismundo's father and king, commits the tyranny of putting his son in prison from his very birth: "he
takes from me my human being" (l. 1487): a patent contradiction. Segismundo is also the crown prince of the kingdom and, by not educating
him, Basilio did *engender* but not *raise* him, that is to say, he has deprived
him of his specifically human character (man's being). To remedy his
first error, Basilio decides to take Segismundo to the royal court in order
to test if he will deserve the crown. Act II of *Life is a Dream* dramatizes,
with concrete, "violent" scenes, the contradictions of each one of the
characters. The prince shows in due course the greatness of his *nature*,
but also the lack of *art* that education provides. The following dialogue
between Segismundo and Astolfo is somewhat enigmatic, but once
again it contrasts the manners of the courtier with those of the natural
man:

> Segismundo: Dios os guarde.
>
> Astolfo: El no haberme conocido
>   sólo por disculpa os doy
>   de no honrarme más. Yo soy
>   Astolfo, duque he nacido
>   de Moscovia, y primo vuestro;
>   haya igualdad en los dos.
>
> Segismundo: Si digo que os guarde Dios
>   ¿bastante agrado no os muestro? (ll. 1351–59).

> (*Segismundo:* God save you. *Astolfo:* Your not having recognized
> me is the only thing that excuses you from not honoring me

6. B. Gracián, *El político*, ed. Arturo del Hoyo (Madrid: Aguilar, 1967), p. 49b.

more. I am Astolfo, born Duke of Muscovy and your cousin.
Let's be equal. *Segismundo:* If I say "God save you," am I not
showing you sufficient appreciation?)

Segismundo greets Astolfo as one man to another. Astolfo, on the
other hand, feels insulted because "God save you" is a greeting among
commoners and he expects the greeting he is owed as sovereign Duke
of Muscovy and "grandee" in the Kingdom of Poland. A servant reminds Segismundo that Astolfo "is a grandee" (l. 1371). The servant understands the word in the courtly sense according to which the
"grandees of Spain" had special privileges above other noblemen. Segismundo understands "grand" in the common meaning of important or
in the purely physical sense of size. For that reason he answers: "I am
greater" (l. 1371). The *grandes de España* enjoyed the privilege of keeping
their hats on in the presence of the king;[7] hence the conflict about
greatness begins when Astolfo puts on his hat before Segismundo (l.
1369), a gesture the prince does not understand, due to his ignorance of
the courtly etiquette.

King Basilio's "violent" gestures—to imprison his innocent son; not
to educate the crown prince; and to deprive his people of their natural
heir—bring about the outburst of violence, the war of succession (ll.
2387–3157). But justice triumphs, and the labyrinth is cleared: Basilio recognizes his son and abdicates formally in his favor (ll. 3157–3254) and
Segismundo, the man-beast, is praised by all as "discreet and prudent"
(l. 3304). A new injustice announces itself when the rebellious soldier
who aroused and led the people's army in favor of the Prince against
the tyrant King Basilio, instead of receiving the reward he expects, is
condemned by Segismundo to life imprisonment (l. 3297ff.). Some critics have seen in the treatment of the rebellious soldier a proof of the
savagery and Machiavellism of Segismundo. In Calderon's doctrine of
the monarchy Segismundo behaves with exemplary clemency, since

7. In fact, when Jerónimo de Barrionuevo says in his *Avisos* that "the king has ordered
some noble to cover himself," it means that the nobleman was elevated to the dignity of a
"grandee."

sedition against Basilio, who was the legitimate king of the country, called for capital punishment according to the law. For that reason even Segismundo, after defeating his father, kneels down before him and asks to be killed, because rising against Basilio has made the prince guilty of treason against the king: "my neck humbly awaits your vengeance. I am prostrate at your feet" (ll. 3245–47).

This brief reading of *Life is a Dream* demonstrates that the word "violent" of the first line, understood in the philosophical meaning of contradictory, is the basic sign of the work with regard to the structure and to the main characters.[8] But the "violent" sign not only explains King Basilio's conflict with his son; it also explains the secondary plot, the story of love between Rosaura and Astolfo. The primary goal of marriage, according to Catholic doctrine, is to have children and to educate them. Basilio has engendered Segismundo, but he has not raised him; he has engendered a crown prince, and has not given him the education that was prescribed in the treatises on the education of Christian princes. The father has made his son into a man-beast, giving him a man's being (nature) "while taking man's being away from me" (lack of nurture), and because of his lack of education a struggle ensues between the prince's congenital magnanimity and intelligence, and the passions of his instinct. The entire third act of the play dramatizes the struggle between reason and passion, until the former triumphs.

Rosaura is a man/woman, noblewoman without honor (sexual honor), a person "without being," since she does not know "who she is," that is to say, she does not know her lineage, which would be the source of her native honor. She has the weaknesses that the scholastics attributed to all women, but she also has a noble soul and virile strength to recover the honor she has lost with Astolfo. Her role culminates when she accepts herself as androgynous, another "violent hippogriff":

> Mujer vengo a que me valgas
> en mi agravio y mi congoja,

8. For a more extensive explanation, see my edition, *Calderón, La Vida es sueño* (Madrid: Eds. Cátedra, 1991), Introduction.

y varón vengo a valerte
con mi acero y mi persona. (ll. 2910–13)

(I come *as a woman* to ask for your help in my distress and grief,
and *as a man* to help you with my sword and my person).
[My italics.]

Her contradiction or violence ends when line 460 ("He is my son and
the King should kill him") is redressed by Clotaldo's admission: "She is
my daughter and that is enough" (l. 3271). As Clotaldo's daughter she is
fit to marry Astolfo; her honor is restored, and now she is truly a noble
woman.

32. A mixture of man and beast

In his first appearance on stage Segismundo is dressed in skins. As a
theatrical image he is a link within the tradition of the "noble savage."
But in *Life is a Dream* the traditional literary image is incorporated into
the philosophical definition of man as rational animal. The man-beast,
irrational man, is a contradictory being. At the same time, it seems as if
Calderón were contradicting himself when later on Segismundo
evinces knowledge of many things, including his rights as crown prince:
"How could you thus betray your fatherland, and hide it from me, since
you denied me this state, against all reason and justice?" (ll. 1300–1304).
But there is no contradiction: all of Segismundo's knowledge is based
on "natural law," which, according to Thomas Aquinas, is inscribed at
birth in all men as rational creatures.[9] Segismundo, naturally magnanimous but abandoned to his instinct, is conceived by Calderón according
to the scholastic and Greek formula: *natura/ars* (nature/education). In
the first monologue Segismundo avers his humanity in contrast with all
the elements of nature, and finds his imprisonment monstrous. In the
face of such injustice he cries out: "Why should I, whose soul is greater,
enjoy less freedom?"

9. See Thomas Aquinas, *Summa Theologica*, I–II, q. 94, art. 6.

Calderón and his contemporaries believed in the mysterious voice of nature. As a result, forms of behavior like cannibalism, incest, and homosexuality were considered unnatural perversions. In *Life is a Dream,* Clotaldo feels his heart flutter upon seeing Rosaura for the first time (ll. 413–426), and since she is dressed in man's clothes he feels a father's love toward "him." Jerónimo de Barrionuevo, a sort of journalist contemporary of Calderón, tells in his *Avisos* (News from the court) the following story:

A son of María de Heredia—she is now in Naples—got married here in Madrid to a daughter of Luis López, named Jusepa. They have been married three years and now María de Heredia writes that they are siblings, for she had him from Luis López, all of them actors. They are separated now after they had two children, both of whom died. One thing is true, and people comment on something very strange: that they repelled each other naturally in bed, and outside of it they cared for each other most tenderly, so that nature seems to have wanted them to know the close parentage they shared.[10]

The characters of the "golden age" are conceived not on the basis of psychological, but of metaphysical and ethical principles. We never know Segismundo's age, and his education takes place, not as psychological development but as a struggle between instinct and reason (the wild animal and man), according to natural law. The text contains two motifs that civilize the prince: beauty and the dream. The first time he sees Rosaura she is dressed as a man; but beauty, even in the young male, restrains the animal instinct of the prince who was intent on killing him, and inspires love.

The other instance toward civilization is the dream. Act II of the play ends with the famous monologue: "For life is but a dream, and dreams are just dreams" (ll. 2186–87). From this moment on, reason fights instinct and triumphs over it, because all unjust pleasure is a foggy dream,

---

10. *Avisos,* February 28, 1657, edited by Antonio Paz y Melia (Madrid: Biblioteca de Autores Españoles, v. 222), p. 65a. Calderón portrays Segismundo with more precise traits than he does King Basilio. While the prince musters the inborn magnanimity of a king, the father does not have the natural grandeur or the wisdom befitting a king. He demonstrates his dignity only when he recognizes his errors and abdicates (ll. 3248-53).

not real life, and only the eternal is the "living fame" (l. 2983). When everyone admires the prince's transformation, he asks: "What amazes you so? What astonishes you, if my teacher was a dream?" (ll. 3305–6).

The other characters in the work can be analyzed in a similar way. We have already mentioned Basilio's and Rosaura's contradictions: a king, professor of astrology, and a noblewoman without honor. Clotaldo, along with his functions as advisor and father, has stereotypical features attributed to the "old man" by the poetics of the golden age. Astolfo and Estrella also embody the conventional features of the gentleman and the lady found in Baroque comedy: they come to fight, he with an army of gentlemen and she with an army of ladies. In their dialogues, he uses the quick rhythm and rash tempo of a passionate young man, and Estrella the slow rhythm and tempo pertaining to a dignified princess. The feminine voice is the voice of control and serenity. Unlike Rosaura, Estrella is not androgynous, but the pure and true woman.

A deeper study of these characters should extend to their interaction, their condition as men and women, kings or vassals, noblemen or commoners. The society presented in the texts of the seventeenth century generally does not reflect the historical conditions of the time. The reason is that the literary work draws not only on the society of its time, but on formulas taken from the classical poets and from traditional philosophy and theology, which had been elaborated many centuries before. The characters in the comedy reflect their personal projects and aspirations, but they also embody the less personal "decorum" or "customs" codified by the commentators of Aristotle's *Poetics* during the sixteenth and seventeenth centuries. For this reason, the social types—with their interaction, and the evaluation of the characters on the basis of their lineage—within the text do not faithfully reflect Spanish society in that period. And the criticism of that society remains on the level of abstract satire without reference to concrete political situations.

A work of art exists as an artifact—painting, sculpture, music, or text. It is a body that condenses a search for meaning. For this reason, the literary characters, in addition to their function in the text as individuals, embody universal dimensions common to other men in fact or in desire—mythical dimensions. Segismundo, the man-beast, represents our perpetual dwelling at the border between the rational and the irrational. Rosaura is androgynous: the desire for the impossible fusion of the lovers, and in general, the desire to overcome differences and arrive at the unifying root of things. This unifying root that intelligence finds in being or in the difference between being and entities, is fixed by the imagination in hippogriffs, centaurs and the androgynous. *Life is a Dream* is not primarily a chain of philosophical messages; it is a work of art where the messages are carried out in actions and images on three levels: (a) the philosophical and theological, or the dramatization of the conflicts of education and rights to the throne; (b) realistic presentation of men and women of this world (struggles for love, honor and power), and (c) fantastic images such as the androgynous, the centaur, and the battle between the titans and the gods of Olympus.

33. *Two modern texts*

Antonio Machado:

Al gran cero

Cuando *el ser que se es* hizo la nada
y reposó, que bien lo merecía,
ya tuvo el día noche, y compañía
tuvo el hombre en la ausencia de la amada.

Fiat umbra; brotó el pensar humano
y el huevo universal alzó vacío,
ya sin color, desustanciado y frío,
lleno de niebla ingrávida en su mano.

Toma el cero integral, la hueca esfera
que has de mirar, si lo has de ver, erguido.
Hoy que es espalda el lomo de tu fiera

y es el milagro del no ser cumplido,
brinda, poeta, un canto de frontera,
al silencio, a la muerte y al olvido.

To the Great Nought

When the *Being that is* made the nothingness
and settled back, as well as it might,
there was night for day and company
for man in woman's absence.

Fiat umbra; human thought appeared
and held up in his hand
the empty, colorless, weightless, cold,
matterless, mist-filled universal egg.

Take the integral nought, the empty sphere—
if you want to see it at all you may stand erect.
Today, as two-footed, not a four-footed beast,
with the miracle of non-being carried out,
poet, propose a song, a borderline song
to death, to silence, to forgetting.[11]

What is involved in the reading of Machado's sonnet? There are clear allusions to the Bible: "In the beginning, when God created the heavens and the earth." "Since on the seventh day God was finished with the work he had been doing, he rested." "Then God said: Let there be lights in the dome of the sky. God made the two great lights, the greater one to govern the day, and the lesser one to govern the night." "But none proved to be the suitable partner for the man. The Lord God then built up into a woman the rib that he had taken from the man" (Genesis 1:2). In some way Machado's sonnet can be understood in its own words, without knowing the biblical narrative of creation, but what kind of understanding would that be? However, the biblical narrative is not sufficient. For the Bible says that God created beings, while Machado's "Being that is" creates nothingness. From the very first line a series of correlative oppositions allows us to detect and classify synonyms for the being that is and for the nought respectively:

11. Antonio Machado. *Poesías Completas.* Colección Austral, no. 149 (Madrid: Espasa-Calpe, 1969), p. 247. Trans. by A. Trueblood: Antonio Machado, *Selected Poems* (Cambridge: Harvard University Press, 1982), p. 223.

Being	Nought
The being that is	nothing
day	night
the lover's company	absence
	umbra = human thought
	universal egg
	de-substantiated, cold
	weightless shade
	hand
	integral zero
	hollow sphere
	stand erect
loin of the beast	human back

The poet is located in a center between the two extremes:

POET: borderline song, silence, death, forgetfulness.

Is Machado's sonnet a humorous parody of Genesis? This question presupposes an interpretation, since we can give the text a humorous or serious meaning only after we have understood it. Before deciding on this point we want to understand, that is, translate into understandable English the sentence "when the being that is made nothingness," a shade instead of the light made by God, and a shade that is synonymous with human thinking (l. 5). Is thinking not akin to light?

"The being that is" seems at first glance to be God. Scholastic philosophers called God the subsistent or pure being. In conventional Spanish, the original language of the sonnet, "the being that is" refers only to God. But, if Machado's being is God, his creation cannot be the primeval one, since day and man already existed when nothingness was made as the night opposed to day, and as consolation for man in the absence of the beloved woman.

The whole mystery of the sonnet depends on the meaning of "The being that is" and "nothing," since all the following lines, up to line 13, are just synonyms of "nothing." The key can be found in Machado's intellectual atmosphere, which for this particular point is summarized in the following words of Unamuno:

Would you prefer some other version of our origin? Very well. There is one which holds that man is no more, strictly speaking, than a variety of gorilla, or orangutan, or chimpanzee, or the like, a hydrocephalic or something similar. Once upon a time an anthropoid ape gave birth to a diseased offspring—as seen from the strictly animal or zoological point of view—really diseased, and if the disease represented a weakness, it also proved an advantage in the struggle for survival. At last, the only upright mammal—man—stood erect. His new posture freed him from having to use his hands to walk, so that he could counterpose his thumb to the other four fingers and thus grasp objects and manufacture utensils; and hands are great forgers of intelligence, as is well known. And the upright position allowed his lungs, trachea, larynx, and mouth to develop the power of articulate speech, and speech is intelligence. The gorilla, the chimpanzee, the orangutan, and their kind must look upon man as a poor sick animal who goes so far as to store up his dead.[12]

This explanation of man's origin gives the precise meaning of the signifier "the being that is": it is not the God of the Bible, but the *élan vital* or the evolution of the species up to the primates, before the leap that culminated in reason, that is, in self-consciousness, in the human ego. That happy, compact, and self-reconciled primate (the being that is) was hit one day by the *notion of being.* For an animal the things that surround it are mere stimuli, whereas man relates to things not as stimuli but as objects of interpretation. With the burst of self-consciousness man found himself as subject in front of things as objects. Seeing other things as objects presupposes a sort of screen on which concrete things rest, and in relation to which they can be named. That screen is the notion of being, absolutely empty, because it is neither this nor that: no-thing, the great nought. The empty being allows us to establish distinctions—the day had night, where night is still the notion of being—because all things (day) are such on the basis of and in reference to the general notion, which is always elusive (night).

12. Miguel de Unamuno, *The Tragic Sense of Life in Men and Nations,* chapter II. Trans. by A. Kerrigan (Princeton: Princeton University Press, 1972), pp. 23–24.

In discovering the object as different from him, man found himself as a subject of his own reflection; the internal division that constitutes irony came about, and there emerged the possibility of a dialogue with ourselves and the capacity for self-criticism. This internal conversation of man with himself is his company in the absence of the beloved woman. The empty notion of being is the created shade, the universal egg, and the hollow sphere that make human thought possible. The hollow sphere of being is the absolute that led the quadruped to look to the sky-heaven, and with an erect posture the loin of the beast *(la fiera)* became the human back. Human thinking is founded on the miracle of the great nought, the no-thing.

But alongside that thinking, which philosophers and scientists cultivate privileging the intellectual function of language, the poet lives at the crossroads of a silence that disrupts the dialogue of two people who used to trust each other, of death, which rends a dear person away from us, and of forgetting—that aloofness that may follow what promised to be eternal love. Silence, death, and forgetfulness are not a purely conceptual emptiness but embers of an absence that hurts.

Machado's sonnet suggests at least the following levels of meaning: (a) the theory of evolution as a referent; (b) biblical allusions that give the text a humorous and possibly ideological density, since the Spanish modernists used Darwin's theory of evolution as a cry of rebellion against the doctrine of creation sustained by the Catholic Church; (c) a parody of the traditional idea of being and of philosophical discourse.

The ideological density of the first twelve lines leads to the true message of the sonnet: the definition of the poetic discourse in contrast to the philosophical one. The poet lives on the borderline, which is the difference or crossroads where personal feeling and the dimension toward the absolute coincide (as Pedro Salinas said, poetry is an adventure toward the absolute). Concepts—being, philosophy, or science—are expressed in nouns; silence, death, and forgetting, on the other hand, are lived and experienced as verbs. Philosophy and descriptive poetry that does not come from the heart is poetry of nouns and adjectives, while the poetry of sincere feeling is a poetry of verbs:

el adjetivo y el nombre,
remansos del agua limpia,
son accidentes del verbo
en la gramática lírica.[13]

(The adjective and the noun, eddies of clean water, are accidents
of the verb in the lyrical grammar).

The same experience of the word converted into verb because the
poet is living in his heart the content of his utterance is also found in the
following poem by Pablo Neruda.

El golpe

Tinta que me entretienes
gota a gota,
y vas guardando el rastro
de mi razón y de mi sinrazón,
como una larga cicatriz que apenas
se verá cuando el cuerpo esté dormido
en el discurso de sus destrucciones.

Tal vez mejor hubiera
volcado en una copa
toda tu esencia, y haberla arrojado
en una sola página, manchándola
con una sola estrella verde
y que sólo esa mancha
hubiera sido todo
lo que escribí a lo largo de mi vida,
sin alfabeto ni interpretaciones:
un solo golpe oscuro
sin palabras.[14]

---

13. Antonio Machado. *Poesías Completas*. Colección Austral, no. 149 (Madrid: Espasa-Calpe, 1969) p. 288.

14. *Las manos del día* (Buenos Aires: Losada, 1968), p. 81.

(The blow: Ink, you that entertain me drop by drop and continue to preserve the traces of my reason and of my unreason as a long scar that will hardly be seen when the body is sleeping in the discourse of its destructions. Perhaps it would have been better for me to have poured all your essence in a cup, and to have thrown it on a single page, staining it with a single green star and that only that stain would have been all I wrote in the course of my life, without alphabet or interpretations: a single dark blow without words).[15]

Taking the texts as complex signifiers consisting of particular signs, the key with regard to Machado's sonnet has been the theory of evolution, a referent without which it was impossible to ascertain the meaning of the two fundamental words of the poem: "the being that is" and "nothingness." In Neruda's poem the referent is the ink that marks in succession the poet's trajectory. The furrow of the poems will be like the scar that lasts after his life—the wound—has vanished. Looking at time as a successive line, the poet dreams of an instant in which he might condense everything he has deployed throughout his life; to spill himself out in a single stain "without alphabet or interpretations"—one dark blow without words. That stain of ink is the dreamed-of nucleus, or the language-essence that precedes articulation in the words of a specific language. The stain of ink and the written lines are two ways of living time: instant or eternity, and trajectory or succession. Saying is unfolding, a discourse that awakens in us the yearning for a condensed and full expression: the saying of the ineffable. Neruda speaks here like *The Cloud of Unknowing* and St. John of the Cross.

34. Reading and the author's intention

Machado and Neruda coincide in expressing two ways in which all humans experience time: as a trajectory, and as an instant. In this sense, the human experience described in their poems, and therefore their

---

15. Our translation.

meaning, is basically the same. But we say "basically" because we hesi-
tate to propose a complete identity of meaning. The poems, meaning
more or less the same, are quite different, as are the attitudes of the poets. Machado is largely ironic, while Neruda reflects a sincere desire to
achieve expressive fullness in a single dab of ink. Both, on the other
hand, seem to coincide in a pessimistic tone. Machado's poetic discourse sings of painful absences, and Neruda expresses fullness with
dark images. I believe that my interpretation of the poems by Machado
and Neruda is objectively valid; on the other hand, my view of the attitude of the poets is simply conjectural, uncertain. Yet, that attitude,
which encompasses both stated aims and the author's apparent mood in
the text, is what we call the author's intention. And the question is: to
what extent should the reader be influenced by the author's declared or
surmised intention?

The issue of intention is a relic of Aristotelianism. The medieval and
early modern writers such as Cervantes (even Fielding in the eighteenth
century) started from Aristotle's principle: "All intellectual agents act in
view of a goal." Consequently, the writer was impelled to write by a
purpose. This principle is associated with the fact that at the time of
Shakespeare and Cervantes writing vernacular literature was not considered a serious activity, much less a profession; thus the authors had to
justify their works of art by claiming a moral intention. Fernando de
Rojas, for example, justifies his work *Celestina* (1499) as a warning to the
young against passionate love and bawds, and apologizes for writing
something marginal to his serious profession: law. Cervantes confronts
the cliché of intention, and in the foreword to *Don Quijote* makes a brilliant analysis of the phenomenon of writing as a struggle between what
the author intends and what he produces beyond his intention.[16]

Those of us who write know that our text is never the faithful pre-
cipitate of our intention, but rather the meeting point of intention and
luck—in the form of ability, inspiration, and even chance. That meeting

16. These ideas summarize my article "El Prólogo del *Quijote* de 1605," in G. Mas-
trangelo Latini, G. Almanza Ciotti, and S. Baldocini, eds., *Studi in memoria di Giovanni Al-
legra* (Pisa: Gruppo Editoriale Internazionale, 1992), pp. 125–44.

point of effort and inspiration is what the reader should look for. But some literary theorists have exaggerated the reader's role against that of the author, and disregard in principle the author's intention, misunderstanding the formula of "the intentional fallacy," which became popular in the United States during the fifties.[17] In historical, philosophical, and theological texts, although the initial intention undergoes changes and specification in the process of writing, the final text generally corresponds to the initial purpose. In literature, the very process of writing a text always shapes and can even modify the original intention of the author. As the plot and the characters develop, a logic is uncovered of which the author may not have been conscious at the beginning, and that logic imposes itself on him. But to the extent that the author discovers his own text while he is writing it, he also discovers his intention. The intention is an integral component of the text.

In all texts, but more particularly in the literary one, the final form is a revelation for the very author who writes it, and successive readings and the dialogue with imitators or critics may lead the author to better understand his own creation. When Cervantes discovered Avellaneda's *Quijote* he gained a new awareness of his own work; from the mirror of the false *Quijote* he understood his own creation better.

The concept of intention, simple at first glance, is quite complex. The poems of a mystic, such as St. John of the Cross, are fervent prayers to God. The saint yearns for identification with God and commitment to God's love beyond anything words can express. In diametrical opposition to that maximum degree of commitment we may imagine an impromptu speech, completely spontaneous and with no preparation or control on the part of the speaker. It is possible, therefore, to pinpoint different degrees of intensity in the author's identification with his own text. Going from a maximum to a minimum of commitment of the authors to their own texts, we can propose the following spectrum:

17. W. K. Wimsatt and M. Beardsley, "The intentional fallacy," in E. K. Wimsatt, *The Verbal Icon. Studies in the Meaning of Poetry* (Louisville, KY: University of Kentucky Press, 1954), pp. 3–18.

Maximum	*Minimum*

Mystical text

Political

Text of love

Text-research

Descriptive text

Formalist experiment

Stream of consciousness

The spectrum does not pretend to be rigid, much less exhaustive.[18] The religious text exhibits the maximum degree of identification, because it is a prayer and total surrendering of the poet to God. Other degrees follow, according to the intensity of commitment that the author feels with regard to his object: the political text, the text of love, the research text, the formal literary experiment (in descriptions of landscape, for example) and improvisation or the spontaneous stream of consciousness.

However, St. John of the Cross gives vent to his religious fervor in images and rhymes that presuppose a deep concern with form and aesthetic enjoyment. And, as we have pointed out, the improvisation of someone who has been thinking and learning for thirty years is conditioned by that accumulated knowledge, never pure stream of consciousness. These paradoxes mean that the author's intention is not given as an isolated fact but, like all human experience, is a moment of man's biography. The aesthetic phenomena that are the well-wrought poems of St. John of the Cross do not contradict his mystical engagement; they are punctual leaps within the trajectory of constant fervor that guided him. Similarly the "free" improvisation of the stream of consciousness is but a discrete act predetermined by the trajectory of knowledge and feelings that we have cultivated in our entire life.

18. This column is not in the original Spanish. I proposed it for the first time in my article "Ortega y Gasset, práctica y teoría de la lectura," in *Homenaje a Juan López Morillas*, edited by J. Amor y Vázquez and A. D. Kossoff (Madrid: Castalia, 1982), pp. 333–47.

In historical, philosophical, and theological texts the author may reflect intentions that he does not express well. In this case the reader should pay attention to the intention in order to give to the words of the text their definitive meaning. At other times, the reader can discover intentions that are not in the text, but can be "inferred" or "surmised" from it. The inquisitorial trials against Pedro Ruiz of Alcaraz, María Cazalla, and Luis de León are full of examples. According to the inquisitors, the words of the defendants could be taken as premises for heretical conclusions, although those conclusions went against their expressed intentions. Logically, in these cases the honest reader will try to respect the avowed intention of the author. In modern literary works authors do not declare their intentions in forewords. Rather they try to mystify the reader. If in general the intention of an author is his text as it is, then text equals intention when intention is not explicitly stated.

To read is not to meekly look for the author's intention, but to display, to ex-pose the text in all its richness as far as the reader can see. However, since the intention leads to the choice of theme, referents, specific signs, and to judgments of value on the part of the author, intention is an essential moment of the text. Reading is not psychoanalysis but grammanalysis—unfolding the density of the words, mindful that the words have or can have a soul.

35. *Knowing, pleasure*

Reading, we have said, is not an act but an activity; therefore, new readings normally reveal to us aspects of the text not noticed in previous ones. There might be an infinite number of personal reasons why we like or dislike a text; what matters, however, is not the subjective reaction but the qualities of the text in order to justify why it pleases or displeases. There is, therefore, an enjoyment based on subjective preferences, and one founded on objective qualities of the text. One-time readers may enjoy a work for the most diverse reasons, but I believe that the explanations given in sections 32 and 33 above allow for a more genuine enjoyment of *Life is a Dream* and of the poems by Machado and

Neruda. Scholarly study brings about the burst of meaning, the revelation of human experience and of the artistic features of the text. This knowledge is pleasure, and pleasure that is not based on understanding is arbitrary, and unacceptable at the university.

As a time-based phenomenon, reading is a dialectical experience: the first reading yields a certain understanding of the text (thesis). The reader then investigates the ideas and forms that precede (sources), surround (context), or follow (reception) the text. This effort, which ostensibly separates the reader from the text (antithesis), actually prepares him for the joyful return to the innocent reading (synthesis). Reading must be "close," attentive to detail before venturing into generalization. But the understanding and enjoyment of detail makes more sense at the end, after the study of background and context, than at the beginning. It is after this understanding that we return to the features of style and structure. Enjoyment at its highest expression follows research. However, as in all dialectics, the effort is guaranteed, but not the success. Poorly guided research, far from leading us to better understanding and pleasure, misguides and depresses us; in this case it would have been preferable to be satisfied with the first reading.

The relationship between close reading and general view from background and context suggests a notion fundamental to the understanding of reading as interpretation: the appropriate distance. In reading "To the great nought," we may speak of Machado in general, of the theory of evolution and creation among modernists, and of Machado's irony, but then we may never get into the text, because of our excessive distance from it. If on the other hand we concentrate on the humorous allusions to the book of Genesis or stay on the formal contrast between the synonyms of being and not being, we still do not read the text, because of an excessive proximity that lacks perspective. The ideal reading has to be located in perfect equidistance from myopia and farsightedness: only the text, but the whole text.

However, if forced to choose, I prefer the broader context to a narrow focus. The most universal signs conform the plot of the text and allow us to incorporate the details, while a concentration on details may impede the perception of the most comprehensive and important signs. This concentration on particular signs leads to one of the plagues of the humanities: fragmentariness, the myriad of partial analyses that produce frustration, not because they are bad, but because they lose the perspective of the whole, so that the reader ends up not knowing where to locate and how to assess these narrow contributions.

The other plague of reading, especially in literature, is formalism. The classification of stylistic and structural features, of opposite pairs, correlations, and parallelisms makes sense only when they are seen as the reverberation of the poetic content. The very same formal structures can generate a great poem or a contemptible tract. That is why some writers may reveal cleverness and subjective talent in the use of language without producing works of art; they do not build the world of meaning that lies beyond cleverness or mannerism.

The third plague of criticism is what I, imitating Ortega y Gasset, would call its dehumanization. Fragmentariness and formalism are already instances of dehumanization. But the most salient one is the failure to pursue the human questions and riddles dramatized in the text. The text in its form is a signifier, but reading takes place in the leap to the signified, and the pleasure is legitimate only on the basis of that leap. At this point the study of literature becomes truly humanistic.

VII Understanding

36. Signifiers and signifieds

In the preceding chapter we have tried to practice and describe the mysterious leap that leads from the first reading, which confronts the text as an ambiguous signifier, into the meaning of that text. Now we need to analyze how that outburst of meaning takes place. The observation that to read is to translate a text into its own language might come across as a joke. But to read is literally to translate a discourse that is more or less obscure (the text as a complex signifier) into one's own discourse, in which the signifieds or meanings of the text become transparent. I speak in the plural of signifiers and meanings, because texts like *Don Quijote* or *Life is a Dream* offer many perspectives worthy of attention, and the idea of finding "a meaning" in them would end up in a simplistic reduction of their richness.

We will now begin another experiment with very simple signifiers: three formulas already mentioned. "I think it good that such singular and, by chance, unheard and unseen things come to be known by many" *(Lazarillo de Tormes)*, "Violent hippogriff" *(Life is a Dream)*, and "When the being that is made nothingness" (A. Machado). What happens within the mind in the process of understanding these expressions? The first sentence is purely informative: Lázaro de Tormes declares his purpose of telling some things that, in his opinion, are important and uncommon. However, in view of what the reader of

Lazarillo learns in the final episode, this sentence cannot be but ironic. We perceive the irony when we find out that what we are told is in fact seen and heard sometimes: the attainment of a dishonorable office, and a wife whose charms, conveniently shared with another man, assure a comfortable subsistence for her husband. The revelation of these two facts is extremely demeaning for the narrator, with the result that it is ironic on two levels. First, the author of the book laughs with the reader at the naïve Lázaro, who boasts of his own dishonor. But on a second plane, perhaps Lázaro, anything but naïve—and, of course, the author with him—may be lashing at the readers as a bunch of cuckolds. For this reason he says that he is no worse than his neighbors. Honor, according to Boethius and the humanists, is "to be known with praise": to have a reputation *(clara notitia),* but a good one *(cum laude).* Lázaro desires that his less than glorious exploits *(sine laude),* be well known *(clara notitia).* In addition, the model of this type of irony (a subject boasting of its baseness) is Erasmus' *In Praise of Folly* (1511). Given the popularity of Erasmus in Spain ca. 1550, a comparison of *Lazarillo* with Erasmus' work helps to understand the concept of irony in itself, and the cultural atmosphere in which both texts emerged, even if the Spanish author had not known Erasmus.

The opening of *Lazarillo,* seemingly obvious and simple because it is a brief anecdote and all its words preserve the same meaning they had in 1554, exhibits, as I see it, at least five layers of signification: the author's irony; the ambiguity of the purported innocence and possible shamelessness on the part of the narrator; the evocation of the traditional idea of honor; the contrast of the new book with the histories of the glorious knights; and the historical relation to Erasmus.[1] To read is in this case to unfold the density of the text, which is revealed to us when we have read the whole book. In the first reading it would be impossible to capture the irony, which is the authentic sense and intention of the first sentence.

1. On the first steps of the Spanish novel in connection with the European novel, see my book *Nuevas Meditaciones del Quijote* (Madrid: Gredos, 1976).

The first lines of *Life is a Dream*—violent hippogriff—require us to know the meaning of the term "violent" in Calderón. Once we know the meaning of the word, not only the first lines but the structure of the whole work become transparent. The burst of meaning, understanding, is the transition from a confused perception to one in which the logical framework of the text is made clear. But, is logic enough to appreciate the artistic character and value of the work of art? Are logic and art not mutually exclusive, at least in many cases? In Calderón the logical coherence, far from thwarting the artistic value, serves as its foundation. Calderón places the core of the drama in the subtleties of reason, which create perplexity in the characters and misunderstandings in their communication. In this way Calderón is a master in the fusion of the logical and poetic discourses.

Machado's sonnet contains allusions perceptible only by those who know the biblical doctrine of creation. Those religious allusions can be parodies with a respectful attitude, or they can be blasphemies in the eyes of a Jewish or Christian believer. The reference to the Bible creates ambiguity, because it is not easy for the reader to dissociate God from the expression "The being that is." This explains why even a specialist in Machado such as professor Antonio Sánchez Barbudo, seems not to understand the sonnet: "What he comes to say is that *nothingness*—that is to say the fear of nothingness, man's suspicion that at the bottom of everything there is only nothing—is the cause of philosophical thinking, and also the foundation of all poetry."[2] Sánchez Barbudo's reading is vague, because he has not found the key to the burst of meaning: the theory of evolution embraced by the Spanish modernists, the often-mentioned influence of Bergson on Machado, and, in this case, probably direct dependency on Unamuno, whom Machado used to call master.

If three isolated expressions indicate the complexities of the leap from the signifier to its meaning, we can only imagine what is involved in reading texts such as *Life is a Dream,* or in themes like "The philoso-

2. Antonio Sánchez Barbudo, *Los poemas de Antonio Machado. Los temas, el sentimiento y la expresión* (Barcelona: Editorial Lumen, 1967), p. 407.

phy of Heidegger," "Structuralism and Marxism," and other possible titles. These last two titles are also texts, although unwritten; they are cultural realities or complex signs with many meanings that converge in a
final one.

A specific text or the title of an investigation ("The philosophy of
Heidegger") is a signifier. This term may remain ambiguous, since it
will be defined in the signified. The signified comprises the following
constitutive moments: referent, meaning, evocation, symbolism, allegory, thrust, intention, and sense.

Referent is the object immediately represented by a word or sentence in the minds of the speakers of a language. The referent of
Lazarillo's opening sentence can be grasped without difficulty: a writer
promises to reveal some far-from-everyday things. However, as we have
seen, the meaning was much more complex than the referent. In the
sonnet "To the great nought," the humor and the ambiguity of the text
arise from the fact that the conventional referent of the expression "The
being that is" is God, while Machado gives to those words a different
meaning. To perceive the distinction between referent and meaning
even more clearly, we may remember the popular sentence: "he's walking on air." The referent faces us with the image of somebody moving
in the air; but the obvious meaning, shared by all speakers of English, is
that the person referred to is happy.

In sentences like "he's walking on air," the referent is almost totally
forgotten for the meaning imposed by common usage. No English
speaker will think of a floating person when speaking in this way of
someone's happiness. But a foreigner who does not master English will
probably wrestle with the referent without capturing its meaning. In
fact, one way to get humor from a sentence is to restore the suppressed
meaning of the referent. Cardinal Mendoza (1428–95) was praised by his
contemporaries as "a very edifying man." The conventional meaning of
"edifying" in Spanish is pious or exemplary, very appropriate for a
priest, and cardinal at that. But the Cardinal was also famous for the
grandiose constructions he had built: the College of Santa Cruz in Val-
ladolid, the Hospital of Santa Cruz in Toledo, and the Cid's castle in

Jadraque, where he had a lover who bore him three children. The word "edifying" hung on a pendulum between the referent (physical building) and the "normal" meaning (pious).[3]

In the example of the "edifying man" a noun is associated with an adjective. But if we associate two nouns in which the meaning is different from the referent we are creating a metaphor. "Our lives are the rivers that go out to the sea, which is death" (Jorge Manrique). Our lives are rivers; this world is the road; life is a dream, etc. In these propositions rivers, road, and dream are metaphors. Although in a metaphor the normal meaning differs from the referent, the latter still keeps a signifying function, because the specific referent connotes and raises particular images and feelings. For this reason, the referents cannot be dismissed in the reading of a text. On the contrary, after ascertaining the different layers of meaning, the reader must return to the appreciation of its specific words, to stylistics. For the text is constituted by these particular words and not by others. Yet, this stylistics is, like close reading, the outcome of a differential movement: not a beginning but an end.

Evocation is the resonance or the presence of a context that has an indirect function within the total meaning of the text. In Machado's sonnet the signifying role of the allusions to the Bible is clear: they create ambiguity about the "Being that is," and also a certain humor, because the reader is easily confused by the enigmatic expression. In the example from *Lazarillo* the evocation of Boethius' definition of "honor" allows the reader to perceive the irony and the complexity of the text. And in *Life is a Dream* the contradictions of the four elements and of the androgynous person evoke a conception of the world as a "confusing labyrinth."

Resonance, or evocation, is an objective dimension of the text, and the ability to perceive it depends on the breadth of the reader's knowledge. However, the greater the freedom given to the reader the more cautious he should be about overinterpretation. One cannot be too careful in distinguishing where the evocative density of the text ends

---

3. Ramon Sender's novel *La tesis de Nancy* (Madrid: Magisterio Español, 1969) is interesting as an analysis of communication in a foreign language, when one does not know the nuances and connotations of words, and referents are taken for meanings.

and the wild imagination of the reader begins. In 1973–74 a polemic exchange took place between Professor Lázaro Carreter (Madrid) and the British Hispanist Professor Alexander Parker. Parker had published his book *Literature and the Delinquent*[4] in 1967 and, when commenting on pranks that the students of Alcalá pulled on Pablos, the protagonist of Quevedo's *Buscón,* he somehow converts Pablos into a Christ-like figure. With this he lent a certain theological density to a novel that, according to Lázaro Carreter—and I agree—is a pure exercise in rhetoric. It is practically certain that the learned Quevedo would remember the Passion of Christ when describing the pranks in Alcalá, and the reader who is familiar with the social and cultural conditions prevailing in Spain when the text was written (ca. 1603), will probably remember it, too; but that simple resonance or allusion does not make Pablos a "figure of Christ." Of course, Parker is very cautious and even admits that Quevedo himself might not have been aware of the parallels that he was establishing between the sufferings of Pablos and the Gospel narrative. The unpleasant polemics might have been avoided with a distinction between simple resonance and symbol.

Some texts, besides the density of their meaning and their evocations, are symbolic. The word "symbol" has several meanings, but all are founded on the etymological one: symbol is co-incidence, condensation. Symbol is the incarnation of a universal truth in a concrete character or image. Segismundo is a symbol of all the human beings whose growth is jeopardized by society or by other individuals—the millions who live in poverty and refugee camps, and cannot dream of knowing the world that surrounds them. All can cry out to our economic and political institutions: "you made me human and you deprive me of my humanity."

Machado's poem is a symbol because it condenses the multiple strata of meaning that we have tried to disentangle. All literary texts can ultimately be called symbols because they are the condensation of the four functions of the human word: emotional, intellectual, sensory, and

---

4. A. Parker, *Literature and the Delinquent* (Edinburgh: Edinburgh University Press, 1967). Lázaro Carreter, "Glosas críticas," in *Hispanic Review* 41 (1973), 469–97; Parker's reply, *Hispanic Review* 42 (1974), 235–39; rejoinder, ibid., 239–41.

structural. As we said in our definition of literature (section 8), a word reverberates most fully as such in a poem. In theater and the novel the message becomes symbol when it is embodied in the actions and dialogues of the characters. Benedetto Croce wrote: "A work of art can be full of philosophical concepts; it may contain them in greater abundance and they may there be even more profound than in a philosophical dissertation, which in its turn may be rich to overflowing with descriptions and intuitions. But notwithstanding all these concepts the total effect of the work of art is an intuition."[5] In the work of art ideas take body and shape in characters and in actions. The work of art is always a symbol, and interpretations are the initial dismantling of the symbol by way of discourses that take apart the well-wrought urn: the co-incidence or balanced relationship of its elements. But the linear discourses that temporarily disconnect the articulated nucleus are only invitations to return to the whole. Critical discourse is purely functional; for this reason it loses its purpose over time, whereas the original text remains vital and unquenchable.

Beyond the objective nature of the work of art as symbol, there are symbolic interpretations because the characters of those works have influenced the collective consciousness of the nation where they were created. In that way, works of the imagination have become historical forces or symbols of national identity. Don Quijote and Don Juan, for example, are considered symbols of the Spanish character. In this case the symbolisms are very subjective, and may be no more than simplistic allegories.

The term allegory is ambiguous. I see three varieties: the allegory of *The Divine Comedy;* that of Calderón's sacramental *autos;* and the parable, whose best examples are the parables of the Gospels. In *The Divine Comedy,* Dante walks from hell to paradise, describing in the course of his journey an imagined cosmos, historical and contemporary characters, his own society, and an experience of love made sublime by distance and death. The only allegorical element in the poem is the image

5. B. Croce, *Aesthetic as Science of Expression and General Linguistic,* pp. 2–3.

of the trip, which stands for the journey of life. But the poem as such is a very complex sign in which the following elements coincide (i.e., they fall together): idea and image, impulse and rhythm, and the process of research that permeates all artistic creation. *The Divine Comedy* is a symbol, not an allegory.

Calderón's sacramental *autos* present on stage philosophical and theological concepts: the faculties of the soul (intellect, thought, will), the forces that fight over man's soul (sin and grace), and the three ages of human history as codified by the scholastics: paganism (the age of nature), Synagogue (the age of the chosen people), and Church (the consummation of history in Christianity).[6] One can speak of all those faculties and powers within philosophy, history, and theology. Calderón gives them a body as characters in a work of art. The allegory in the autos is constituted by the fact that the preexisting theological ideas condition the characters and their actions; in other words, the idea controls the symbol. But in turn, Calderón makes art insofar as he gives life, personality, and dramatic movement to those ideas: he transforms them from abstract concepts into symbols.

A parable represents allegory in the strict sense, and it has two parts: a story or myth with its main characters, and a subsequent interpretation. But the typical thing about this interpretation is that it does not unfold the conventional meaning of the words of the story; instead, it gives to those words meanings from a private—and therefore arbitrary—code. In this case, the reader can understand the text only if he knows that code. The parable of the prodigal son in Luke's Gospel describes the father's behavior toward the faithful son and toward the careless one. The obvious reading is that one can have ungrateful children, that the father is always willing to receive all of them, and that siblings can be jealous of each other. What we could never derive from the story as such is that the father is God, and that the celebration he throws for the returning son represents the joy of God over the repentant sinner.

6. See Ciriaco Morón Arroyo. *Calderón. Pensamiento y teatro,* 2d ed. (Santander: Sociedad Menéndez Pelayo, 2001), pp. 122–36.

Don Quijote as a character condenses many human experiences. When Unamuno makes him the symbol of man in search of glory, he is in fact converting him into an allegorical character. Dulcinea condenses different forms of experience in Cervantes' novel: a literary experiment in which the author parodies the traditions of courtly and Platonic love; an experience of creativity according to the imaginative abilities of Don Quijote and Sancho, since each one creates her according to his respective world of references, and some other possibilities. Unamuno forgets about the passages referred to and makes Dulcinea synonymous with glory. Instead of respecting the complexity of the text he kidnaps it according to his own private code. When Unamuno wrote his *Life of Don Quijote and Sancho* in 1905, he was obsessed with the problem of glory and immortality, and did not read Cervantes' text in its objective articulation.

While the work of art is symbol, allegory is an intellectual discourse that reduces the symbol in a specific direction alien to the codes which are shared by the whole community that speaks a language. But the question arises: does not all interpretation reduce the complexity of a symbol to a merely intellectual discourse? Is then all interpretation allegory? The difference between interpretation and allegory is that the former deploys the conventional meanings of the language, while the latter reads into the text meanings from a private code. The Spanish poet Gonzalo de Berceo (thirteenth century) portrays himself as an exhausted pilgrim who arrives at a meadow crossed by four rivers, pristine with fragrant grasses and cooled by the shade of trees. The meadow and the pilgrim's arrival form a poetic scenario; the interpreter or reader can ask if that landscape resembles that of other medieval poems or if it has some symbolic value. But when Berceo identifies the meadow with the world and the rivers with the four gospels, he is using a private code, an allegory that no reader with any mental discipline would apply to a text. Interpretation, the reading that aims at understanding, is not allegory but ex-position or reflective unfolding of the text itself, not an imposition of external meanings upon it.

Incorporated into the objective content of the text is the author who makes himself visible in his optimistic or pessimistic attitude, his reticence, and his concentration on one aspect or another of the work of art. The author's presence is a new level of meaning that we can call "thrust." A text charges in one direction or another. The poem by Neruda interpreted in the preceding chapter contrasts the experience of time as a line or trajectory with the instant of eternity in which all segments of time coalesce. The following poem by Jorge Guillén expresses the same experience:

> *Perfección*
>
> Queda curvo el firmamento
> Compacto azul sobre el día.
> Es el redondeamiento
> Del esplendor: mediodía.
> Todo es cúpula. Reposa,
> Central sin querer, la rosa,
> A un sol en cenit sujeta.
> Y tanto se da el presente,
> Que el pie caminante siente
> La integridad del planeta. *(Cántico)*

> *Perfection*
>
> Curved, the firmament remains
> Densely blue, above the day.
> It moves toward the encircling
> Of magnificence: Midday.
> All is a dome. Quietly
> There at the center rests the rose,
> Subject of the noonday sun.
> And so much does the moment lend
> That the traveling foot can feel
> The completeness of the planet.[7]

7. Trans. by B. Howes. In J. Guillén, *Cántico. A Selection*. Edited by N. T. Di Giovanni (London: André Deutsch, 1965), p. 155.

The referents in Guillén's poem are different from those in Neruda's but the meaning of the two, what they say about time and eternity, is the same. The thrusts, on the other hand, charge in opposite directions: Guillén appears in an attitude of celebration; Neruda in one of doubt and longing—a mystic sense of life in Guillén, a tragic one in Neruda.

One must not confuse thrust with intention, although they in part overlap. The intention is frequently declared by the author and conditions many signs of the text, because the author chooses them in view of his aim. The thrust, on the other hand, is an objective drift or nuance within the text, what the words say, and the way, temperature, and tempo with which they say it, in addition to, and sometimes in contrast to what the author intends to say. If intention is the control of the message on the part of the author, thrust can be described as the mood that the text betrays. This experience is common in everyday conversation, where something "escapes" our mouth that we did not mean, or when we do not make ourselves clear. In these cases the text drifts opposite to our intention. In chronicles and literary texts written under censorship the thrust is the series of messages contained in the possible meanings of the words, although they actually may not be explicitly formulated. However, while these remarks seem valid to me, the reader should be very wary of excessive subtlety in reading, because he may be overinterpreting. Intention and thrust overlap when the author accepts his text with all its elements, regardless of the degree of awareness with which he introduced those elements.

The ultimate ideal of reading arises from all the levels of meaning described: the sense of the text. Sense is the fusion of all the aspects analyzed so far—referent, meaning, resonance, symbol, allegory, thrust, and intention—and of the social and historical significance of the text. *Don Quijote* is a web of sense in all the ways described, but it is also considered the first modern European novel, a text that appeals to readers beyond the beliefs and cultural conditions of Spain ca. 1600, a possible symbol of the defeat of Gothic knighthood with the rise of the bourgeoisie, etc. Sense is the translation of the text into a reflective discourse—interpretation—and the insertion of the text in the world in which it arises and in the one that it opens up. For the work of art rewrites the whole history of art, locating itself at the center of that history. The sense of the work as social and historical reality is a fundamental moment in the understanding of the text, the culmination of reading.

37. *Sources, parallelisms, and irony*

Through which means does the reader pass from the signifier to its precise meaning or meanings? First through knowledge of its sources. In the example of "violent hippogriff," the structure of *Life is a Dream* has become clear to us by recovering the scholastic meaning of the word "violent." Scholastic philosophy is the source of Calderón's text. The immediate question is whether someone who does not know that meaning of the key sign can understand Calderón's play. To which we must reply: in the sense of an ideal reading, no. But besides the ideal reading there are many legitimate ones that do not aim at such degree of precision. Also, remembering that reading is a social phenomenon, a reader who does not know philosophy can be helped by a professor's explanation or by the footnotes of a good edition.

Another example where the source provides the clue for understanding is found in the first lines of *La Celestina* (1499). Calisto, the protagonist, tells Melibea that he feels as happy before her as the saints in heaven, but with a difference: "that they *purely* live in bliss, and I enjoy *mixed* with the fleeting torment that your absence will cause me." Some editors, unaware of the theological context of these lines, have developed subtle fantasies on the mixture of body and soul in man, or on a supposed "mixed love," of which there is no trace in the text. The theologians said that the joy of heaven "is *pure* of all *mixture* of sadness and of all that can distress us."[8] For Thomas Aquinas earthly happiness was "mixed" because it is always limited, and is accompanied by the assur-

---

8. "Quanto etiam illa delectatio est magis pura ab omni permixtione constristantis, aut sollicitudinis alicujus molestantis" (Thomas Aquinas, *Summa contra gentiles,* book III, chap. 63 [Madrid: BAC, 1952], II, p. 242).

ance that it will end. By contrast, eternal happiness is "pure" of this fear. Incorporated into its source, which is its cultural context, Calisto's sentence becomes diaphanous.

The examples mentioned demonstrate that in some cases the sources of a literary text are indispensable keys to understanding it. Does this mean that knowledge of philosophy is a prerequisite for understanding literature? The literary text and the philosophical source are both expressions of the same culture; thus, philosophy explains the literature, and literature documents the presence of a certain philosophy in a given place and time. But philosophy explains while literature only documents. Therefore, the study of philosophy is preferable in education to the study of literature, because philosophy serves as background for the literary text, while literature only attests to the presence of philosophy, but can only help indirectly in understanding it and even in understanding literature. Literature is complex because of its symbolic character, whereas philosophy, privileging the intellectual function, is clearer, and clarity is the ideal of interpretation.

In the two cases mentioned, the sources have a positive relationship with the text that is founded on them. But there are also key sources, even if they do not constitute the ideological background of the text. This phenomenon occurs when a text criticizes or parodies its social environment. If we want to understand an author's criticism of his society and the fairness and value of that criticism, we have to contrast the text with the reality that is being criticized. In this case the source of the text is social history, which the literary work will usually present in a stylized manner, selecting features that suit the author's purpose. However, since stylization inevitably implies impoverishment of reality, the reader should contrast the stylized image given by the literary text with the historical reality in all its complexity; otherwise, the literary text, taken as history, will give a slanted and falsified view of everything. This kind of simplification has occurred in pseudo-Marxist criticism and, in general, in mechanistic applications of methodological fads.

Another type of dependency on sources is the parody of written texts. By reading some books of chivalry parodied by Cervantes we discover humor and irony in many passages of *Don Quijote*. But when the text that begins as parody turns out to be a work of genius, then it contains within itself the main clues for understanding it. For the important thing about *Don Quijote* is not that its battles resemble those of Amadís or Tristán, but rather that in all of those scenes Cervantes dramatizes a human experience which is our own: the dwelling at the border between the sound perception of reality and the paranoia of illusion. The bookish background of the work of genius may be interesting, and research cannot dispense with it, but the true background is the human experience displayed in the work. The only key sources to *Don Quijote* are the philosophical concepts of man and cosmos that conform Cervantes' ideology.

This last example forces us to distinguish key sources from simple parallel precedents. Erudition sometimes tries to scour history for motifs or images which resemble or are related to a certain character or idea. The right appreciation and use of sources does not advocate the accumulation of related motifs for the sake of accumulation; on the contrary, parallelisms that do not provide clues to the text divert from it and from sensible reading. The study of sources can degenerate into resentful deconstruction, when the scholar finds a sort of pleasure in denying originality to the author he is reading. The experience of writing tells us that a text may be original even if it consciously elaborates on some material accepted from sources.

After knowledge of the sources, the second means of understanding is the parallel. In *Life is a Dream* we have described numerous "violent" scenes, and by means of parallels within the same work and others by Calderón the irony of the first lines became clear. The parallels allow us to find the articulation of the structure, the defining features of the characters in their respective roles, and the most repeated signs of the text. These parallels document the *intentio operis,* i.e. the text in its objective articulation.

The third means of understanding is irony. The text invites the reader to reproduce certain experiences. It is irrelevant whether those experiences be real or purely imagined. The literary work does not necessarily narrate facts; it deploys possibilities of human behavior. However, some experiences to which the text invites us are patently impossible, or are so strange that the reader may legitimately doubt their plausibility. In a fantastical text in which animals or extraterrestrial beings speak, the superficial framework is not realistic, although a realistic signified may lurk in that framework or signifier. In Julio Cortázar's story "Letter to a Lady in Paris," small rabbits sally forth from the poet's stomach, which stain and mess up the clean apartment the lady rents out. Since it is impossible to accept that rabbits come out of someone's stomach, the text is pure fantasy. But the fantastical surface is a parable that reveals the outburst of the writer's freedom vis-à-vis the laws of dictators. Because it is a parable, my interpretation is personal and might be arbitrary; however, the historical situation of exile and Cortázar's well-known ideology dissipate in great measure the personal aspect of my reading and make it at least plausible. The writer's biography reinforces in this case the content or intention of the text.

In the fantastic text it is easy to distinguish the surface from the deeper layers; but the difference is not always so obvious. In Cela's *The Family of Pascual Duarte,* some see Pascual's savagery as realistic—even as a resonance of Spanish savagery in the Civil War—while others consider his actions so weird that they can only be fantastic as well. What is narrated in *Pascual Duarte* is a gray line that calls our attention to a fundamental aspect of understanding: to understand is to decide whether a described experience is possible or impossible. When we do not consider it possible we attribute it to the author's ironic intentions. The reader intervenes therefore in the text he reads, and judges whether or not he should take it in a conventional or an ironic sense.

The source, the parallel, and irony are the means through which meanings burst open for us. But the means of understanding are not yet the understanding.

38. *Identification and distance*

To understand a text is to capture and to formulate its meaning. This phenomenon unfolds in three moments: acceptance, reinsertion, and judgment. To understand is, in the first place, to accept a message. Writing is an invitation, and understanding reproduces in ourselves those experiences to which the text invites us. This is proven by the fact that when we do not see reality behind a text, we find it unbelievable, or else we sift what can be real from the fantastic framework, as in Cortázar's story. In the face of a text, the reader performs two movements: one of acceptance or identification, and another one of re-insertion of the message into its own context away from the reader. To see how this double movement operates we take Plato's doctrine of ideas as an example.

Any notion, such as humanities, emerges on the background of more general notions, such as disciplines, knowledge, and sense. It is impossible to speak of any concrete thing without seeing it inserted in broader notions. But where do the more universal ideas come from? Do we not limit ourselves to the idea of the humanities? Every time we say something, we actually say two things: the concrete statement, and the background on which this statement is founded. Man is a rational animal, animals are vegetative like plants, and physical compounds like the stone. In saying "man," we are referring also to animal, living, and being. That background, which is simultaneously present and elusive in our mention of man, is what Plato called the ideas. Therefore, we all share with Plato the experience of the universal ideas; on this first step he has not been and cannot be surpassed because he described the unalterable structure of the human mind. We have understood the doctrine of ideas by discovering them in our mind, and therefore realizing our obligation to accept Plato's analysis.

However, we locate ideas in our minds, while Plato located them in heaven. He did so because in his conception of the world the ideas were absolute realities existing without matter. We no longer share that view of the physical world; hence in the doctrine of ideas we separate the acceptable experience from the unacceptable explanation. But rejecting Plato's metaphysics and pushing it back to its time is a way to understand it. In this second moment, to understand is to re-insert a text into its context and background. All hermeneutics is a glance into a distant structure from a contemporary vantage point; it brings the past closer to us by making it present, and pushes it back from ourselves by uncovering its own logic and milieu.

But this double movement of identification and distancing is carried out in the world of sense that constitutes our existence. Understanding is ultimately judgment in view of this sense. We choose to study a certain book because we hope to receive information, guidance, or pleasure from it. Hence, the last step in understanding a text is the judgment about its value. The criterion for this judgment is the truth of its ideas, and if it is literature, its aesthetic dimension. But does this judgment of value harmonize with the ideal objectivity of rigorous knowledge?

Understanding, like reading, takes place in acts of punctual revelation within the framework of our existence, that is to say, with mediation, corrections, and constant searching. The punctual acts of revelation happen within the habit of our intellectual life. As human reality, understanding possesses an ethical dimension together with the cognitive one. The first moment, the methodical acceptance of what is understood, presupposes a willingness to listen and a desire to understand. The moment of re-insertion, when something is unacceptable because we do not share its context, presupposes an opening toward, and understanding of, the environment in which the rejected message was written. And the moment of criticism presupposes a reader's view of reality. The ideal of understanding implies more than the strictly cognitive moment; it implies all that we connote when we say that a person is wise or reasonable. This open attitude toward acceptance gives us the strength to reject without hesitation any text that spreads lies or illegitimate interests, be they personal or national.

39. Perspective, ideology

To understand a text is to discover its density (a text is an eddy with layers); and density refers to the internal signs of the text and to its insertion in its context. But the selection of both signs and context depends on the reader's perspective, which is the result of his education or competency (native and acquired ability, degree of attention while reading, the level of interest that the reader has in the topic, etc.), and of the interests that drive him. This perspectivism, with its different constitutive moments, is what we usually call ideology, and it becomes particularly conspicuous when the ethical dimension of understanding is considered.

Perspective is the creative contribution, or the emission contributed by the receptor in his reading of a text. The phenomenon of communication is summarized into four moments, according to this commonly accepted outline:

Message

Emissor—Receptor

Code

In its formal simplicity the outline is not false, but it can also lead to confusion for an excess of clarity. To begin with, when an author "emits" a book, he has corrected it several times in a continued effort to best describe the topics he is studying, and to express them in the clearest possible language. I have stated several times that to write is an effort to learn; to emit is to receive. One does not understand the "emission" unless its passive moment, the aspect of reception, is duly emphasized; the emissor is the first receptor of his own message. And in turn, it is necessary to put equal emphasis on the active and creative dimension of the reception. Everything said in this and the previous chapter about reading and understanding demonstrates that to read is to work, starting with a certain attitude, context and purpose. Attitude, context and goal constitute ideology.

Ideology is the reader's position. In general, the term "to understand" is usually shorn of its ethical moment, while we tend to forget the cognitive dimension of ideology. But the separation of the two dimensions blurs their role. Ideology can be described as a segment that stretches from the most honest ignorance to the blindest fanaticism. We locate the desire for the best possible degree of objectivity in the ideal center of that segment. We want to keep our personal ideals in check so the text, as Ortega y Gasset said, shines by itself in its multiple reverberations. In our reading we try to let the text speak. Thus, even with the most determined intention of bringing the text and not ourselves to the fore, there will always be desire, goals, and a non-transferable personal perspective: our preparation and interests.

The greatest degree of objectivity, of course, lies in making the text the center of attention and not disrupting it for any purpose other than the display of the text itself. But we all know that even with these intentions our level of knowledge and the aim for which we read open a specific path in our reading, which leaves many aspects of the text outside of our focus. The limitation of perspective is a form of ideology.

In history more than in any other discipline, one thinks about the relationship between ideology and objective truth. On what basis do we embark into a possible reconstruction of some historical events? We confront each topic from a background of knowledge and interests, which conditions the questions we pose to the text, the signs that we find most important, and what we extract as final message. These epistemological phenomena apply also in science, where some definitions—and especially evaluations—of facts, and the timeliness of research projects are conditioned by a structure of education and interests, which in general constitute what was traditionally called the *a priori* of knowledge.[9]

The *a priori*, or ideology, is the basis of perspectivism in the sense that our knowledge is limited. But perspectivism is not subjectivism.

9. For an analysis of personal perspectivism in science see Michael Polanyi, *Personal Knowledge,* especially ch. VI: "Intellectual passions" (pp. 132–202). On the apriori conditions of the seemingly most simple propositions see J. R. Searle, *Expression and Meaning,* p. 80.

My personal ideas in this book intend to reveal an object that everyone is invited to see for himself. My perspective is valid to the extent that it can be accepted by others, and this co-participation is possible because we all live in the framework of meaning that makes communication possible. There are as many readings of *Don Quijote* as there are readers. Not one of them can replace another; but those readings may agree on essential points, and in no case do they need to contradict each other. Thus perspectivism has nothing to do with relativism.

40. *Learning*

Reading is the effort to understand a text, but without a guarantee of success. The yardstick for measuring success or failure is to share our reading with others and see if they find it compelling. We can only propose a reading, not prove that it is right, and, of course, we are certain that our reading does not exhaust the meanings of the text. It follows that the ultimate criterion for assessing the value of a reading—indeed, of any contribution in the humanities—is dialogue. The clearest criterion of the correctness of an interpretation is its potential for explaining the largest possible number of signs in the text. From that totality we can appreciate the positive value of more partial contributions, and find the criterion for uncovering wrong interpretations. The most brilliant interpretation is wrong if it runs contrary to a single sign of the text. In *Don Quijote*'s story of the captive (I, chaps. 38–40), Zoraida abandons her good and exemplary father in order to convert to Christianity. Cervantes maintains the traditional thesis that conversion (the supernatural bond) must take precedence over any human respect (natural bond); this fact alone—which is borne out by many other signs—shatters the imaginative but unfounded thesis about Cervantes' relativism, which is surreptitiously identified with his modernity.

The creative moment of reception becomes obvious in the analysis of learning. To learn is to receive; but how much effort is required for this reception that sounds so passive? Every reader will remember some book that he has found difficult to understand or has not understood at all. What does it mean to not understand? It means listening to a text without finding the clues that bring about the leap from the signifier to the meaning. Communication takes place in a triangle (taking for granted the sharing of a common code): speaker who points to a reality, and listener who, while listening to the speaker, looks at the same reality. Reality is the vertex of the triangle. When we understand, the words we hear lead us to the vertex, and when we do not understand we hang on the speaker's word and see no-thing; the vertex, reality, disappears, and a line of dependency between speaker and listener is established. In this case one learns words by rote without penetrating into the things the words point to. It happens on an individual level when we do not understand a concrete text, and on the social level in all forms of epigonism and scholasticism, and in the repetition of fashionable jargon.

The reason for not understanding something is lack of preparation. To understand requires a willingness to listen (ethical attitude) and the proper cognitive background. This background is a certain level of knowledge in the field of the text that is being read. However, if we already share with Calderón the background that allows us to understand *Life is a Dream,* can we learn anything new from the work? And in reference to other disciplines, if we need to know theology in order to understand the difference between "pure" and "mixed" in *Celestina,* it seems that reading, rather than leading to learning, leads to retrieving and updating what we know in advance. Learning, on the other hand, is to acquire new information or to assimilate ideas that we do not have.

In order to unravel the mystery of learning it is necessary to analyze the notion of code in the outline of communication mentioned above. To understand and to learn presuppose knowing in advance something about what is being learned. But, if in reading or listening we already share everything, then we learn nothing. The difference between the words "something" and "everything" should not be taken in a quantitative sense, but as a strictly human, qualitative phenomenon. As I see it, the mystery of learning follows these stages:

1. Actualization. If we read a book of history or philosophy and understand it so thoroughly that we do not learn anything new, that book can still actualize what we knew only in the way of habit. It pulls things to a new degree of consciousness and probably in a new context, where old ideas are seen in a new light. If it is wrong to limit the analysis of human experience to acts forgetting habits, it is equally wrong to forget the decisive role of acts. We may know very well Ortega y Gasset's *Invertebrate Spain* or *The Dehumanization of Art,* but in a new reading we actualize the habitual knowledge, discover new stimuli and relationships, and get new ideas that lead to a new vision of reality. This experience shows that by studying we can always learn more about what we already know; hence the need for both professors and students to work constantly if they want to maintain a worthy level of competency. In intellectual life one cannot live off dividends from old investments.

2. At a second stage, the common code is the experience of the world (as explained in section 20) that we share with all men in what we have called the language-essence. Within this nucleus we begin to distinguish ourselves along lines of specialization, and then we share specific codes with people in the same field. Learning, the transition from ignorance to knowledge and expertise, takes place as the insertion of particular information into shared universal codes. We insert what we receive into universal structures and decide if the new concept is acceptable or not. What we call preparation or ability to learn, takes place (a) on the general level of communication, because student and teacher share the code of first principles of the mind and of common sense; (b) within the concrete disciplines, by sharing the basic notions of those disciplines; and (c) on the post-disciplinary plane, by the leap into generalization. As an example of this type of leap we can take the list of the basic problems of linguistics and history listed in Chapter II. They contain my general vision, which I propose to the reader as objectively valid, and the crucible of their validity is whether they cover the basic questions asked in linguistics and history.

3. "Common sense" is the shared consciousness of what is possible and what is not. The sense of the possible and the impossible allows us

to discover the ironic meaning of a message. Many texts cannot have the normal meaning conveyed by their words; they have to be ironic or allegorical because what they say cannot be real. Irony proves that before and beneath every verbal communication, there exists a shared agreement about reality from which we determine that many expressions cannot be understood in their literal sense.

4. Learning, as the insertion of specific contents within principles that provide the appropriate background, describes the reception of external contents (from a lesson or a book). But there is also learning by looking directly at reality. In this case, one learns by discovering the different aspects of a thing, drawing its map,[10] or disentangling the different meanings of a word, always mindful that one must reinsert all the partial aspects into the whole. This way of learning is imaginative, both for the scientist and for the humanist. Assuming that two scientists are equally familiar with what is known in their field, the original mind will offer new ideas, while the less creative one will stop at what he learned. The fusion of the ability to receive with the new content takes place in two ways: subordination and association. To learn is to connect by subordination (universal-particular) or by association (parallelisms between the different arts in the concept of Baroque), by creating, and by regularly updating what we know.

41. *Ideal reading and legitimate readings*

The kind of reading defined in this chapter and in the previous one is the ideal of the scholar who is devoted to research and teaching. But very few people embrace this profession. Readers in general do not read many books, they do not read regularly, rarely re-read, and they can pay only superficial attention to the text. This kind of everyday reading enriches one's vocabulary and the ability to express oneself, it reveals facts or at least problems, it may help the reader become a good conversa-

---

10. On the potential for concept maps in the process of learning, see F. González and J. Novak, *Aprendizaje significativo. Técnicas y aplicaciones*, pp. 86–120 and 190–95.

tionalist: it is, therefore, legitimate, but not ideal. Someone who has read *Don Quijote* only once may have more brilliant ideas on the book than those of a misguided scholar, but that is pure chance. It is also possible for a non-specialist to interpret a book after only one reading better than the specialist does. But, allowing for all possible exceptions, a text, an intellectual trend, or a historical period, are usually understood best by those who study them as specialists. There also exists the narrow-minded specialist who reads only about "his" author or century. Contrast and comparison are a way of learning; so in order to be a good specialist in our field we must get out of it.

I find two differences between the ideal and the merely legitimate reading: first, the ideal reading is also meta-reading; it studies the questions raised by the phenomenon of reading. Secondly, the ideal reading makes the text the center of attention, while other types of reading obey the reader's interests and taste. The ideal reading is an answer to the call of the text in its content and structure. But a text is a complex and open reality; consequently, one can legitimately pay attention to certain components and forget others. We can approach Ortega y Gasset's *The Revolt of the Masses* in the full sense that I have called ideal reading, but it is legitimate to read the book for a specific paper on Spanish populism in the twentieth century: the difference between a people as symbol of the continuity of the country, the psychology of the multitudes or masses, the "masses" in the pejorative sense of an insolidarious or passive crowd, the "masses" in Ortega's specific sense, etc. In this case, rather than focusing on the text, we extract the signs that interest us for our own intellectual endeavor. As we see, there is room for many legitimate aims in reading a book, even if they do not respond to the text as a whole.

However, while recognizing the legitimacy of those approaches, it is necessary to extol in unmistakable terms the value of the ideal reading over the merely legitimate ones, especially at the university, where the humanities should be a bastion of intellectual rigor against subjectivism and relativism. In this book, of course, whose basic image is the crossroads where all differences emerge and converge, we cannot distinguish readings in any mechanical way. It is always necessary to recognize the imbalance between ideal and reality. Recognizing the validity of concepts in the abstract, we cannot be, nor do we want to be, their mere incarnation; in most topics we can only aspire to the legitimate reading.

Related to the two forms described is the notion of innocent reading. This concept has to be linked with those of intuition, spontaneity, and the dichotomy between act and habit. Human intuition, as we have said, is hermeneutics; spontaneity is always mediated. In the same vein, the innocent reading is the one achieved after the greatest struggle, when we divest ourselves of subjectivism and the text reveals to us the beauty of its style, the finest traces of irony, and the seriousness of scenes that make us laugh at their surface. Only after rigorous research can we enjoy *Don Quijote* in a mood of simplicity.

The last two chapters have allowed a definition of reading as the effort to understand a text. Effort: study, a biographical and social phenomenon, research. To read is to understand; the center of reference is the text, not the imagination or the reader's wishes. The reader's response should be an attitude of openness to listen to the text. However, that opening contains the inevitable perspectivism imposed by our limitations. To understand is the burst of meaning, whose result is knowledge.

VIII Knowing

> ∞ *Man's greatness comes from knowing he is wretched: a tree does not know it is wretched.*
>
> (Pascal, *Pensées*, p. 59)

42. Concepts versus images

What does it mean to know *Don Quijote*, World War II (1939–1945), the essence of man, God? These questions chart in all its complexity the problem of knowledge in literature, history, philosophy, and theology, and the basic problem is how the ego (the knowing subject) confronts the object to be known.

The literary work (poetry, novel, theater) touches on reality in different ways, while criticism or philology focuses primarily on the text created by the writer, and through it on the reality it presents. History presents an interesting paradox: in literary criticism and in philosophy understanding is primarily the reproduction on the part of the reader of the human experience displayed in the texts. The understanding of history requires that reproduction as well, but only to a certain extent, since the historical events remain at a distance from the reader. Nothing is more disturbing than World War II, but for all our efforts to empathize with the victims of the war, we no longer die or suffer in it. What tore apart so many bodies and souls is for us a text constructed on the basis of other texts down to the original documents. The common phrase "history repeats itself" is true only in part. To the extent that men share certain universal characteristics and attitudes with human beings of all times and places, history repeats itself. But history also has a dimension of complete otherness: the unrepeatable events. Wars recur, and so they are a repeated phenomenon, but the fighters and casualties are always new.

Naturally, we cannot reproduce Garcilaso's experience when he was writing a sonnet of love, or Kant's when he was writing his analysis of knowledge, but the understanding of Garcilaso and Kant implies the direct experience of love and knowledge on the part of their reader. In history, on the other hand, the dimension of otherness predominates over the dimension of sharing. Human time, as we said above, is "eternal tradition," the nucleus of our existence in its present, which projects itself into past and future. The segments past, present, and future are dimensions of the ego at any given time, but they are also independent magnitudes separated from the ego and independent from it. The pure future without connection with the present is utopia, while the pure past already fixed in its rigidity as past is the subject of mere information, and its bearing on the present is at best indirect; for this reason Aristotle wrote this sentence on poetry and history: "The Historian relates what has happened, and the Poet represents what might happen— what is typical. Poetry, therefore, is something more philosophic and of higher seriousness than History; for Poetry tends rather to express what is universal, whereas History relates particular events as such."[1]

To be sure, history can also be understood only from the universal side of human experience; the understanding of events (particulars, pure past) requires understanding of the concepts (universals, eternal tradition) involved in the formulation of the events. The word "nation" is used today as it was used at the University of Paris in the thirteenth century, but if we were to interpret the texts of the university about the different nations with the modern idea of nation we would sorely misunderstand those texts. Nation as a contemporary reality is the name that comes from the evolution of, and revolutions in, what used to be called "Kingdom," "the Crown," "Republic" (as a group of citizens).

1. Aristotle, *Poetics,* chap. IX, Trans. L. Cooper, p. 31 (Bekker, 1451b5-7).

The modern idea defines the nation as a society resulting from the fusion of several ethnic groups that share a certain tradition, culture, and, in many cases, the same language. Without clarity on these universal concepts it is impossible to understand the historical facts. The subject of history is those particular facts in themselves insofar as they are different from the present. And yet, even in history, we understand the past only to the extent that we share a world with its protagonists, empathize with the victims of crime, and admire the exemplary feats. The segments of past, present, and future converge and diverge in the difference: the present in its three dimensions. The pure other, or fixed past continues to be fluidly bound to the flow of the "eternal tradition."

No discipline confronts the other, or The Other *par excellence,* as clearly as theology. What do we say of God when we talk about God? How and how much does Dante's *Paradiso* reveal of the Christian heaven? Throughout history, these questions have received answers ranging from an optimism that makes of God little more than a bigger and wiser old man (anthropomorphism), to the affirmation of a complete otherness. The theologian Karl Barth wrote that when we speak of God we do not really know if we are speaking of God or blaspheming him. Between these two extremes, Catholic theologians established the doctrine of the analogy of being. The concepts that we use in speaking of God are a call to the absolute Other, whose being is infinite and therefore incomprehensible to us. But human intelligence, image of God, is capable of communicating with God through language, so that man shares with God in the world of meaning. This partnership makes divine revelation possible, and since God's word is His Son, the shared language has taken physical form in Christ—the incarnation of the Word—who has established a new communion and communication between God and His creatures. Theology is enlightened and reflective faith, a perfect blending of speculation and prayer. The miracle of a mystic writer such as St. Teresa of Avila (1515–82) resides in her ability to say the ineffable. In section 6, I have adduced Heidegger's basic idea on language: language calls. There is hardly a better proof of this thesis than the mystical text.

When St. Teresa speaks of God, she moves and invites us toward God. And when Dante describes paradise, he does not represent it as it is, but he takes us with him to knock and scratch at its doors.

The idea of knowledge as a dialectics between representation and the call toward the absent other, or The Other, helps to explain and surpass the inveterate distinction between the experience or the phenomenon on the one hand, and the "thing in itself."[2] This distinction refers us to the mysterious physiological process that takes place in the brain between the moment when the eyes see colors, surfaces, and shapes, and the moment when the human being (not just the eye or the mind) says: desk. This is a key issue in cognitive research, but the analysis of the relationship between brain and knowledge presupposes an idea of knowledge or must lead to it. Certainly the neurological conditions and the physiological process are not knowledge, and it is knowledge that we are trying to define here.[3]

For us the difference between a phenomenon and a thing in itself rests on a vain illusion about our ability. We dream of being gods who comprehend reality (things as such) and, since the dream is but a dream, we fall into extremist despair: we know only appearances. A prerequisite to overcome the dilemma is to realize that knowledge is neither command nor exhaustive representation of a subject, but dedication to research. If I talk about the Socialist Party, the Baroque, or the theory of knowledge, I do not speak of appearances versus pretended things in themselves; I speak of the Party, the artistic school, and the philosophical problem in their reality, yet mindful that the better I know the topics,

2. As is well known, Kant, based on a rather mechanistic distinction between sensitivity, understanding, and reason, distinguished experience from knowledge, attributing to the senses the perception of phenomena or appearances, and to knowledge the imposition of forms from the perspective of the subject who gives names, and therefore, rises from the sensory impression to the essence. The union of phenomenon and essence needed a point of intersection: the *Urteilskraft*, or moment of distinction. Obviously, we can't enter into discussions of this type here.

3. This is the subject of a dialogue between the neuroscientist Jean-Pierre Changeux and the philosopher Paul Ricoeur in *What Makes Us Think*. Chapter III, for example, deals with the neuronal model and the test of experience (pp. 70ff).

the better I see how little I know about them. All knowledge is a discourse, a formulation in language, which is at the same time limited presence and invitation to the absent and elusive reality. But both the representation and the experience of distance are moments of "the thing in itself," not appearance vs. true reality.

Another fuzzy image of knowledge derives from the confusion between acts and habits. To know is an act: to perceive a reality or the meaning of a text. We praise an individual by saying that he or she knows a lot. This convention became widespread in societies with a predominantly oral culture, in which to know was to carry data in one's head and the ability to display them in appropriate circumstances. These common images obscure the idea of knowledge. For Aristotle knowledge was already an "intellectual virtue," a habit or permanent quality, not the momentary act of assimilation of meaning, and still less the oral display of what we know. In order to understand knowledge it is necessary to abandon the image of the memorizer and of the "brilliant speaker without notes." The oral culture of peoples without writing or of real or potential demagogues is a culture without roots. Of course, the preceding statements should not make us forget that all human behavior takes place in acts. The habit of knowledge must be constantly revitalized with acts of knowledge or momentary revelations. Knowledge is a dynamic fusion of acts and habit, acts that proceed from the habit, and enrich the habit in turn. For this reason, oral communication, in which the punctual predominates over the habitual, must be integrated into writing, where habit predominates over the acts and, by producing a text open to correction, generates true knowledge.

From the experience of writing we learn not only that our own text, the fruit of research, is independent of its author, but also that it becomes a teacher to its own author. To write is both to teach and to learn at the same time. And when the book has become completely independent of the author, he can reread it, remember many things that he had forgotten, and continue adding ideas in each paragraph, because he perceives more and better aspects of his topic. But, although it is true that we forget many things we knew when writing our own texts, it is also true that at least some of that knowledge remains with us as a habit that can be retraced in an "improvised" oral presentation.

From the preceding observation one can derive several preliminary conclusions for our topic. We begin with the distinction between orality and writing. To know is not the ability to recite the names of all the rivers and all the Visigothic kings of Spain; it is to understand the meaning of rivers in geography, in history, and as natural resources, and why between the years 415 and 711 there were thirty-three Visigothic kings in Spain who reigned an average of fewer than ten years each. In fact, the large number of kings is very important for knowing the life and institutions of that monarchy. For this reason, the memorization of at least the names of the most important kings cannot be dismissed as rote versus meaningful learning; after all, without actual (and in this example factual) knowledge there is no habit either.

Orality and writing are mutually related as yet another instance of difference. Oral communication takes place in the words, presence, and gestures of the speakers. The words convey meanings, presence adds to or subtracts from the words a special authority, and gestures give precise meaning to the words. When someone looking at deficient work says, "Good job!" the tone in the presence of the product determines the ironic intention of the remark. As opposed to oral communication, writing presupposes the absence of the speaker and does not have the advantage of the gesture that accompanies the words. The result is the common assumption that writing is a more vague and weaker vehicle of expression than oral speech. But in the stylistic features, the exclamation and question marks and other rhetorical devices, writing also makes the speaker present: "The style is the person."

However, in their deeper relationship orality and writing are more than just different degrees of expressive power; they are two different ways in which reason operates. The written text registers a dialogue between the writer and three partners: the writer himself, the topic on which he is writing, and his potential readers. But, once that first draft is recorded, the text remains as an objectified discourse independent from its author. As such, it teaches its author and bids him to correct and rewrite. Why, after all, do we correct the very text we wrote yesterday, maybe just half an hour ago? Have our ideas changed so suddenly? The text invites correction because it is an effort to reveal reality, and the more we work on a subject, the more sides it offers us, and allows us to express those sides in better order. Correction is the honest response to the call of reality, and an effort toward a clearer expression of our ideas and a better organization of our text. But the criterion for judging the clarity of a discourse is how it reflects the reality to which it points. And the criterion for the good or bad organization of a text is whether the order of its paragraphs reflects the articulation of the reality under investigation. To correct is, therefore, the decision to be faithful to things as they are, although here again success is obviously never guaranteed.

In contrast to writing, in oral discourse the sentence, once uttered, is hard to retrieve; the only possible corrections extend to the limits of our memory. Oral speech, given the scant possibilities of correction, is generally more imprecise than the written text. But not always: knowing is, like reading, a biographical phenomenon, and in our lives everything is mediated. An individual who has written all his life will bring to bear in his oral improvisation all the precision attained in his writing: he may speak "like a book."

The crossroads between orality and writing shows that knowing is an open process, a continuous education. In classical Latin the present tense "I know" was expressed with the form of the past: *novi,* "I got to know." It looks as if they were saying: "I am through with the effort, and master the subject." We would be tempted to use the verb in the form of gerund or in a sort of potential mode: "I am trying to know," "I may know." At the same time, this intimation of modesty is as removed from relativism as one can be. Scientists do not feel close to exhaustive knowledge of the universe, but their limited knowledge finds useful applications. The same approach should be taken in the humanities. The most exhaustive study of a topic is an outburst of new lines of research. But knowing is, in one of its aspects, synonymous with ability: application and praxis. Every step from habitual knowledge to concrete acts is taken as a response to a need. To know is to possess the ability to do something.[4]

Knowledge is always knowledge of reality, that is to say, of truth. With regard to truth it is also imperative to distinguish the concept from vague or distorted images. The passage from the signifier to the signified in isolated sentences such as "shoot the breeze" or "he's on top of the world" can be very well analyzed and will never really be in contradiction with the clarification of the idea of truth in more complex and realistic situations. An example of a real and complex situation in the humanities is the question: when do I really know *Don Quijote* or, to continue with the example analyzed in Chapter VI, *Life is a Dream*? And since the humanities cannot be reduced to literature, when can somebody be considered competent regarding the questions posed by the other humanistic disciplines? In all of them there is a moment of acquisition that takes place at random, and a moment of reorganization. Both moments are necessary in attaining knowledge, but it is the second one that leads to the authentic transparency of reality and organized discourse. As the old rhetoricians used to say, invention must be controlled by disposition. All serious and rigorous knowledge is systematic.

43. *Toward knowledge*

Up to now we have described the phenomenon of knowledge from the point of view of the subject who aspires to know, but the object of knowledge also determines the process of knowing. To know a short poem by heart is quite different from knowing Shakespeare's work. From the perspective of the object, to know is to reveal things as they are. To know a complex reality such as "man" is to arrive at an organ-

---

4. The famous joke "those who can't do, teach" is frivolous, because, as we shall see later (Chap. IX), teaching, real teaching, is an important form of action.

ized body of propositions that reflect the largest possible number of man's characteristics. Subjects of this type must obviously be approached from different angles, which constitute distinct fields of research. Less complex than "man" is a topic such as "philosophy and literature." Even so, the first step in the study of this question would be to determine how the different philosophical disciplines relate to literary discourse and the different literary genres, and vice versa. Seen from the object, the first step in the acquisition of knowledge is classification.

To classify is to pay attention to the differences and similarities of things, and to give names according to the common characteristics and differences discovered. Plants, for example, were first classified according to their types of leaves, like the arches in architecture. Biology and the social sciences began with classification.[5] Starting from there science has always worked by way of formalization, that is to say, the application of mathematics. From physics to literary structuralism, mathematics has been the language of science.

After classification, science advances by enlarging with instruments the field of perception of our senses. Since the seventeenth century, the telescope and the microscope have been decisive tools behind scientific progress. In general, knowledge in whatever field is a penetration into reality beyond the surface. In physics and chemistry, analysis finds similarity or identity where the simple sensitive impression does not perceive them. For this reason, comparison is a means of knowledge that begins by highlighting similarities among things in order better to see their differences, and in this way save and perceive their independence in their mutual dependence.

The third aspect of science is finding the cause-effect relationship. It is the key feature of the scientific method. All types of classification that do not help to predict the behavior of things are not scientific. Technology is founded on the possibility of that prediction on the basis of laws discovered through the cause-effect relationship.

5. See Ernst Mayr, *The Growth of Biological Thought. Diversity, Evolution, and Inheritance* (Cambridge MA: Harvard University Press, 1982), pp. 195–208.

The humanities begin, like the sciences, with the moment of classification—literary genres, philosophical disciplines, turning points in history, etc. In the humanities reading is the effort to scrutinize a text beyond its surface, an operation analogous to the microscopic search in science. Where the method of the humanist departs from science is in the linear relationship cause-effect. In the humanities we transit between different aspects or sectors of the same reality, and explain each one of them through their mutual involvement and insertion in the whole. The cause of World War II was probably the decision of one or a few individuals. But "the causes" were a set of ideas and facts—a context or atmosphere (Dilthey's *Zusammenhang*)—that drove those individuals to such a decision. In the humanities, instead of drawing conclusions from premises, we discover different aspects of the subject through mediated intuition and relate those aspects to the nucleus we are trying to clarify. As I have repeated, the process of knowledge is not linear, as the outline of thesis, antithesis, and synthesis may suggest, but an exploration within a sphere. In the process of research we may be forced to abandon the initial hypothesis and, of course, the answers that loomed as probable at the beginning. Research, after all, starts with a hypothesis, ready to accept the outcome of the research, even if the initial hypothesis must be discarded. The process takes different forms in each of the humanistic disciplines.

Linguistics is open to formalization and, consequently, to science, when it studies the objective structure of language. Grammar will find many exceptions called idioms, locutions, or irregular verbs; but in general it formulates rules that are universally valid (with the exceptions just mentioned). However, beyond all grammar and grammars is language as man's essence. In this area a generalizing discourse is attained with the help of what we have called mediated intuition, in which classification manifests itself only in the way in which we order the presentation of general ideas. As we have seen, Heidegger's lecture, "Language," is basically an intuitive leap, but it is organized according to this outline: Language is the home of man; language speaks; language calls;

language is the difference; language is the articulation of the reality or being of things; language is the peal of stillness. The relationship between a linear discourse and a circular one comes about because speech or language as man's essence always floats on the same nucleus, while the languages, as systems of signs, are lines or rigid structures.

In history the problem lies in how to organize our narrative text with the help of documents that can never be complete and are subject to various degrees of manipulation and censorship. Even contemporary testimonies about concrete events are already filtered through the ideology or the ignorance of their authors, which may include intentional omissions or erroneous views of the context in which the events took place. Also, especially for older times, the documentary record is slight and fragmentary, and the historian is forced to guess and build many aspects of the historical reality on the basis of his own knowledge and ideology. However, the number and condition of the documents do not eliminate their objectivity or that of the historical knowledge; the problem lies in defining objectivity in a realistic way so as not to fall into relativism for harboring unrealistic expectations. Objectivity in the vision and evaluation of reality is conditioned (a) by an interest that moves us to select certain facts; (b) by the limits of our ability to see, to insert the facts in a context, and to interpret them; (c) by the particular goal that prompts us to that study—the pleasure of knowing, research into history as "guide for our lives," or curiosity about the past to the extent that it provides perspective for the present.

Another fundamental point in historical construction is causality. Collective history is made by the direct decisions of a few individuals. However, the individual who makes momentous decisions for a society depends in turn on it, and the decisions revert on that very society. Both individualism and socialism would be simplistic positions with regard to the causes and meaning of historical events and decisions. We do not explain the Reformation by pointing to Luther's discontent with clerical celibacy, but we do not explain it either by generalities about social conditions in Europe in the sixteenth century without taking Luther's career and ideas into account.

Of course, the historian's ideology influences the selection and evaluation of facts. Sometimes this has led to historical cover-ups and attempts to rewrite history. The important thing for the historian in this case is to restrain his impulse to judge, and try instead to reconstruct the dialogue that led to the events (conflict, war) by putting himself in the perspective of each one of the actors (contenders). With this attitude, the history of the Inquisition, for example, will aim at retrieving the documented facts and the *honest* arguments that led to the infamous tribunal. The dishonest arguments need only be recounted, since they are not based on any logic. Historians often read the ethical justifications of some protagonists of history as pretexts for the defense of hidden interests. But the example of the Inquisition prevents us from being so clever. Even if Ferdinand the Catholic, "the Aragonese fox" (Ortega y Gasset), was guided by interest and thirst for power in establishing the tribunal, many inquisitors sincerely believed that they served God when they contributed to the eradication of heresy. And even if they had all been criminals interested in the death of the Judaizers (not the Jews, but the Christian converts accused of practicing Judaic rites, and therefore of heresy) and Protestants, the fact that they justified their crimes with moral reasons shows that morals were the ultimate criterion of value in that society. History is the recovery of the structure of collective life and the hierarchy of its values, even if these were rarely put into practice.

In philosophy, knowledge has taken the form of systems, which are holistic visions of reality in connection with the science of each epoch. The different paradigms of thought influence the vision of reality and many practical corollaries of that vision. Perhaps the greatest revolution in philosophy has been the step to privilege the future over the past in the understanding of human life. The past is race, biology, and social and economic heritage; the future, on the other hand, is a personal project in view of our past and present circumstances. Superiority or inferiority founded on blue or crimson blood disappears when each person is seen as his or her own child. "Each one is a child of his own works" (*Don Quijote*).

Theology is, at least formally, the most rigorous form of knowledge, because it must be as precise as is humanly possible. Most Christian theological concepts are contradictory at first glance: God: one and Trinity; Christ: God and man; a God who dies on the cross to redeem man's sins. In the moral order, there are inalterable idealistic principles that are never perfectly assimilated or practiced even by their most ardent defenders. Christianity is the religion of love, even for one's enemies, but in history it has often been imposed on others by the sword and with the harshest persecution of dissidents. Other aspects of "the agony of Christianity" (Unamuno) are: the contradiction between freedom and discipline; Divine Providence and the suffering of the innocent; sacrifice and happiness, etc. That agony was felt not only by the man in doubt, Unamuno; it was also experienced by the great mystic St. John of the Cross in his "Dark night of the soul."

These seeming contradictions demand from the theologian a special degree of accuracy in his reflection and consequently in the text that expresses it. Erasmus and Vives laughed at scholastic subtleties, but they avoided them at the cost of ignoring the central questions of theology. They proclaimed a moral application of Christ's teachings without speculating about the Trinity of God or the Incarnation of the Son, but somebody must reflect about these mysteries if belief in them is to make sense. And who is going to do it if not the theologian?

The medieval philosophers distinguished between two levels of knowledge: the sensory and the rational or intellectual. Kant and his followers fixed the modern theory of knowledge on three levels: knowledge by the senses, by the intellect, and by reason. I do not recall anyone who has made the distinction between knowledge as the mysterious biologico-psychological process from sensation to designation, and knowledge in the phenomenological sense, as we are analyzing it here. We do not know how we pass from our impression of the color green to the idea of the tree. Humanistic analysis begins at the tree, at the end of the biological process. Starting there, one can have knowledge on three levels: (a) a vague presence in which we count on things: I go down a corridor and pay fleeting attention to the walls so as not to walk into them; (b) I can become especially conscious of the wall for some special features, and may pronounce its name and some judgments about it; (c) I am an architect and have been called to study that wall. For the architect the simple name "wall" has a pregnant meaning inaccessible to the passer-by. Levels of knowledge are for us (a) impression, (b) a more or less general notion of a subject, and (c) serious idea after doing research on that subject. Of course, the problem is how to apply to *Don Quijote* what seems so obvious about the wall.

44. Literary knowledge

Among the humanistic disciplines literature raises the greatest suspicion about the rigor of its methods and knowledge. The reason is that language in the literary text is more complex than in the other disciplines, and consequently there is greater danger of subjectivity and fragmentariness, that is to say, of paying attention to aspects of the text whose function in the whole is not clearly visible. In the second part of *Don Quijote,* for example, when a dress is mentioned, its color is almost always green. May this fact have some symbolic value? Assuming that somebody does a thorough research and suggests possible meanings of the motif "green" in *Don Quijote,* how would it help for the ideal reading of the text as a whole? The difficulty of defining the very subject of literary study leads to doubts about the educational value of literature. And, certainly, the rampant subjectivism and playful postures conveyed by many interpretations of texts raise legitimate doubts as to the usefulness of its study.

Up to circa 1830, the classical literatures were studied as examples of taste and as the roots of European culture. Instead of analyzing the texts in their own structure and inserting them in their context, anthologies were compiled with fragments that were considered exemplary in their form or content. When the study of vernacular European literatures—and of comparative literature—was introduced at the university in the nineteenth century, it was in search of the "national soul." Philology was then a useful tool, since it aimed at knowledge of one's own history and, therefore, of one's own collective being. In Spain, the *History of literature* by Amado de los Ríos (1861–65) emerges in that cultural perspective, and Unamuno, in his essays *En torno al casticismo* (1895), resorts to literature in order to find the features of the "Castilian soul." These ethno-psychological perspectives of culture are relegated today to folklore and regional literatures. The great national literatures are questioning the inherited canons and probing the very idea of literature as religious or social commitment, as game, or as instrument of power.

For about one century comparative literature was conceived as the study of the influence of one nation on another. Today this branch of the humanities is the study of the very concept of literature, and of the phenomenon of writing and reading as the background for the comparison of specific languages. The enjoyment afforded by the different languages with their respective powers of expression is founded on the clarification of that universal background. For this reason, the general reflections on literature and literary knowledge today are taken from any language; the flavor of the concrete style is a result, not a beginning. The extraordinary intellectual experience of translating is founded on that identity and difference of the universal background on one side, and the specific nuances of each language on the other.

Literary knowledge begins with written texts. The ideal method with respect to texts is: attention to the basic signs (analysis), generalization on the content and meaning of the text, and evaluation of its qualities. Generalization and evaluation seem to contradict the leitmotiv of this book: to know is to investigate, not to master. But, forgetting about mastery and other forms of utopia, repeated study and thinking about certain subjects take us to higher levels of knowledge than improvisation or cursory attention to those subjects.

Assuming that my reading of *Life is a Dream* (see sections 31 and 32) is correct—i.e., helps readers to better understand the play—the different motifs mentioned in the interpretation can be classified into four categories: fundamental signs, structure, characters, and meaning. The fundamental signs have been "violent" (with its synonyms monster, wonder, labyrinth), man-beast (and "androgynous," woman-man, noblewoman without honor). In these signs of the text even more universal ones are revealed, such as philosophical and theological ideas on the structure of the cosmos and the obligation of parents to educate their children after bringing them into the world.

These signs explain the structure and the two plots of *Life is a Dream:* the story of Segismundo and his father, and of Rosaura and Astolfo. The reason for the conflict between Segismundo and Astolfo is the inheritance of the Kingdom of Poland. Around this motif, Calderón expresses his ideas on monarchy, more or less the ones prevailing in seventeenth century Spain.

The characters are individuals inserted in certain groups and in a specific society. The portrayal of characters points in two directions: on the one hand, they act as individuals, but they also incarnate social roles according to an internal sociology of the text. Segismundo, Basilio, Rosaura, and Clotaldo, besides being individuals, are king, prince, male and female, and they are all noble. The characteristic of being king and prince gives them certain rights and exclusive obligations as opposed to the vassals, and the characteristic of the nobleman also gives him obligations and privileges not enjoyed by the commoners. In *Life is a Dream* Segismundo rebels against his father. After defeating his father in battle he kneels before Basilio and asks for punishment for his sedition. Basilio, instead of killing his son, transfers the crown to him with the words: "Let your feats crown you" (l. 3253). The scholastics recognized three ways by which a nobleman could become a legitimate king: the right of heredity, of conquest, and of election. Segismundo becomes king by virtue of both conquest and heredity. Subsequently, since Segismundo recognizes that the uprising was illegal, he rewards all those who were loyal to his father, and punishes the soldier who mobilized the army in his favor. There is no pardon for the seditious commoner.

This sociology that governs the text generally corresponds to what was thought about the monarchy at the time. But the war of Catalonia in 1640 proves that in the real society of Spain in that period the seeds of rebellion were about to burst. Calderón fought as a soldier in that war. If we did not know that *Life is a Dream* had been published in 1636, knowing Calderón's involvement in the war, we would conclude that it had been inspired by the speeches of Pau Claris to the parliament of Barcelona in 1640:

Just because the eagle is sovereign among the birds, that did not stop nature from arming lesser birds with claws and beaks. For the afflicted vassal it is the same thing whether a government surrenders out of malice or out of ignorance. For us, gentlemen, these are the effects; we do not dispute the causes that way. We must no longer fan ourselves when we should defend ourselves, and think that it is not only temporary convenience, but rather the obligation which nature has given us.[6]

The "illegal" rebellion of the play musters striking parallels with the rebellion in self-defense instigated by the priest Pau Claris. And the rebellion against kings was not confined to Spain; on January 30, 1649, King Charles I of England was beheaded.

After deciding which are the fundamental signs, we use them to describe the structure of the text and the traits of its characters, and to judge its value and meaning.

Where does the worth of *Life is a Dream* as a work of art lie? Is it a worthy member of the Western canon, as is expected of a classic? In my view, the quality of a literary text must be assessed on the basis of four criteria: originality, truth, complexity, and formal perfection. Originality is the most conspicuous quality when it comes to appreciation. However good a text may be, if it is not original it will at best be seen as an epigone within a school.

Truth is fundamental, to the point that Heidegger defines art as "Truth setting itself (in)to (a) work." "Setting itself into a work" means taking form in an artifact that is the temple, the statue, the painting, the literary text, or the musical piece. And "setting itself to work" means

---

6. Francisco Manuel de Melo, *Guerra de Cataluña* (Madrid: Biblioteca Universal, 1878), I, pp. 140–41. Our translation.

that the static artifact is dynamically linked to the creative artist (and his society), and to its receptors (and their respective societies) who accept and preserve it. The work of art convokes two societies (the emissors and the receptors) to a common celebration. Through this power to bring together men into a common belief and celebration, the work of art embodies and reveals truth.

The literary work brings forth the truth, but it is an old proverb that poets lie, and today "fiction" is the common name for all narrative genres, from the novel to the folk-tale. There is no contradiction between fiction—using the name in this general sense—and the truth of the literary work as such. The adventures of Don Quijote never happened, and bunnies never sprang from Cortázar's stomach. If we call those adventures and the tale of the bunnies the surface of the text, that surface was indeed invented by the writer. But the imaginary fictions reveal possibilities of human behavior that range from the deepest love to the most refined hypocrisy, from the hero to the scamp. The expression "imaginary fictions reveal" means that the text is like an eddy of water that allows us to see deeper layers below the superficial tale. Yet the image of the different layers is too physical and mechanistic, for the depth of a text—what the medieval writers called the kernel behind the bark—is embodied in the only thing there is in a text: its surface. The kernel is the surface or signifier, which is pregnant with its meaning waiting to be unfolded by the reader. In fables where animals speak, and in fantastic tales the distinction between the fictional surface and the truth of the work of art is quite obvious.

However, since truth is universal, in the final analysis the superficial fiction—the set of referents—is what makes each text or work of art the unique work it is. The meaning of "violent hippogriff" is contradiction, but contradiction can be expressed in many ways; in *Life is a Dream* it is embodied in the powerful image of a horse raised to cosmic dimensions. This particular referent (the hippogriff) ultimately gives its mythical and artistic character to the philosophical message, and indicates the world of references of the author. Consequently, knowledge of the literary text should penetrate into the deeper truth (significance and meaning), but then return to the innocent reading of the surface, to stylistics (referents, the world of the author). The innocent reading of a text is a return; paradise regained. And at the end, even this joyful return to the stylistic niceties of a text we love ends up in a feeling of partial failure. Literary analysis culminates in the need for yet another reading.

The third quality of a literary work is complexity. If we only intend to express the truth, the best way to do it is to write an essay or a treatise on the topic we want to clarify. What I am saying in this book on the power of language and on the limits of our knowledge is dramatized by Cervantes in chapters 44–46 of the first part of *Don Quijote* in the discussion on the barber's basin, the helmet of Mambrino, and the forms of doubt and deference to authority that Sancho shows when he invents the basin-helmet (I, 44). Cervantes dramatizes doubt by embodying it in characters whose interests are based on their respective social classes. He does not offer a detailed view of the problem of truth, but he gives it life in dialogues, battles, and humor. In Cervantes' chapters, language displays its emotional, intellectual, sensorial, and structural potential, while in the essay we give preference to its intellectual function. The use of language in its four functions is the basis of the complexity of the literary text.

The last criterion of the quality of the literary work is the perfection of form. Of course "last" in this context should not be understood as less important than the other criteria. The distinction between surface and depth can in general terms be equated with form and content. Applying what we just said about the referent as the essence of each particular text, we may affirm that the literary work is nothing beyond its form, a form with density, a content structured in language. In more specific terms, richness, elegance, and clarity or stylized precision constitute the quality of the literary text.

45. Literary knowledge and reality

Once again, if our reading of *Life is a Dream* is correct, then we as philologists, in addition to knowing Calderón's play as a textual and historical reality, have gained knowledge of its social and cultural background. After all, when Calderón wrote his work, he was not studying Calderón's plays, but reality itself, which he endeavored to deploy in his texts. For this reason, the critic who intends to know a text should go beyond it to the same reality that stimulated the author. To begin with, the title of the play, "Life is a dream," is a radical statement about human life. Can the critic eschew discussion of that statement? As we see, the text confronts the reader with a basic philosophical question, and that is reality, not textuality.

Another example: Segismundo's drama arises out of the premonition read by King Basilio in the stars when Segismundo was born. When we report on the astrological beliefs of the seventeenth century in order to understand the conflict we are still in a textual world. But with the astrological referent Calderón displays the drama of determinism versus freedom in human existence. The drama of destiny and freedom is as enigmatic for us today as it was for Calderón. Only the surface of the dilemma has changed; if in the seventeenth century the terms were stars versus free choice, in our time the genetic code has replaced the stars, but the mystery is still with us.

Life is a Dream confronts us with hierarchies and with criteria of ranking that place the individuals in a certain social layer. The question of reality for us is this: if we still have criteria of social discrimination, how do they differ from those of Calderón and how have these differences come about?

The preceding considerations lead us to conclude that we understand a literary text only when we understand the reality that constitutes its theme. The purely formalist analysis that does not penetrate into that reality is merely a game, not knowledge.

Humanistic knowledge in general and literary knowledge in particular must be systematically organized. To a great extent, the success or failure of studies on *Life is a Dream* or *Don Quijote* will depend on the structure that we build with their signs. I have suggested an outline with four coordinates: fundamental signs, structure, characters, and meaning. Other parameters, and better ones, are also possible; the best outline will always be the one that allows us to clarify more signs and make the text more transparent. From this we may conclude that humanistic knowledge lies basically in classification and construction. Classification is the order in which we see and present the articulation of the signs, according to their range of signification in the totality of the text. The decision on the importance of each sign will depend on acuteness of our vision. In any case, humanistic study is construction, and deconstruction is a parasitic function that feeds on the humble builders.

A text—except in the case of authors who have written only one book, such as *Celestina*—is usually one among several texts written by the same author. Juan Ramón Jiménez maintained that all of his poems were fragments of one alone, which he called "the work." The complete works of an author constitute a text which, though not written, serves as the foundation of all the written ones, and therefore, justifies the construction of a scholarly discourse about "the work of" Calderón or any other writer. Writing is, like reading and knowledge, a differential interplay of acts and habit. If writing is a lifelong dedication, each text is conditioned by the preceding ones, and possibly by those that follow it; consequently, in reading one text one must keep in mind the parallelisms or contrasts with others by the same author.

Beyond the "work" of an author there might be a "school" to which he belongs. Terms such as "school" and "movement" were used in the nineteenth century as categories for the classification of literary history: in the Spanish Golden Age (another classificatory term) the poetic school of Salamanca was distinguished from that of Seville, and in comedy, historians speak the schools of Lope and Calderón. Eventually, the terms "style" and "generation" were introduced. The study of style was expounded by Heinrich Wölfflin's works on the Baroque, and "generation" became a household term in Spanish literary history when Azorín grouped his contemporaries under the rubric "Generation of '98." There is no room here for a broader history of these concepts, but they must be mentioned in any theoretical discourse on literary knowledge.

School, movement, style, or generation, are but layers on which the text is founded. The change of name of these underlying notions indicates that the categories of literary history are also subject to history. The important thing for us is that every isolated text, already complex in itself, reflects strata of meaning that come to it from its background. The attempt to know concrete texts must also study such general concepts, and since they are usually quite vague, it is necessary to apply extreme caution in describing them and their variants. The relationship text-context brings us back to the relationship between the universal and the particular—Heidegger's difference—as the basic structure of knowledge.

Historical and literary knowledge can become banal in spurious manifestations. One of them is pure erudition, which does not insert the concrete text or event into its background, or which enumerates isolated data without leaping into a universal context. To describe the plot of a text, to count the characters, and to add some subjective observations on each play by Lope de Vega, is at best raw material for getting to know Lope de Vega. Knowledge begins when constants are discovered that allow a universal thesis on the art of structure and character in Lope. Any conclusions on Lope are, in turn, specific knowledge that will acquire still greater meaning if we achieve, through the study of several authors, conclusions about constants in Spanish theater of the seventeenth century. There is no real knowledge of individual things *(De singularibus non est scientia),* Aristotle said in an aphorism that is often forgotten by historians and philologists. Knowledge of individual things is disorganized information, a prerequisite for real knowledge at best, which must be universal and systematic.

The concentration on the individuals in history and literature leads to one of the most worrying deficiencies in history and literature: fragmentariness. There is no knowledge without some general conclusions on a subject, and no intellectual maturity without engaging in value judgments. At the same time, the humanist must fight, in himself and in others, premature generalization and irresponsible evaluation. The goal of study is to learn, not to proclaim theses. The work of the humanist sways on this pendulum between honest caution and honest audacity: one must dive into facts and have the modesty to jump to universal conclusions. In this leap we deploy our ignorance together with our knowledge. To expose is to be exposed.

The important thing for understanding the structure of knowledge is the idea of man (Chapter IV) that has guided our reflections. There is no linear step from the particular to the universal, and vice-versa. It is always a spiral around a center. In this upward spiral we swing back and forth between erudition, generalization, and judgment, without forgetting that reality is simultaneous and that our linear thinking is the penalty we pay for our limitation. Again, humanistic discourse is the pursuit of the different lines contained in the articulated nucleus.

Philosophical knowledge does not inspire the same doubts about its status as literature. We may have some misgivings about the usefulness of the topics, but philosophical texts are generally studies of reality. *The Modern Theme* (1923) by Ortega y Gasset is about the relationship between spontaneity and rationality. In it Ortega, following Georg Simmel, asserts that the cultural values for which we give our lives originate as a "secretion" of life. We may accept or reject this thesis, but with it the author invites us to think for ourselves about human life in its aspects of vital impulse, and the values that sprout from that vital impulse, and then control it in turn. We may study the rhetoric of Ortega's book, and discover the ways in which style shapes the content, but the main thing is the content.

What I have said about philosophy appears also valid for theology. If we start with faith in God and in the precepts of the Church, theological discourse has the same character as the philosophical: use of the word in its intellectual function, and phenomenological demonstration. Documents can prove superficial facts; thought, on the other hand, is an invitation on the part of the emissor to share in the glimpse of reality. If we do not believe in the theologian's premises, then the theological problem becomes a philosophical one: the existence of God, the possibility for our mind to prove the existence or non-existence of God, the sense or senselessness of different religious confessions, and many more questions that we tend to avoid.

The reflections of this chapter allow for some conclusions that I consider applicable to knowledge in general, and to the humanities in particular:

1. Knowledge is a body of objectified learning.[7]

2. Knowledge in each one of us is at the same time a presence and an absence, a little bit of mastery and a lot of research into the other.

3. Knowledge is the insertion of specific contents into a universal context and/or background.

4. Things are forms linked with other beings in a chain of sense. Knowledge is the vision of those things in their mutual insertion or causation.

5. To the extent that we perceive the things inserted in their chain of sense, all knowledge is system.

---

7. Karl Popper distinguishes three worlds of knowledge: the broad field of reality; personal knowledge; the world of knowledge stored in libraries. The latter he calls the third world, which is the true repository of knowledge. A work becomes objectified and thus a tenant of the third world even for its own author. See K. Popper, *Objective Knowledge*, pp. 106–52.

IX Usefulness

◯ℨ *The aim of every step in the cultural progress which is man's education is to assign this knowledge and skill he has acquired to the world's use.*

(Kant, *Anthropology*, p. 3)

46. The useful

As noted in Chapter IV, man is inherently social, which means that he contributes to the well-being of others, and benefits from them. The study of the humanities can be justified only if they are useful to those who cultivate them and to society at large. Of course, it all depends on the definition of the useful.

Usefulness can be understood as a series of concentric circles. The innermost one refers to the necessities that keep us alive. Then there are broader circles of realities that are useful in a less immediate and short-term way. Faced with the urgent needs of every day—natural disasters, refugees, slave children—it may seem immoral to spend money on knowing if there was some form of life on Mars thousands of years ago. The most urgent need is to respond immediately to a crisis that in a few days can cause or save many thousands of human lives. But *Don Quijote* is also located in some circle of useful things, for even if it did not bring Cervantes much more than the parsimonious patronage of Cardinal Sandoval y Rojas, in our time it is a goldmine of revenue for publishers in some parts of the world. And as for Shakespeare, he "was an immense financial success as a playwright and died affluent."[1]

1. Bloom, H., *The Western Canon*, p. 119.

The example of *Don Quijote* or of the economic import of Cervantes and Shakespeare, enhanced by cinema in our times, puts us on guard against simplistic conceptions of the useful. How useful is the study of literature, philosophy, or theology? By exploring *Don Quijote* and *Hamlet* most of us will not prepare ourselves or our students for writing similar masterpieces and best-sellers, but we will prepare ourselves and the students to do justice to those works by reading them as they deserve to be read. And to read well is to be able and eager to listen—another kind of usefulness.

The most conspicuous circles of the term "usefulness" would be: urgency, necessity, pleasure, and education. Urgency: to give food, shelter, and clothing to the needy. Necessity: to improve the conditions of life, health, and communication among all human beings, as technology improves food, medicine, and the instruments of communication and travel. Pleasure: the art of making meaningful use of free time. Reading is an obvious course in this regard. And finally, the maximum service: education. The humanities are useful insofar as they educate us. The sciences also educate, but in a different way.[2]

Founded on the wide range of meanings of the term "usefulness," Unamuno wrote:

Art, science and the purest theoretical work contribute to the improvement of industry. Kant, Hegel, Schopenhauer, Goethe, Schiller, Beethoven, Schumann, have created current German industry in greater measure than people generally think. The sentimental, romantic or idealistic German has turned out to be the most pragmatic of men; 1848 prepared the way for the era of Wilhelm. Basically both theory and praxis go together.[3]

Unamuno's statement can be understood in two ways; the first and decisive one is that an original and well-organized culture displays itself in

2. Even speaking of circles, the need to describe them in linear succession imposes a sort of central vs. superficial, greater vs. lesser importance. In view of what we will say in chapter X about the role of education for human life, education is human food and vice-versa.

3. Unamuno, "Discurso en los Juegos Florales de Bilbao." [Speech at the Juegos Florales in Bilbao.] In *Obras completas*, VI, 340–341.

all fields of social activity. While Roentgen was discovering the x-rays in Wuerzburg, the masterly Teubner editions of the Greek classics were appearing in Leipzig. In a secondary and derivative sense, the cultural prestige of a nation eventually gives it an edge in the competition for the export of its products.

A few years later, Unamuno became famous for another sentence: "Let the others invent." "The others" were the Europeans and North Americans as opposed to the Spaniards. The sentence is still quoted by many in Spain as proof of the frivolity of some intellectuals in the face of serious problems that affect their nations. But, as Unamuno explained several times, far from advocating the retreat of the Spaniards from scientific research, he was inciting them to be creative in the field for which they felt gifted. Spaniards should strive for invention in science and technology, but if they were more gifted for poetry and religion, it would show in their works. In this way, while Spain would enjoy the scientific and technical inventions of others, the latter should also be able to receive something from the Spaniards.

In 1921 Eugenio D'Ors wrote that history has progressed along two principles of order and hierarchy: the warrior in the past, and the principle of work in our days: "Between the social idea of war and the social idea of work there is no room for a social idea that is properly bourgeois, because this—as Eduard Berth has pointed out—is characterized already in its definition by an absurdity: the subordination of the public interest to matter; in other words, the radical negation of the idea of order."[4] D'Ors then cites an idea of Bertrand Russell: "The dreamer of a new religion or of an unheard of artistic form for which utilitarian remuneration is unthinkable, shall always find, according to the Cambridge master, a niche in the world. However, it will be good that, as it fits the principles of justice, this niche be exceptional and very narrow and thorny."[5] According to D'Ors, any room left for leisure in a society of workers will be exceptional and difficult to justify.

The question is whether the creation of a religion or a new art form

4. "La idea social." In *Nuevo glosario, I (1920–1926)* (Madrid: Aguilar, 1947), p. 401.
5. D'Ors, op. cit., p. 402.

can be considered leisure. And furthermore, today both work and leisure present problems. Work is a problem, because of the difficulty of getting a job—depending on countries and junctures—and because of the very conception of work. The life of the worker was not humane throughout the history of Christian Europe. But at least, since Pope Leo XIII confronted the issue of work in his encyclical *Rerum novarum* (1891), there has been a Christian doctrine of labor in which the product is not an impersonal artifact, but the life and work of a human being inseparable from his family. Today for the most part the religious and human dimension of production is relegated to the back burner, and work is measured primarily in terms of productivity. Hence, work is not stable, families are obliged to uproot and move, and many workers are forced to change not only workplace, but even profession several times in their lives. The alienation of the worker for the sake of higher productivity is the most alarming example of man converted into a tool.

Leisure is a problem in the form of unemployment for those who seek work, and as a void in the mass of relatively young retirees who, given current averages of life expectancy, need to fill their free time. Psychological studies show that being occupied prolongs mental and physical health, and contributes to a healthy and balanced longevity. Of course, the dichotomy leisure-work is not as clear as it appears at first glance. People in rural and poor societies imagine the happy "gentleman" who, sustained by his inherited wealth, "does not lift a finger." That image has been real only in exceptional cases. Man's work, from which neither the pauper nor the millionaire is spared, is having to fulfill ourselves in an attitude of equilibrium, joy, and hope. In this task leisure can be torture, and work pleasure. That is why Unamuno demanded compassion for all, including "the poor rich people."

47. In praise of teaching and learning

All the words that express the phenomenon of education point to an influence that guides individuals through a particular path and guards them from deviations. This influence is not a mechanical impact of the educator upon a passive subject, but the subject's free decision to accept the norms and values proposed to him. Values, like ideas, can only be proposed and accepted, not imposed. The linguistic principle that the emissor is receptor and vice-versa, is valid not only for linguistics but for education as well. Naturally, in the first stages of life we receive in a more passive way, but from the age of twenty-two, more or less, our life is in our own hands. However, even in the period in which we are more passive than active, the reception is still an activity of the learner. And when we are basically active, the reaction to the stimuli will be determined by our context and projects, but the passive moment does not disappear; we are still dependent on the external stimuli, which sometimes may come by chance and mark a turning point in our lives.

The usefulness of the humanities becomes visible first and foremost in education. Beginning with the most superficial facet, the humanities produce teaching positions for many people from elementary schools to the university. It has always been recognized that education never ends. Even when the university and society did not pursue research as a goal, it was assumed that what was learned in school led to practical application, and praxis was in turn the best way to learn: practice makes the master, says a German proverb. If this is old wisdom, today the pace of innovation in research and the possibility of knowing the new results immediately, exacerbate the need to live in an attitude of perpetual learning. Whoever does not ride the fast-speed train of technical innovation cannot have a secure job for very long. Private Master's programs, summer universities, and courses and seminars within companies respond to this need for continuing adaptation. Certainly, most of those courses are not in the humanities, but the humanities will also be cultivated to the extent that public and continuous education of adults is strengthened.

Compared with the cruel conditions prevailing in the world of labor, a professor at any level of schooling, but especially the university professor (and here I include all areas of study), lives almost on a utopian planet. The first reason for this privilege is that to be a professor is not a job but a vocation, and work brings such pleasure that we count our hard work as leisure. It is common to hear the humanist express admiration at getting paid for what he does with such delight. It is this very satisfaction that often leads the humanist to underestimate the value of his contributions to society.

Many professors achieve what every working individual should come to enjoy: satisfaction and pleasure in their work. Some teachers seem to be transfigured when they enter the classroom, and they project an air of happiness over it. Yet, there is no denying that the professor's life is monotonous and solitary. In general, it is not a lucrative career, although it can be—in an honorable way—through participation in the textbook market and other related activities, such as writing in newspapers.

Another privilege of a professor's life is freedom. He is probably the only worker not formally tied to more than ten hours of class and office hours per week. To be sure, he is tied to the laboratory or may still be writing at eleven P.M. on Sunday, but he can break for coffee with a friend at eleven A.M. on Tuesday. This freedom, of course, is not an arbitrary concession or lack of accountability; it is required by the nature of intellectual work, which can only be regulated by the struggle between the will to work and inspiration. The proof is found in the scarce results produced by those research institutions—here I refer specifically to the humanities—in which the scholars have to be present for a fixed number of hours. Naturally, in this as in everything else, freedom implies the possibility of doing nothing or doing the wrong thing, and we never lack a percentage of "idle kings," who wrote their last paper for the tenure review. The best thing that can be said in these cases is that their crime is their punishment. There is no sadder image than that of the sexagenarian professor with his notes yellowed by time, and who goes to class like a prisoner to the gallows. On the other hand, the majority who honestly do research and probe the quality of their teaching makes the failure of the minority who abuse their freedom insignificant.

To the vocational satisfaction one must add the joy of dealing with man's highest legacy: the masterworks of culture, including the drama of scientific research, which, as we have said, becomes humanities with the passage of time. The greatest misfortune that Don Quijote foresaw for his story was that it might need "commentary." Spaniards may legitimately comment on the work of Cervantes as a landmark in the awareness of their collective identity. Beyond the national reference, we may comment on it as a model of perfection for all mankind and, in a more professional sense, as a way of helping students to understand and enjoy a masterly text. Aesthetic enjoyment, as stated in section 35, depends on our ability to unveil more secrets of the works of art. The humanities are, therefore, not only useful, but also necessary to elevate our receptive capability toward texts on the aesthetic, ethical, and social levels.

This praise of teaching seems to be founded on petit-bourgeois values: personal vocation, individual freedom, and aesthetic sensitivity. Nothing can be farther from the truth; the teacher and professor embody and carry with them the most important function of society: education. To learn how to read and write is to contemplate reality through some traits with particular shapes that we call letters. The person who teaches children to associate meaning (to see reality) with those traits is the miracle worker who removes the scales from a child's eyes and gives him light, as Christ did to the blind man. The profession of elementary school teacher is not appreciated by society as it should be, and yet I would measure the civilization of a society by how it appreciates its elementary school teachers, the miracle workers who give sight to the blind.

The secondary school teacher no longer performs the miraculous leap of the primary grades, but he guides and tolerates the children of his peers in their adolescence, the crucial moment in a person's development. And the college and university professor proposes to the students ideas and values in the only opportunity they have to live and interact in a worldwide atmosphere. The college student comes from his home and high school, a relatively narrow environment, and after college he will settle again in the limited environment of his profession; the years at the alma mater present the unique opportunity of being in dialogue with partners from different parts of the world. The college and the university are a sanctuary of universality in contrast to the limited environments in which we generally live. The fact that the college professor is the mentor of the individual in this unrepeatable circumstance, gives to the professor's work a decisive social and political momentum. He does not make legislative decisions as the politicians do, but through the search for truth in his field of teaching and research he fosters the sensibility that produces honest and competent politicians.

The work of the university professor consists of teaching and research. In principle, there should be no conflict between the two activities; without doing research it is practically impossible—with all respect for the rare exceptions—to be a competent teacher, and the need to formulate ideas in the classroom raises new questions for research. Of course, conflicts may arise for something as simple as timing. One who is teaching Medieval literature while writing a book on Unamuno may not reread the Medieval texts with due attention or be up to date on the latest scholarship about them. But this imbalance is anecdotal, and simple common sense can overcome it.

The American college offers the student a great deal of personal attention: psychological, financial, academic, and career counseling. Here a gray area opens up in which professors who do little or nothing in research justify their sterility with their frequent interaction with the students. In this way we have come to accept a conflict between research and teaching that splits the two faces of the profession. In my view this dichotomy is theoretically untenable, and deleterious in practice.

Nobody should underestimate the need for a professor to be available to the students as partners in the same search and dialogue. What is more, a professor should lend his time to all students regardless of whether they are in his department or he is on their committee. It is also true that, since the ultimate responsibility and merit of learning rests with the student himself and learning is a life-long enterprise, a teacher who stimulates the love of learning is excellent, even if he does not contribute to the advancement of knowledge. But in order for this teacher to remain competent in his subject, he must at least keep abreast of the contributions of other scholars. In the final instance, however, the student is in college to receive an education, to become professionally competent, or in the case of a few, to start a career in research and teaching. A professor who wants to fulfill his obligation to these students must be up to date in his field and, if he can, add something original to it.

Good teaching consists of four moments: competence, enthusiasm, immediate preparation, and generosity. Of the four, competence is the most indispensable one, and—once again, with rare exceptions—the only way to be competent is to do research; consequently, the professor who does not do research cannot be a good teacher. Students of mathematics and the sciences must learn principles of algebra, geometry, and calculus, in order to understand other questions. In these fields, which repeat centuries-old theorems and laws, it may be possible to be a competent and inspiring teacher without doing research. But in the humanities, beyond the data and facts, all discourse is construction and, consequently, creation. Creative work may lead us to realize that we are not original, but this realization can still be an original conviction based on the practice of research. We must embark on the personal effort of creating, even if we discover that we are not Menéndez Pidal in philology or Heidegger in philosophy.

The excitement of discovery arouses enthusiasm. We are not responsible for our creative powers, but we are for avoiding complacency in every respect and at every moment. Of course, it is easier to maintain enthusiasm in youth than in later stages in life. The "old professor" is not old so much in age as in attitude. Old is the man or woman who has arrived at unalterable views and positions, and for whom there is nothing new under the sun. Knowledge and language, we have repeated, are not the representation of realities that we master, but arrows that point to, and call us toward the real. To maintain this conviction and act accordingly is a sign of mental youth.

Competence and enthusiasm constitute what we would call long-term preparation. But in addition, a professor needs to prepare each one of his classes. Many years ago in Munich I used to listen with great admiration to my revered teacher, the great theologian Michael Schmaus. Some days I noticed that he was wavering, using vague language, and was not finding the right sentence to end the class. He had not prepared that lecture as he had prepared others to which we were accustomed. I experienced how even the most prominent thinkers need immediate preparation for each meeting. It is the only way to connect one class with the preceding ones. Good order is an inherent moment of meaningful learning.

The fourth quality of good teaching is generosity. The classroom is a social institution, but the student and the professor are unique individuals; they both need the balance of what we have called in section 20 the professional role and the personal recognition. And in this relationship the professor can be a role model for the values of loyalty, attention, consideration, understanding, and good manners.

48. *Other career opportunities*

A career in law has many possibilities for employment, while philosophy or history offer few avenues outside of teaching. However, in societies whose cultural offerings are richer every day, careers for humanists exist and more can be created. To begin with, we have analyzed the humanities in a very strict sense: language, literature, history, philosophy, and theology; but we have also emphasized that the field does not have such precise borders. The humanistic disciplines exist because creation in all fields pre-exists. We explain St. Augustine, Kant, or Cervantes; but consistent with our stance against mechanistic distinctions, we observe that the levels of creation and criticism cannot be separated in a rigid way. Cervantes includes in *Don Quijote* reflections about the quality of literary work; and it can be said that in general the most penetrating and illuminating literary criticism comes from those who combine theory with the experience of creation: Goethe, García Lorca, Torrente Ballester, etc.

Artistic and literary creation not only provides the texts with which the critic makes his living; it also generates and moves large amounts of money. The successful novels and plays, the ones made into movies, the scripts for television series, the poetry of love and protest written for professional singers: these are all necessary literary forms for the entertainment industry, the one that perhaps accounts for the largest transactions of money in the world.

In the American universities programs in creative writing, while recognizing the subjective condition of literary production, teach students to improve their texts by discussing them with their professors and peers. The programs also pay attention to the commercial aspect of writing by putting students in contact with agents. In this cultural network a few succeed with their creations, but those few rise out of the many who also aspire, and collaborate in less glamorous roles.

The publishing industry demands readers and correctors of style, people who revise translations and call attention to inconsistencies in the bibliography, in proper names, and in other aspects of a book. Those who have published books know how much they owe to the query of the editor who faced them with the inaccurate date or the fuzzy sentence.

Another area of employment for the student of humanities is journalism. The range of topics covered by the press is so wide that specialists are needed for the different sections of newspapers and magazines. But the special pages on opinion and culture—including literature, history, essay, religion, and entertainment—require humanistic competency. Above all, journalists need a deep knowledge of the political and cultural history of their nation in order to avoid simplistic theses or the shameless posturing with which they cover up ignorance or resentment. The journalist exerts so much influence in our societies that he has taken the role traditionally accorded to the intellectual. This power, in order to be responsible, demands the corresponding degree of study and thoughtfulness.

Another source of jobs for humanists is regional and local history. There are positions in cataloguing, conservation of, and research into, local archives and museums. And public libraries require competent personnel for the services they provide.

A form of cultural enrichment today is tourism. A trip that wants to be more than the tasting of a new beer requires some information about the places to be visited, and that information is basically history, literature, and art. We must be aware not only of our immediate surroundings, but of the whole world, which today is within reach of television and the airplane. And just as our trip demands that we know the culture of other countries, foreign tourism in ours demands cultural services for which the humanities provide the most pertinent background.

One may of course ask if it is a worthy goal for a Master of Arts and Letters to be a tour guide. To which I would answer that a worthy goal is anything that helps one to practice what he has learned, stimulates one to learn more, and is a gratifying job-vocation. The listing of possible careers does not bind any individual to a specific one; on the contrary, it may liberate him by suggesting viable alternatives. In tourism one can be a waiter, a guide, a writer of tour books and therefore researcher, promoter of tours based on that research, and several other things. The humanities educate, but they have to be applied where their services are needed, and today the areas of travel and leisure need such cultural services.

Eventually, in a society with growing numbers of retired people, adult education will increase in proportion. Adults of all ages would probably attend courses and seminars on the structure of human life (as biography), on communication between parents and mature children, on love and its desirable manifestations in families, where the desire to say a kind word to a wife or child is sometimes repressed as embarrassing. And these courses would not be given only with the discourse of the natural and the social sciences, but with a truly humanistic approach, and with a rigor that surpasses easy moralization and "how to" gimmicks.

The studies of philosophy and theology educate with a comprehensive vision of life as a calling conditioned by concrete possibilities; they analyze freedom as guided by obligation, and the ego as a solitude open to others. The philosopher and the theologian, besides being professors, in many cases also help as social workers providing psychological and pedagogical services. They must be familiar with scientific research in psychology, a demand that is inherent to the interdisciplinary character of philosophy and theology.

With regard to religion, studies show that its practice contributes to prolong human life and to maintain the mind creative and alert. This practical value alone would make religion commendable, even if there were no other reasons to embrace it. But, of course, for one who professes faith in God and prays for perseverance in that faith, it is insulting to put religion on a par with exercise and low cholesterol. Religion is the conviction that a personal God exists and sets the ideal rules of human behavior, and that in this way human life, in spite of the most incomprehensible injustices and atrocities, still makes sense. The magazine *Business Week* of August 23–30, 1999, included a section titled "Twenty-one ideas for the 21st century." Number six of these ideas is religion, and the article by Karen Pennar begins with the statement: "Religion will endure, affirming our vulnerability." The author also anticipates that what Andrew Dickson White called the "history of the warfare between religion and science" will give way to cooperation in the search for truth.

But, since religion is so vulnerable to all sorts of impurity in the form of fundamentalism, fanaticism, and destructive and self-destructive cults, it should be a subject of the most rigorous study. An educated person in our society should at some point learn about the following topics:

1. The fact of religion in human life; religion and anthropology; the main religions.

2. In view of the differences between religions, can there be a definition of religion as such?

3. Religion as a biographical and personal phenomenon; religion as feeling, as rituals, belief, religion and biography; religious education as

an aspect of the individual's insertion in the family, that is, the role of family tradition in one's religious confession, and the power of that tradition to let that confession appear as the most reasonable one.

4. Christianity: history and varieties; the Bible, as the most prominent book of Western civilization. Christianity: ideal doctrine versus historical development. Peace and war; the division of the Roman Empire, and the grudge between Latin and Greek Christianity; Latin Christianity and the modern European Union; Christians, Jews, and Muslims.

5. Catholicism and Protestantism: the wars of religion and the cultural impact of religion in the different European nations.

6. Religion and ethics: universal brotherhood, and behavior toward the other in business, politics, the workplace, etc.

Some parents contend that religion should be left to the decision of the individual when he can make it himself. But life is a process of development in which the individual is dependent on others. Education means to raise a son, not only as a body that is fed but as a full human being. In this idea of education parents instill their values, including religion, from the moment of birth. If we force a child to study mathematics because we know it is necessary, why should religion be slighted in the child's education?

From a historical point of view, religion is at the basis of constructive doctrines, transcendental events, and of inexplicable outbreaks of barbarism in the past and in our own time. Spain and Portugal in Southwestern Europe, Venice and the Austrian Empire in the South East, with Italy in-between contained the advance of Islam. The wars in Bosnia and Kosovo in 1996 and 1999 have brought to our attention the deep-seated hatred still existing among neighbors in the name of religion. And though Europe is healed of almost all the wounds of the religious wars that followed the Reformation, the unending conflict between Catholics and Protestants in Northern Ireland is a sad reminder of their lingering impact.

Scholastic theology, as the theoretical formulation of medieval and early modern Christian doctrine, provides both the ideological clues and the semiotics for understanding the classical European literatures of the sixteenth and seventeenth centuries, including Cervantes and Shakespeare. The ideas on man, woman, and cosmos influence both the characterization and the structures of novels and plays, and the criteria of evaluation of individuals and behavior follow the same principles. Obviously students of the humanities should learn more about religion than they do now, and it is necessary to train teachers for this task.

49. Intrinsic usefulness

After outlining some practical applications of the humanistic disciplines, we need to return to man's image as center and articulated nucleus. Usefulness is understood as the practice of an acquired skill. But the humanities are a center, and all applications should be justified as a circular path that originates in the center and returns to it. The first and final function of the humanities is to guide the individual who lives with and from them, in other words, to help us grow internally. In this function of promoting personal growth, our native language occupies the first place.

The study of our native language is necessary to express ourselves well, both orally and in writing. The art of good expression implies grammatical correctness, precision in the choice of words, and fluidity in the sentences, avoiding loose words that are completed by gestures or interrupted by grunts—indices of poor discourse. Good expression implies adaptation to the cultural level of the receptor, display of as many aspects of the topic as possible, and logical organization of the material. In this experience, teaching a subject to non-specialists, or writing for a general public, forces us to polish our style. With a specialist it is enough to mumble something, and he will immediately understand us; but in teaching we do not speak to specialists, and the important thing is to make ourselves understood by the person who is not well versed in a topic. Surprisingly, when we practice this philosophy, far from lowering the level of the discourse, we benefit by better understanding the subject under discussion. The one who mumbles is the first victim of his own game; the hallmark of a great teacher, on the other hand, is clarity, which is achieved by putting the ideas expressed into universal structures reproducible by the listener or reader. The first step toward understanding, as stated in section 38, is to accept or to reproduce the communicated experience.

Good speaking can have more subtle secrets, one of which is the euphemism. As opposed to the curse word, courteous speaking can educate and create an atmosphere of pleasure among the speakers. As funny as a swear word may seem to be, the listeners probably forgive it but do not like it. The writers of treatises on courtly manners posited good speaking as a distinctive feature of discretion. The curse word is in most of us a spontaneous outburst, and among the minority who use it in literary works, a mannerism. Sometimes shy and well-mannered writers who do not curse in their conversation will do it in their writings, contributing to the un-education of their society.

In addition to one's native language, it is immensely useful to know foreign languages, especially now that we are citizens of "the global village." To know a second language broadens our mental horizon, allows us to move freely in dialogue with more people and in another culture, and enhances the chances of finding better jobs. With the same degree in business, getting a job in a bank or in a multinational company will depend in many cases on knowledge of a foreign language.

Of the modern languages, English is today the universal *koiné,* as Latin was for many centuries. In the United States, after English, Spanish is by far the most widely studied second language, and it keeps expanding. In theory, it is possible to establish criteria as to which foreign language is more or less useful, but in practice it does not make sense, and to suggest rankings would be quite anti-humanistic. Chinese, Russian, and Arabic, spoken by many millions of people, will prove advantageous to those who know them, but the minority who may know Sinhalese and Nepali will also be in demand.

The desirability of Greek and Latin is a subject of discussion in any effort to devise an ideal humanistic curriculum. Greek civilization is still operative in ours as the paradigm that shaped its basic principles. The relation to the world on the basis of the idea of being; the dichotomy of subject and object; the structure of our grammar; the basic principles of mathematics; the ethical discourse including the names of virtues and vices; aesthetic, literary, and political categories, and the roots of the scientific and medical lexicon: all these elements maintain, or rather are, the presence of ancient Greek culture in our own time. But this does not mean that high school students or those in scientific and technological careers should spend years studying a language they will never use. Greek culture should be studied not as language but as culture, that is to say, by reading in translation its most important works: *The Iliad* and *The Odyssey*, because they have been the model of epic poetry, the most prestigious literary genre in the West; *Oedipus Rex*, by Sophocles, because it has been the model for tragedy; Plato's *Symposium*, because there we find a theory of love that has pervaded medieval mysticism and the literature of courtly love in the Renaissance and the Baroque; Aristotle's *Nicomachean Ethics*, because it is the unsurpassed codification of ethical discourse in the West, and its terms constitute today the moral lexicon of our own languages—virtue and vice, action and habit, meaning of life, magnanimity, kindness, wisdom, happiness, etc.

Every college student of any school and department should take at least one course in Greek culture. Doctors and scientists may have an interest in the language, since their terminology derives, in great measure, from Greek. Of course, the decision on the level of dedication beyond the required course rests on the individual, but even if few students attend those courses the college still has to offer them. While the student is limited and, like his professors can allow himself a lot of ignorance, the university is the repository of objective knowledge—the "third world" in Popper's terms—and is obliged to make it available.

What has been said about Greek applies, for the majority of students, to Latin, though for a different reason. As a cultural paradigm, Latin culture derived from the Greek. On the other hand, Latin is not only more present in Western civilization; it was its core until very recently. Spinoza's *Ethica* (1677) and Newton's *Principia* (1687)—to mention just two modern classics—were published in Latin. Recognizing that there are many legitimate levels of competence in any field, if a professor of humanities wants to move freely in the Western tradition before 1700—and in many important texts of the eighteenth and nineteenth centuries—he must read Latin.

In addition to our natural languages, there is mathematics, the universal language that codifies the structure of the physical and social reality, and even of poetry. Literary and artistic expressions that come freely and spontaneously from the heart exhibit a structure that can be formalized in mathematical formulas and statistics. Mathematics—and computer science—is a language derived from and connected to the natural one; consequently, it is not opposed to the humanities. To the extent that mathematical language consciously or unconsciously conditions our lives, its knowledge is inevitable for an educated individual. In this context, the role of the computer as a prodigious but double-edged machine is obvious: the convenience it offers for writing and publishing has ied in some cases to an explosion of verbiage; but for the responsible user it facilitates correction, and therefore fosters concision and precision.

The expanded access to information in our world increases the need for translation. Translation has a mechanical aspect that today can be carried out to some extent by the computer. But "artificial intelligence" depends on the natural one for its birth and working, and for the interpretation of its results. Anyone who has practiced translation knows the intensity and quality of intellectual commitment it elicits. Translation enriches the intellectual experience of the translator at least in two ways: (a) the connotations of words and the nuances of expression in the different languages make us aware of the nature of language; (b) the struggle for expressing the foreign content with accuracy and elegance in our mother tongue is—at least has been for me—the best workshop for learning both the foreign and the native one by becoming aware of nuances not noticed before.

With regard to the usefulness of history—including cultural history—the study of our nation is a necessary condition for being responsible citizens. Spanish history has been darkened by the so-called "black legend," spread all over Europe on the basis of the writings of three Spanish dissidents: Bartolomé de las Casas, Reginaldus Montanus, and Antonio Pérez.[6] Passionate reaction in Spain led to the fabrication of laundering myths, and the reaction to the Franco dictatorship has resulted in a political rewriting, not only of recent but also of past history. In this case, only honesty and extreme rigor in distinguishing facts from subjective attitudes can mend the wrongs. What I am saying about Spain applies of course to most countries.

Cicero called history the teacher of life. History is a teacher, first because it removes from us the illusion of novelty. It is a sober truth that, with different protagonists (the unrepeatable other), the same human passions struggle over and over (history repeats itself). Secondly, history is a teacher because in it we can learn the lesson *sic transit gloria mundi* (thus passes the glory of this world); whether it is worthwhile to lose one's soul (and sometimes the body) for the sake of power and money. We might in this way liberate ourselves from stressful greed in order to cultivate the legitimate ambition of developing our potential and helping others achieve the same goal. History teaches us to avoid errors, because it displays the alternatives that have already been tried in certain situations. Whoever delves into the results of war will end up detesting war.

However, history is the teacher of life mainly as the density of our consciousness. The more history we know, the larger our vision for both present and future. And, as a teacher, history is also a student of life, that is, it remains anchored in the present. We approach the Inquisi-

---

6. "Black legend" is the name given to the falsification of Spanish history by the political propaganda of Spain's religious and political enemies—the British and the Dutch in particular—since the sixteenth century. The Spanish friar Bartolomé de las Casas accused his fellow Spaniards of merciless cruelty in the Indies. Reginaldus Montanus, a Sevillan monk turned Protestant, denounced "the arts of the Spanish Inquisition" (*Sanctae Inquisitionis hispanicae artes aliquot detectae* [Heidelberg, 1567]), and Antonio Pérez, who betrayed King Philip II after being his secretary, and sold secret information to England and France, contributed to the demonization of the Spanish king and Catholicism. Schiller's *Don Carlos* (1787) is a good sample of the spread of the legend in Europe. See William Maltby, *Black Legend in England; the Development of anti-Spanish Sentiment 1558–1660* (Durham, NC: Duke University Press, 1971).

tion, colonization, and political wrangling of the past as examples of assaults on freedom, property, and rights, issues that we face in our time. The past needs interpretation, and the interpreter cannot free himself of his perspective. And finally, we devote our attention to history in view of future projects.

Classical languages are a fundamental aspect of the historical dimension. Western culture, we have said, is in its origin Latin culture. The Greek metaphysical and aesthetic traditions, and the Bible on which Western culture are founded, were transmitted to us in Latin. Recalling what has been said about Greek culture, the intensity of dedication to the classics must be decided by the need and will to assimilate the legacy of the past, but without letting it become a straitjacket that makes us blind to the present and future.

Philosophy is the ultimate reflection on reality and on the meaning of life, especially for those who do not profess religious faith. Although few can make a living with it as teachers, philosophy is inherently useful, because we all philosophize in a more or less creative way. The ideas of those who have thought more deeply or who have known how to express their thoughts more poignantly clarify the world in which we dwell. In addition, philosophy constitutes the background of Western literature and art. As we have seen in our analysis of *Life is a Dream*, it sometimes provides the clue for understanding the literary text. In several plays by Shakespeare a sister is amazed at the conduct of her brother, and cannot explain how offspring of the same mother and blood can be so different. The motif makes sense on the basis of the scholastic doctrine of the "indirect" influence of the body upon the soul. Shakespeare's image of woman (*"mulier: mollis aer,* a piece of tender air"— *Cymbeline*) similarly reflects the influence of philosophy on the portraiture of the literary character.

Theology is a reflection on the belief in the existence of God and on the immortality of the individual. All linguistic and historical meaning is founded on the ultimate meaning of life. The book of Job says that man's life on earth is a struggle (Job 7:1), but if in the end we die like any other animal, only those sacrifices made for our loved ones are worthwhile. I accept with Unamuno that our personal behavior usually will not change regardless of whether we believe in God or not, but the tone and color of our life will probably change. Unamuno analyzed the "tragic sense of life" as the anguish of the individual who yearns for God and immortality but cannot be sure of their existence. By contrast, the mystic writer Teresa of Avila (1515–82) lives in the presence of God and from that bedrock looks at the world with love, distance, and freedom, all in proportion to how things bring her nearer to God. In contrast to Unamuno, Teresa of Avila incarnates a mystic sense of life. In fact, one perceives the tragic tone in Greek culture when compared to the mystical one in Christian discourse. Greek culture, which does not rest on belief in the immortality of the soul, or in freedom as opposed to destiny, exhibits a tragic sense, while Christian discourse is basically mystical, since God the father and "logos" gathers all things into a nucleus of meaning. Christianity is logocentric. Even St. John of the Cross, who experiences the pain of the dark night of the soul, rests on "the living flame of love."

The mystic sense of life is the ultimate foundation of the humanities in a positive sense. St. Thomas Aquinas holds that all natural perfection acquired in this world will be preserved for eternity in heaven. But many people cannot believe in God and the other world, and both believers and agnostics need to live on earth in the most civilized way possible. In this sense, the humanities can be useful in two ways that we may call the pragmatic and the aesthetic. The pragmatic position highlights their value as a vehicle of communication among individuals and collective bodies, and communication implies respect and rejection of violence.

Regarding the aesthetic aspect, we all recognize the pleasure of good conversation, of understanding art, music, and poetry. In the twentieth century, social and cultural progress helped to extend to the masses the pleasures that were previously the privilege of a few. Cinema, art, television, journalism, theater, travel, and sports enrich man in the aesthetic dimension.

The pragmatic function of the humanities is not always visible, and rarely has a perceptible impact in facilitating communication and in curbing violence. The aesthetic function is hopelessly mixed with subjectivism, and therefore suspected of arbitrariness. Hence the precarious position of the humanities in the face of studies that look more directly practical. This is why, although the academic study of the humanities flourished with agnostic positivism, we spontaneously place their supremacy in the Middle Ages. Today, even if religion were an illusion, the pragmatic and aesthetic functions justify the humanities. For, if there is no Heaven, we should preserve the earth from becoming Hell. As the Spanish poet Blas de Otero said, "Who knows if there is more, but we know there is less."

X Value

Granted that we cannot do anything with philosophy, might not philosophy,
if we concern ourselves with it, do something with us?

(Heidegger, *Introduction to Metaphysics*, p. 12)

50. The personal self

Heidegger's statement about philosophy can be extrapolated to the humanities in general. In order to show how humanistic discourse can be intellectually rigorous I have analyzed Calderón's *Life is a Dream* and in a less direct and comprehensive way *Don Quijote*. In the preceding chapter I have pointed out several things we can do with the humanities, but what we do with them must be founded on their objective value, that is, on what they can do with us. And what they can do, when cultivated as "rigorous knowledge" (Husserl's idea as alpha and omega) is enlighten us about the basic questions we face as human beings: personal identity, collective identity, communication, the sense of human life, and creativity.

What good is it to study *Don Quijote*? It narrates the adventures of a knight who has gone crazy. In scholastic philosophy, on which Cervantes based his idea of man and of the literary characters, the intellect operated in two functions: wit and judgment. Wit is imagination, creativity; judgment, on the other hand, is the ability to control and organize the content gathered by wit. Wit speculates in the realm of ideals and possibilities, whereas judgment sees things in their concrete reality. The two functions described by philosophers as operations of the mind, were codified in rhetoric as "invention" and "disposition" respectively.

Cervantes describes Don Quijote's madness with the expression: "he lost judgment," which means that the knight's intellect was left only with wit. By losing judgment, the "ingenious knight" replaces the perceived reality with an illusion he carries within himself. The entire first part of *Don Quijote* consists of adventures which follow a common pattern: the knight sees a reality—the windmills, the inn, young women, mule drivers; he substitutes the illusion of his mind for what he sees and hears; as a result of the falsification, he goes to battle and loses; and finally, instead of blaming himself, he resorts to a wonderful means of self-consolation: he blames the enchanters. As a human experience, reproducible by all of us, don Quijote is the loner, the withdrawn person who, instead of looking at the people around him, attacks them on the basis of his prejudices. From his imagined world he mistakes windmills for giants and inns for castles, as we do when we look at the world from a deep abyss of shyness or resentment, which make us suspicious of everyone and everything.

For lack of judgment, don Quijote embarks on adventures in which he is defeated and beaten. But in his defeats, far from acknowledging his errors and blaming himself, he accuses the other, the enemy-enchanters. In this resource of self-consolation Cervantes also reveals a pattern of human behavior. When a reviewer criticizes a book as mediocre or bad, the writer usually consoles himself by feeling misunderstood or the victim of a conspiracy. Of course, writers *are* sometimes victims of conspiracy, but the healthy approach is to listen to the criticism and to denounce enemies only when all other explanations for the criticism prove futile. In his introverted and illusory world, don Quijote is also fanatic. Based on absolute principles (wit) that he does not contrast with reality (judgment, discretion), he attacks flocks of sheep or illegally liberates galley slaves. The feature that redeems don Quijote is that in his madness his native goodness is also loosed, that goodness that was both natural and acquired in the tranquil life of his village, with the priest, the barber, and neighbors like Pero Alonso.

Cervantes has created in Don Quijote a radiograph of the human ego at the border between reality and desire, life as a crossroads between legitimate hope (truth) and self-deceiving illusions (dreams). In *Life is a Dream* Calderón describes Segismundo as a man-beast. As we said, "beast" stands for the man who has been engendered and not educated. Segismundo is every person denied human rights. If that person is conscious of his rights, he suffers while questioning heaven and earth, and if he is not even conscious, if he is not able to question, he simply suffers the injustice. Segismundo is that large percentage of humanity that lives in absurd criminal dictatorships; the refugee; the one discriminated against and persecuted; the hungry; and the one who cannot hope to develop his potential for lack of means. All of them can ask the Western bourgeoisie: why, having a greater soul (than the animal), do I have less freedom?

Machado's sonnet "To the great nought" describes not only human experiences, as the older texts do, but the modern probing into the structure of the mind, and the contrast between the abstract emptiness of the concept "being" and the painful emptiness of death, silence, and forgetting. In the sonnet Machado hints—only hints—at the beautiful topic of the difference between the philosophical and the poetic discourses.

The first theme of the humanities is the problem of the self, our identity at the crossroads of reality and illusion. Where is it that legitimate expectations end and paranoia begins? Is realistic happiness possible, and where does its secret lie? How does each one of us answer the three questions formulated by Kant: What can I know? What ought I to do? What may I hope? Philosophy answers those questions with rational discussion, describing the universal characteristics of man in his nature and behavior. To speak of philosophy in general terms may oversimplify a vast field that comprises several disciplines, as we have seen in section 10. Of these disciplines, the most relevant one is ontology, which studies the very constitution of the self. The ontology of human existence includes ethics, which studies the criteria of equilibrium or alienation that condition our lives. These abstract words, equilibrium and alienation, simply express the crossroads from which at any moment we may take the route that leads to fulfillment or to drifting without aim.

Life is a play performed without rehearsal; a mistake once made cannot be undone. However, since life is a play performed without rehearsal, if an error cannot be taken back, it can and should become a spur for change. What does not make sense is to dwell on the error and to cut off one's future with narcissistic lamentation about the past. The only healthy repentance is change, to open new routes, using our errors as warnings against childish pride in our accomplishments. In order to develop its potential an individual must demand the utmost of himself, but must accept himself even if he is the last one in the crowd, a position that someone in society has to occupy. But we already know that men cannot be lined up from first to last. Each individual has an irreplaceable and unrepeatable mission, and in that mission each person is always number one, or a failure if he does not fulfill it.

For the believer in a providential religion the world has meaning because God exists, and it has different meanings depending on whether God is thought of as father or as judge. Only confidence in divine providence provides the basis for a joyful humanism, which incites generosity in imitation of God who is most generous *(maxime liberalis),* as St. Thomas Aquinas says. But in our pluralistic societies any religious confession must engage in dialogue with all men and women on the basis of purely rational principles.

The first of these principles is personal balance. The kindness or wickedness of our acts usually, though not always, flows from our basic attitude toward life. This is the meaning of Machado's lines: "And more than a man who knows his doctrine, I am, in the good sense of the word, good." The more vital and free the good person is, the more easily he or she creates or accepts rigid laws and discipline when they make sense, as poets shape their free-ranging creation into strophes with mathematical structure. On the other hand, the dogmatic individual is the slave to the commonplace, whose vote is mortgaged by party discipline or who may be trapped by terrorist slogans. Rational ethics, as the reflection on the principles of man's behavior, is the new religion of mankind in a society that is no longer held together by a single religion or by religion at all.

Aesthetics also has a very practical value. We tend to limit aesthetic enjoyment to reading or to museum visits while on vacation; as such, aesthetics is associated with leisure. This association led Kierkegaard and Marx, each in his own way, to talk of aesthetics with disparagement. The study of aesthetics is justified as a way of making sense of, and giving meaning to, free time, especially now that a longer life expectancy promises us many years of healthy leisure. The ideal, however, is that men enjoy not only their vacation but their work, which takes the longer and better part of their lives.

The humanities are sometimes justified on the grounds that man, supposedly dehumanized and reduced to a mere number by scientific rationalism, needs to put a coating of beauty and intuition onto his life. This premise and its conclusion are in my opinion unacceptable, or at least insufficient. Humanistic discourse is not intuition but hermeneutics; mediated, rigorous research. And although we have not discussed the topic in detail, of all the humanistic disciplines only literature has historically been associated with beauty. But the notion of beauty and its relationship to literature needs a precise clarification in a work on aesthetics or literary theory. From our idea of man as an articulated nucleus, the aesthetic is a dimension of the human, inseparable from the scientific and the ethical. The aesthetic is the search for truth insofar as this search is displayed in an imaginary artifact: "Truth setting itself (in)to (a) work" (Heidegger). The opposition between aesthetics and science is based on a reductive concept of aesthetics, and can only broaden the gap between the "two cultures."

If philosophy studies how the self relates to the world around it by way of knowledge, literature deploys the same relationship, depicting individuals whose egos cover a spectrum from the firm stance of the fanatic to the one who dissolves in its environment. Calderón's *Life is a Dream* (1636) is at times compared to Descartes' *Discourse on Method*, published in 1637. However, Descartes' doubt is "methodical," postulated by reason, not truly felt and lived. Descartes' human self has a solid consistency and questions only the data of the senses. Calderón, on the other hand, questions (through Segismundo), not the information of the senses but the very consistency and identity of the ego. Many modern texts, from Rousseau to Sartre, present characters that dissolve in intimate anguish and perplexity. Descartes did not doubt the solidity of the soul, while Ganivet and Unamuno saw the purpose of life in the creation of a soul for ourselves. Literature dramatizes Kant's three questions by presenting characters and stories that display perspectives of life, either in the form of superficial reactions or of radical attitudes: the tragic, the mystical, and the nihilistic sense of life.

The self—analyzed in philosophy and dramatized in literature—conquers his identity ultimately through his faith or lack of faith in God. With God, happiness, suffering, victory, and defeat get their respective place in a structure of sense. Without God, joy and pain are real, but life in general is semblance and "as if." That is why Unamuno postulated God as a rock on which to stand: "Because if you existed, I also would truly exist."

51. *Collective identity; culture*

The humanities constitute what we call the cultural tradition of a people. In the definition of man we have pointed to our roots in time or history, and our present is a whirlpool that includes both past and future. In order to live consciously and with self-assurance in our own country we need to know its history as our own human space. In modern democracies, where we all participate in government through our vote, it is fundamental to know the country we are in, which is ultimately the result of our thoughts and actions. This knowledge of history has nothing to do with memorization of past dates and glories; it is simply the extension of our present in the direction of past and future. Such knowledge, which involves both acceptance and criticism of our own society, constitutes the pedestal from which we can react to foreign visions of our own country. Those visions derive mostly from their image of our history, and they affect us—sometimes quite directly—through attitudes that may have practical repercussions on our lives. In view of the influence of history, we may understand the following words of a Spanish historian, which otherwise may sound hyperbolic: "When the children grow a little older and are ready, I will go one or two years to your home as a preceptor, and will teach them the science of sciences, life and thought in action: history."[1]

Language and history transformed into culture become the symbol of our national identity. In 1915 the French Hispanist Georges Cirot wrote: "*The Lusiadas* symbolize in their immortal lines the heroism of a race and assure the Portuguese a homeland."[2] In Spain, we need only remember Don Quijote, Sancho, and Don Juan. Around 1900, in the wake of the Spanish-American war, some writers converted these literary figures into representative symbols of a pretended Spanish national character. This ethno-psychological discourse is debatable to say the least, but one thing is undeniable: whether we identify with those literary characters or reject any similarity to them, the works in which they appear constitute a legacy that most Spaniards proudly accept as theirs. The impact of that legacy is such that a Spaniard who today rejects the slightest impulse of imperialism cannot but feel proud in St. Augustine, Florida, or at the California Missions.

If between approximately 1850 and 1920 (from the first steps of literary history to the heyday of the avant-garde), attention focused on works and characters as national symbols, today, when all forms of nationalism are unworthy of a sound mind, we label certain works of art "treasures of mankind," and include Shakespeare and Cervantes in a universal canon. From this perspective we broaden our view to embrace the whole world and see the humanities as a search for cultural contributions and the very idea of culture beyond national borders. This is easy to do with regard to art, science, and any accomplishment not tied to a particular language. Literature, on the other hand, is embedded in one specific language, and as a result, will keep on shaping the distinctive features of collective identity, even though global integration is advancing.

1. Emilio Castelar to Adolfo Calzado, August 23, 1874, in *Correspondencia de Emilio Castelar, 1868–1898* (Madrid, 1908), p. 12.

2. "Chronique," in *Bulletin hispanique*, 36 (1915): 67.

Usually culture as a collective legacy is associated with nationality; but there are other possible criteria on the basis of which we embrace a collective identity, such as race, religion, profession, political credo, and social class. The "cultural politics" of fascism, communism, and capitalism, and the obsession with identity of Latin American literature in the twentieth century, bring home the role—with some accompanying risks—of the humanities in shaping "imagined communities" (B. Anderson).

52. *Communication*

The third fundamental topic of the humanities is communication. Literature presents every imaginable variety of interpersonal communication: love and hate, shyness, hypocrisy, and loyalty. In 1959, the prestigious Hispanist Arnold Reichenberger published an article, which for many years was required reading for all students of the Spanish *comedia*. In it he said that the two fundamental topics of the Spanish classical theater were honor and religion.[3] Religion aside, honor has been a basic topic in theater and literature in general. Honor is the sense of duty that the honorable person feels even in his most intimate privacy. It is, therefore, a secular ethics that links men as men, regardless of religion or any other criterion. A secular ethics without religious references finds in loyalty the bedrock of human communication. In fact, we can deceive a person only if that person considers us loyal. Truth and lie are, therefore, not two poles with the same range. Truth stands by itself while the lie feeds on truth; it is truth's parasite.

With all the caveats that befit grandiose generalizations, it is safe to affirm that European poetry has had basically two topics: love and satire, or, in more contemporary language, love and protest.[4] And furthermore, the meaning of love has not changed since the Middle Ages.

---

3. "The Uniqueness of the Comedia," in *Hispanic Review* 27 (1959): 303–16.

4. Of course, there are other themes, too. I am only highlighting the most pervasive ones. Death, for example, has been a recurring theme in poetry, but most of the poetry of death is love poetry.

From the Mozarabic *jaryas* (eleventh century) to the latest pop, love is a feeling of devotion and desire for requital, always genuine, and therefore sincere. In real life it is possible to confuse love with some counterfeits: sexual attraction toward another body devoid of true interest in or respect for the person, or simple vanity where we are more interested in appearing attractive and enjoying the illusion of our own importance than in loving the other. Sexual and selfish love is what the medieval theologians called concupiscent love, because in it the lover seeks only his own gratification. True love, on the other hand, is focused on the beloved. But it also asks for correspondence; this is why the literature of love abounds with laments of absence or ingratitude. And since genuine and sincere love is so difficult, there is also a rich body of irony and satire with respect to love.

In modernity, a lot of literature, from poetry to the essay, has analyzed love and its many falsifications. We have already mentioned two: sexual desire and selfishness. Love can also be timid, jealous, and submissive in the sense of asking for protection. Since the eighteenth century, perhaps the most frequent satire of love has been to portray it as a mask for interest. In our time, satire has highlighted sex without love. Cela's works, for example, are notable for a cynical presentation of love. At times that vision is confused with realism, but it is not realistic; rather, it is subjective and arbitrary, as it fails to do justice to the nuances of human experience. In general, contemporary literature and cinema dwell on man's perpetual dream of love, and the disillusion brought about by its rareness and fugacity, and its inability, even in the best of cases, to satisfy our infinite yearning. Maybe this is why we sorely miss dear persons when they die, and do not pay sufficient attention to them while they live. We all love Beatrice and Laura, apparently because they are the perpetual promise.

Love and its falsifications bring to mind Don Juan Tenorio. The first Don Juan (in *El burlador de Sevilla* [The Trickster of Seville, ca. 1625]) neither loves nor practices the art of seduction. He deceives Duchess Isabela by impersonating Duke Octavio, her true betrothed. Under the cover of darkness, Don Juan has formally married her by pronouncing the sacramental words of matrimony before consummating the sexual union. At that time, although the Church had at the Council of Trent (1545–1563) prohibited clandestine marriages, they were still a common topic in literature. Certainly even a secret contract had to be entered into freely, so Isabela's marriage to the masked Don Juan could not be valid in the eyes of the Church, since she thought she was getting married to Duke Octavio. But in the imprecise theology of *El burlador* the union is given as valid, for at the end of the play Don Juan dies, and Duke Octavio marries Isabela as a widow: "Since Isabela is a widow, I want to marry her" (ll. 2855–56).

When Don Juan arrives in Tarragona from Naples, he marries the fisher Tisbea with another private promise. This time, however, the sacrament is void because Don Juan is already married to Isabela. The trickster then seeks to possess Doña Ana de Ulloa by impersonating her lover, the Marqués de Mota, but she discovers his ruse and rejects Don Juan, who so far has not displayed any charm. On the contrary, since Doña Ana is noble and would be unable to marry the Marquise if she had lost her virginity with another man, the only statement Don Juan makes before dying is that he did not dishonor her: "Saying before his end that he did not owe any honor to Doña Ana because she recognized him before he could deceive her" (ll. 2846–49). This testimony, and of course, her status as virgin, makes the noble woman fit to marry the Marqués de Mota. Don Juan "the trickster" is the opposite of the man in love who refuses to deceive or take advantage of his lover.

José Zorrilla's Don Juan Tenorio (1844) has all the traits of a liar, a scoundrel, and a criminal. But he does fall sincerely in love with Doña Inés, and true love compels him to behave differently with her than he does with any other person, including his father. The mere memory of Doña Inés civilizes Don Juan and, in the end, in scenes that are perhaps theologically absurd but of great theatrical effect—the cemetery, the tolling bells, the last dialogue before the judgment of the souls—love saves Don Juan in the last minute of his life.

The literary text is a stage on which the most diverse ways of human conduct come into play. It is neither a book filled with advice, nor a court in which vice is punished and virtue rewarded. Instead, the literary text dramatizes the need to be on guard against falsification, and displays examples of madness, cruelty, and heroism—the heroism of the exceptional feat, or the one of the daily routine. The moral of the literary work lies not in proposing guidelines or in giving counsel, but in analyzing possibilities of human behavior, in dramatizing the problems that concern us in our most intimate life, and create happiness or misery in our family relationships, in the groups to which we belong, and in our society in general.

History is a theater of communication: loyalty and infidelity, colonization, slavery, discrimination, absurd wars, and tense truces. For the humanist it is enlightening to discover the history of how the facts have been justified. In many cases the perpetrators of criminal acts have explained them with pseudo-scientific or pseudo-ethical pretexts that made them appear moral.

Nothing needs to be added on the communicative function of language. We live, we move, we are within language. Rhetoric is not the art of persuasion, and of disguising falsehood as truth. It is the description of the constitution of our existence as communication. Rhetorical figures are the classification of existential experiences from the side of their expression. Within the philosophical disciplines, logic studies reasoning: the possibility of dialogue; ontology, our openness to ourselves and to others, which is essentially the same thing; and ethics studies our behavior, always in connection to others.

Theology, as a reflection on collective beliefs, tends to stress the dimension of community among the adherents to a particular faith. Religions have been the strongest unifiers of individuals into the shared confession, and the strongest sources of exclusion of the "infidel." As instrument of exclusion religion has caused and justified horrible crimes. In Christianity the idea of the mystical body implies an actual sharing of the same nature, grace, and merits; a sort of material—not purely symbolic—communication between all members, which imposes on each individual a responsibility for all of the others. This is the meaning of the Catholic "communion of saints." Even though salvation and condemnation are personal, there is no salvation outside of the church, that is, outside of community. According to Rivera de Ventosa, Christian humanism, despite all the evils that Christians may have committed, is a universal embrace.[5]

53. The sense of life

One fundamental theme in literature has been religion, whether it takes the form of prayer or blasphemy, mystical commitment or sarcasm. I have already mentioned in Chapter III that the word "literature" is too abstract; there are concrete works and each one with few exceptions is grouped under universal categories called literary genres. The classical epic is the narration of wars of the gods as they related to humans; the lyric poem celebrates, doubts, implores, rebels against, or submits to God. Some theatrical works such as *Hamlet* or *Damned for Despair* (attributed to Tirso de Molina), dramatize religious experiences with tragic results that raise questions, since Christianity in its abstract perfection excludes the possibility of tragedy. For Christianity lives in and from the confidence that the greatest natural disasters, human injustice, and family dramas, are foreseen by the Divine Providence of God the Father, who loves the victims of these occurrences more than we do.

However, the abstract perfection takes flesh in the Christian believer, who faces evil and unjust suffering, the greatest source of tragedy in this world. For if tragedy is the experience of a dilemma with no way out, our perplexity as Christians does not find its way in the face of the massacres of innocents, perpetrated daily because of hatred, rapacity for money, or political interests. The belief in God makes the question more vexing; for if there is no sense in life, anything can be expected. But believing in God, we ask him why he permits so much evil. That is

5. *Visión cristiana de la historia en sus textos.* Suplementos Anthropos, n. 26 (Barcelona: Anthropos, 1991), pp.12ff.

why literature has dramatized the cries and doubts of so many people, and philosophy and theology have dealt so deeply with the problem.

Intimately tied to the question of the religious meaning of life is the attitude of the individual toward the world. There is, therefore, a psychological dimension linked to religion: the affirmation, the negation of meaning, and the tedium of relativism and cynicism. A person with a living faith in Divine Providence will not succumb to despair. On the other hand, one for whom the world makes no sense will not only question the purpose of all that surrounds him but will probably cringe through life in a vacuum. The tedium of living is one of the most frequently described experiences in literature. It is anguish, the melancholy of Shakespeare and Calderón, Unamuno's tragic sense of life, nihilistic existentialism, the groundless life and text of the post-modernists. Schopenhauer is the most conspicuous proponent of these attitudes in philosophy. But of course, these attitudes are still preferable to the reckless self-assurance of the fanatic. Literature, history, and philosophy present us with a gamut of human possibilities among which we can choose the one we prefer, along with alternatives that enlighten us by contrast. Inspired by Unamuno's tragic sense, and in contrast with it, I embrace St. Teresa's of Avila's mystic sense of life: "The soul is not a dark thing."

54. Creativity

Every branch of knowledge or human action requires creative talent. But even if scientists and inventors use their notebooks to reflect upon the process of their discoveries, the main subject of their analysis is the reality investigated, not the process of discovery. The analysis of creativity in a comprehensive phenomenological sense belongs to the humanities. Many historical and literary texts are studied for their reflections on the method of researching and writing as much as for their content. The best example I know of this fusion of creation and critical consciousness is *Don Quijote*. This book is the story of a knight and his squire. But next to them there is a third character: Miguel de Cervantes, who enters his own work by displaying the experience of writing and the drama of inventing an extensive fiction that is the child of "the intellect," not of wild fantasy. It is easy to plan the structure of a short story, but immensely difficult to invent and organize (invention/disposition, wit/judgment) a long fictional story with many episodes and characters—especially for Cervantes who had no model for such a project. This is why Cervantes voices his bewilderment in the face of the strenuous effort.[6] Cervantes' book is not just a novel but a treatise on how to invent a novel as well. His theoretical reflection on the creative process of the novel appears in the prologues, in the commentaries by various characters about the narrative as such, and in the author's commentaries about the doubts of the fictitious author Cide Hamete Benengeli.

From chapter IX of the first part to chapter LIX of the second, Cide Hamete is the author, and Cervantes a "historian" who paid for the translation of the book. Beginning in chapter LIX of the second part, when Cervantes finds out about the spurious *Quijote* published by a pseudonymous Avellaneda he casts aside all masks, and even though he still speaks of Cide Hamete, he vindicates the paternity of his characters and text. Who is Cide Hamete? Is he perhaps just a joke? In every act of writing there are two people writing: the one who inspires and the one who copies while looking upward for inspiration. Cervantes was the first to unfold the ramifications of this experience. Until the prologue of *Don Quijote*, poets had invoked the muses or Christ. Cervantes finds the muse within himself, and describes writing as the collaboration of Cide Hamete and his translator, the inspirer and the inspired. This collaboration assumes the character of a struggle between

6. "It is said that in the original manuscript of this history one reads that when Cide Hamete came to write this chapter his translator did not render it as the Moor had written it, with some sort of complaint against himself for having undertaken such a dry and limited history as this one about don Quixote, always feeling himself restricted to talking about him and Sancho, never daring to venture out into any digressions or more serious and entertaining episodes" (*Don Quixote*, II, 44. Trans. by J. Rutherford [New York: Penguin Books, 2001], p. 776).

desire and ability. *"I would like* this book, as a child of the intellect, to be the most beautiful, the most noble, and the most discreet we can imagine, but *I have been unable* to contravene the rule of nature."[7] From this experience onward *Don Quijote* contains an array of voices that seem to belong to different authors. But there is only one author: the one of flesh and bone, Miguel de Cervantes, tax collector by profession and writer by the grace of God. Only he discovered that talking and writing are the crossroads of effort and inspiration. We dwell in the difference where talking is listening and teaching is learning.

This is not the place to present statistics concerning the many poems in which the awareness of writing is as abundant as the writing itself. Of course, what has been said about meta-literature in literature is applicable to all the humanistic disciplines. Can we think of a philosophy that is not meta-philosophy?

55. *Faith in the humanities*

This book has focused on academic disciplines: linguistics, literature, history, philosophy, and theology. We have taken it for granted that, in order for us to write history, historical reality must exist, and that literary texts must exist to make reading possible. But we have mentioned art, literary creation, and history as reality only in passing. On the other hand, to determine the value of the humanities by the light they shed on our most decisive questions we have referred to works of creation (*Don Quijote* and *Life is a Dream*), not to the academic disciplines that

7. The italics are mine. "Prologue" to *Don Quijote.* The available editions of *Don Quijote* in English—from Walter Starkie to John Rutherford—translate "hijo del *entendimiento"* as "child, or son of *my brain."* This translation misses the meaning of a key sign placed by Cervantes in the first line of his text. "Entendimiento" is the intellect, the superior faculty of the soul in scholastic philosophy. The books of chivalry are the product of wild imagination without judgment. Against these books Cervantes seeks to write a "child of the intellect": a long fiction in which all episodes are verisimilar, that is to say possible according to the laws of nature. Some episodes may be strange and improbable—the meeting of two brothers in an inn after twenty years in which they had lost track of each other—but these meetings by chance are still naturally possible and provide the basis for *admiratio,* one of the purposes of literary creation.

have been the main subject of our analysis in this book. Have we suc-
cumbed to a colossal fallacy in order to support our cause? I do not
think so. The researcher who reads a literary or philosophical work does
not truly read if he does not penetrate into the reality explored and
dramatized in those texts. For this reason I have criticized fragmentariness, formalism, and the dehumanization of criticism (Ch. VIII). *Don
Quijote* is *Don Quijote* when it has been made transparent in an enlightened and enlightening reading. Therefore, the best reader is the one
who succeeds in exposing the masterpiece, and that means to allow the
work to speak to us. We professors look at reality via ancient and modern classics, because from them we receive the most rigorous visions of
that reality.

However, here lurks another possible fallacy. In our phenomenology
of reading and understanding we have stressed the need to return to the
past and learn the language in which the classic texts are written. For
this reason we devoted so much space to the expression "violent hippogriff" in *Life is a Dream*. On the other hand, we are now highlighting
the contemporary relevance of the classic texts. No contradiction exists
here, either. The classic, just like everything human, retains a lasting value, but it also has sides that belong irretrievably to the past. As Heidegger said, language brings things closer to us, and calls us to their own
distant location.

Humanistic discourse is not linear but spiral: it always circles and surrounds the same nucleus. But this nucleus is articulated: thus it too, has
pathways, or better, hidden galleries. The humanities do not stress the
aspect of progress, but rather the entrance into the gallery and the return to the classics because of their lasting value. But society has progressed since Cervantes and Calderón; in spite of the inhuman cruelty
that still exists, the progress of human rights is beyond debate: equal opportunities for women and men; the condemnation, at least in theory,
of racism; the suppression of the death penalty and torture in civilized
codes of law; and the establishment of international tribunals that judge
crimes against humanity by national leaders. What makes a classical
work a dated piece are those elements that were typical of their time,

that is to say, the social discrimination that they reflect and generally endorsed, and the pseudo-science (from biology to law) that justified that discrimination. Instead, what makes a classical work modern is the presence of individuals seeking sense, the rebellion against injustice and commonplaces, and the invention of new values in both form and content, with which we can identify.

Well-intentioned efforts to make Cervantes and Calderón (and Shakespeare for that matter) "modern" must ignore fundamental aspects of their texts. A classic has a permanent value, but it is anchored in a specific historical moment. Because aspects of the present and the past cannot be distinguished in a mechanical way, a reading of the classics places itself in what is permanently valid while pushing back to its epoch the unacceptable residue, the purely other. Hermeneutics is the crossroads of the search for the objective structure of the text as other, and the pulling of the text toward us as a mirror of permanent truth.

If we have been able to prove that humanistic knowledge can be rigorous and that it deals with those themes that preoccupy us twenty-four hours a day from the cradle to the grave, it seems only fair to conclude that the humanities are central to our lives, and should thus be the root disciplines of any educational curriculum. They are the moment of introspection that allows us to know ourselves, and in that way stimulate our betterment and our self-acceptance with our limitations.

The discourse of the humanities grapples with man as the nucleus that precedes any distinction, and therefore in the essential unity of the ethical and the cognitive. But the human totality is a biography in which man opens his way as he wanders. Phenomenology as method emphasizes research over mastery, the journey over the comfortable inn. Understanding is an effort to understand, and knowledge little more than the accumulation of questions.

Humanistic discourse is the humble discourse of truth, but it is not weak. Its humility is based on the fact that, instead of trying to influence, it only invites the partner to share perspectives on things. Consequently, the discourse of the humanist is exactly the opposite to that of the preacher, the politician, the lawyer, and the salesman. All of these speak with a certain interest in mind, and attempt to trap the listener. The discourse of interest may be true, but is prone to lying. The humanist, on the contrary, looks and simply points toward what he sees. Antonio Machado had an intuition of this: *"Your* truth? No: *truth;* and join me in searching for it. Keep your truth to yourself."* In the humanities, the ultimate criterion for ascertaining if we are right or wrong is dialogue. If I publish this book, it is because I believe that I have perceived truth, outlined several of its problems and tentacles, and done so in a systematic way. But important points—perhaps the most important ones—may have escaped me, or I could be so confused that the whole book could be a mistake. Again, Antonio Machado: "In my solitude, I have seen very clearly some things that were not true." Only the reader can reassure the author or suggest better ways to deal with the question of the humanities.

This attitude rejects dogmatism but is not relativistic. It promotes the enthusiasm of the search, and the mature acceptance of limitation and error. This is the way in which the humanist can take a critical attitude against all apparent falsification, and against the language of special interests and of power. The humanities are a strong discourse that survives as a force beneath ephemeral fads or even legitimately urgent necessities. The latter demand our immediate attention while the humanities lie submerged in values that gush up from hidden paths and glance at a distant dawning (*"cauce oculto y madrugada remota"*—García Lorca).

Ortega y Gasset denounced the ungratefulness of the mass man toward the heroes that through science, technology, and liberal democracy paved the way for our comfortable existence. We vow our highest respect and gratitude toward scientists and toward science and technology. Their theories and artifacts are human efforts, make our lives longer and more comfortable, and are beautiful objects. But the humanities are more important. The engineer works ten hours every day to improve the mobile telephone and the computer program, and the economist develops promising models to increase exports. But the engineer and the economist are men and women who twenty-four hours every day need clarity with regard to their personal and collective identity, their communication (with those closest to them and with society), their creativity, and the meaning of life. Ingratitude toward science and technology is based on innocent oblivion, because they do not affect us in our deepest core. Today the threat of nuclear war appears more remote than in the decade between 1962 and 1972. But even then, at the mention of the nuclear threat people reacted like Don Juan: "We'll cross that bridge when we come to it." On the other hand, love, fear in the workplace, our relationships with our children and friends, and the questions about the sense of human existence demand our unremitting attention. Thus the humanities, far from being a bulwark against science and technology, profit from them but search for the ground in which science and technology gain their meaning. Instead of the two cultures, we need the culture of the difference, which keeps us aware of their convergence and divergence.

Life develops as a series of acts conditioned by our abilities, circumstances, and ideals, but never predetermined by these three parameters (section 20). As a result, no system can guarantee correct behavior, and, now and then, the "good" among us commit inexplicable acts. But the more we accentuate the ideals of attention, consideration, understanding, and courtesy, the greater the probability that they will be put into practice.

We may conclude that the greatest value of the humanities lies not in what we can do with them but in what they can do with us.

♋ Bibliography

Andrés Martín, Melquíades. *Pensamiento teológico y cultura*. Madrid: Sociedad de Educatión Atenas, 1989.

Aristotle. *On the Art of Poetry*. Translated by Lane Cooper. Ithaca, NY: Cornell University Press, 1975.

———. *Nicomachean Ethics*. Translated by Terence Irwin. Indianapolis, IN: Hackett, 1999.

———. *Metaphysics*. Translated by Richard Hope. Ann Arbor, MI: The University of Michigan Press, 1975.

Ashby, Eric. *Adapting Universities to a Technological Society*. San Francisco: Jossey-Bass, 1974.

Atkinson, R. F. *Knowledge and Explanation in History: An Introduction to the Philosophy of History*. Ithaca, NY: Cornell University Press, 1978.

Bataillon, Marcel. *Erasmo y España* [1937]. Translated into Spanish by A. Alatorre. México: Fondo de Cultura Económica, 1965.

———. *Défence et illustration du sens littéral*. London: Modern Humanities Research Association, 1967.

Bird, Alexander. *Philosophy of Science*. Montréal & Kingston: McGill-Queen's University Press, 1998.

Bloom, Harold. *The Western Canon. The Books and School of the Ages*. New York: Riverhead Books, 1995.

Bourguière, André. "La centralization monarchique et la naissance des sciences sociales. Voyageurs et statisticiens à la recherche de la France à la fin du 18e siècle," *Annales, Histoire, Sciences Sociales* 55 (2000), 199–218.

Cadalso, José. *Cartas marruecas* [1789]. Edited by José Tamayo. Clásicos Castellanos, no. 112. Madrid: Espasa-Calpe, 1967.

Calderón de la Barca, Pedro. *La vida es sueño*. Edited by C. Morón Arroyo. Madrid: Cátedra, 1991.

Cano Ballesta, Juan. *Literatura y tecnología*. Madrid: Orígenes, 1981.

Caro Baroja, Julio. *Razas, pueblos y linajes*. Madrid: Revista de Occidente, 1957.

Cassirer, Ernst. *The Logic of the Humanities*. Translated by C. S. Howe. New Haven, CT: Yale University Press, 1961.

————. *Symbol, Myth, and Culture.* Edited by D. P. Verene. New Haven, CT: Yale University Press, 1979.

Cerrillo, P. y García Padrino, J. *Hábitos lectores y animación a la lectura.* Cuenca: Universidad de Castilla-La Mancha, 1996.

Changeux, Jean-Pierre, and Paul Ricoeur. *What Makes Us Think. A Neuroscientist and a Philosopher Argue about Ethics, Human Nature, and the Brain.* Translated by M. B. DeBevoise, Princeton, NJ: Princeton University Press, 2000.

Cohen, R. S., and A. I. Tauber, eds. *Philosophies of Nature: The Human Dimension. In Celebration of Erazim Kohák.* Dordrecht: Kluwer Academic Publishers, 1998.

Condorcet, Marquis de. *Tableau général de la science qui a pour objet l'application du calcul aux sciences politiques et morales.* En *Oeuvres Completes,* vol. XXI, Paris, 1804.

Croce, Benedetto. *Aesthetic as Science of Expression and General Linguistic.* Translated by D. Ainslie. New York: The Noon Day Press, 1960.

Culham, Ph., and L. Edmunds, eds. *Classics: A Discipline and Profession in Crisis.* Lanham, MD: University Press of America, 1989.

Curtius, Ernst R. *European Literature and the Latin Middle Ages* [1948]. Translated by W. R. Trask. New York: Harper & Row, 1963.

Danto, Arthur C. *Connections to the World.* Berkeley: The University of California Press, 1997.

Dilthey, Wilhelm. *Introduction to the Human Sciences. An Attempt to Lay a Foundation for the Study of Society and History.* Translated by R. J. Betanzos. Detroit, MI: Wayne State University Press, 1988.

D'Ors, Eugenio. *La ciencia de la cultura.* Madrid: Rialp, 1964.

Eco, Umberto. *A Theory of Semiotics.* Bloomington, IN: Indiana University Press, 1979.

————. (with Richard Rorty, Jonathan Culler, and Christine Brook-Rose) *Interpretation and Overinterpretation.* Edited by Stefan Collini. Cambridge: Cambridge University Press, 1992.

Fernández Rañada, Antonio. *Los muchos rostros de la ciencia.* Oviedo: Nobel, 1995.

Ferrater Mora, José. *Las palabras y los hombres.* Barcelona: Península, 1972.

————. *Cuatro visiones de la historia universal.* Madrid: Alianza, 1982.

Freud, Sigmund. *Civilization and Its Discontents* [1930]. Translated by J. Strachey. New York: Norton, 1962.

Gadamer, Hans-Georg. *Truth and Method* [1960]. Translated by J. Weinsheimer and D. G. Marshall. New York: Crossroad, 1992.

Galilei, Galileo. *Dialogues Concerning Two New Sciences.* Translated by H. Crew and A. De Salvio. Evanston, IL: Northwestern University Press, 1968.

Garrido Gallardo, Miguel A. *Estudios de semiótica literaria.* Madrid: C.S.I.C., 1982.

————, et al. *La crisis de la literariedad.* Madrid: Taurus, 1987.

Goethe, J. W. *Conversations with Eckermann.* Translated by W. Wood. New York: M. Walter Dunne, 1901.

González, Fermín M., and J. Novak, *Aprendizaje significativo: técnicas y aplicaciones.* 2d ed., Madrid: Ediciones Pedagógicas, 1996.

González de Cardedal, Olegario. *El lugar de la teología.* Madrid: Real Academia de Ciencias Morales y Políticas, 1986.

Graham, Loren R. *Between Science and Values.* New York: Columbia University Press, 1981.

Granger, Gilles-Gaston. *Pensée formelle et sciences de l'homme.* Paris: Aubier-Montaigne, 1967.

Heidegger, Martin. *Being and Time* [1927]. Translated by J. Macquarrie and E. Robinson. New York: Harper and Row, 1962.

———. *An Introduction to Metaphysics* [1935]. Translated by R. Manheim. New Haven, CT: Yale University Press, 1964.

———. *Letter on Humanism* [1946]. Translated by F. A. Capuzzi and J. G. Gray. In M. Heidegger, *Basic Writings.* Edited by David F. Krell (New York: Harper & Row, 1972), pp. 193–242.

———. *Poetry, Language, Thought.* Translated by A. Hofstadter. New York: Harper and Row, 1975.

Hume, David. *A Treatise on Human Nature.* Edited by L. A. Selby-Bigge. Oxford: At The Clarendon Press, 1968.

Hummel, Pascale. *Histoire de l'histoire de la philologie. Étude d'un genre épistémologique et bibliographique.* Geneva: Droz, 2000.

Husserl, Edmund. "Philosophie als strenge Wissenschaft," *Logos* 1 (1910–1911), pp. 289–341. Translated by Quentin Lauer, New York: Harper & Row, 1965.

Iser, Wolfgang, *The Act of Reading: A Theory of Aesthetic Response.* Baltimore: The Johns Hopkins University Press, 1978.

Jaeger, Werner. *Paideia: the Ideals of Greek Culture.* Translated by G. Highet. Oxford: Blackwell, 1954–61.

Jovellanos, Gaspar M. de. *Memoria sobre la educación pública,* en *Obras escogidas.* Edited by A. del Río, Clásicos castellanos, no. III. Madrid, Espasa-Calpe, 1966.

Kant, Immanuel. *Critique of Pure Reason* [2d ed., 1787]. Translated by N. K. Smith. New York: St. Martin's Press, 1965.

———. *Anthropology from a Pragmatic Point of View.* Translated by M. J. Gregor. The Hague: Martinus Nijhoff, 1974.

Kerr, Clark. *The Uses of the University.* Cambridge: Harvard University Press, 1963.

Koch, Sigmund. *Psychology in Human Context. Essays in Dissidence and Reconstruction.* Edited by D. Finkelman and F. Kessel. Chicago: The University of Chicago Press, 1999.

Kockelmans, Joseph J., ed. *Phenomenology: the Philosophy of Edmund Husserl and Its Interpretations*. Garden City, NY: Doubleday and Co., 1967.

Kristeller, Paul O. *Eight Philosophers of the Italian Renaissance*. Stanford: Stanford University Press, 1964.

Kroeber, A. L., and C. Kluckhohn. *Culture. A Critical Review of Concepts and Definitions*. New York: Random House, 1952.

Laín Entralgo, Pedro. *La aventura de leer*. Colección Austral, no. 1279. 2d ed., Madrid: Espasa-Calpe, 1964.

———. *El problema de la universidad*. Madrid: Cuadernos Para el Diálogo, 1968.

Lakatos, I., y Musgrave, A. *Criticism and the Growth of Knowledge*. Cambridge: Cambridge University Press, 1974.

López García, Dámaso. *Sobre la imposibilidad de la traducción*. Cuenca: Universidad de Castilla-La Mancha, 1991.

Malmberg, Bertil, *La lengua y el hombre. Introducción a los problemas generales de la lingüística*. Translated into Spanish by J. López and K. Lindström. Madrid: Istmo, 1966.

Marías, Julián. *Antropología metafísica* [1970]. In *Obras*. Madrid: Revista de Occidente, 1982, vol. X, pp. 1–217.

———. *La persona*. Madrid: Alianza, 1996.

Martin, Rex. *Historical Explanation: Re-enactment and Practical Inference*. Ithaca, NY: Cornell University Press, 1977.

Marrou, Henri-Irénée. *De la connaissance historique*. Paris: Editions du Seuil, 1954.

Millán Puelles, Antonio. *La formación de la personalidad humana*. Madrid: Rialp, 1963.

———. *La estructura de la subjetividad*. Madrid: Rialp, 1967.

Montaigne, Michel de. *The Complete Essays of Montaigne*. Translated by D. Frame. Stanford: Stanford University Press, 1965.

Morón Arroyo, Ciriaco. *Calderón. Pensamiento y teatro* [1982]. 2d ed. Santander: Sociedad Menéndez Pelayo, 2001.

Morón Arroyo, Ciriaco, and Manuel Revuelta, eds. *Fray Luis de León. Aproximaciones a su vida y su obra*. Santander: Sociedad Menéndez Pelayo, 1989.

Nicol, Eduardo. *Metafísica de la expresión*. México: Fondo de Cultura Económica, 1957.

Nietzsche, Friedrich. *Untimely Meditations*. Translated by R. J. Hollingdale. Cambridge: Cambridge University Press, 1997.

Novak, Joseph D. *See* González, Fermín M.

Nozick, Robert. *Philosophical Explanations*. Cambridge: Harvard University Press, 1996.

Ortega y Gasset, José. "Prospecto del Instituto de Humanidades (1948), in *Obras completas* (Madrid: Revista de Occidente), 1964, vol. VII, pp. 11–24.

———. "Boletín N. 1 del Instituto de Humanidades. In *OC*, vol. IX, pp. 439–46.

————. *An Interpretation of Universal History*. Translated by M. Adams. New York: Norton, 1973.

Panichas, George A., *The Critic as Conservator. Essays in Literature, Society, and Culture*. Washington, D. C.: The Catholic University of America Press, 1992.

Pascal, Blaise. *Pensées*. Translated by A. J. Krailsheimer. New York: Penguin Books, 1966.

Petrarca, Francesco. *Opere*. Edited by M. Martelli. Florence: Sansoni, 1975.

Polanyi, Michael. *Personal Knowledge. Towards a Post-Critical Philosophy*. Chicago: The University of Chicago Press, 1962.

Polo, Leonardo. *Curso de teoría del conocimiento*. Pamplona, Universidad de Navarra, 1985.

Popper, Karl. *Objective Knowledge: An Evolutionary Approach*. Oxford: Oxford University Press, 1972.

Putnam, Hilary. "To think with integrity," in *Harvard Review of Philosophy* 8 (2000), 4–13.

Quintilian, *Institutio oratoria*. Translated by H. E. Butler. Loeb Classical Library, n. 124–27. Cambridge: Harvard University Press, 1980.

Revuelta Sañudo, M., and C. Morón Arroyo, eds. *El erasmismo en España*. Santander: Sociedad Menéndez Pelayo, 1986.

Ricoeur, Paul. *The Conflict of Interpretations: Essays in Hermeneutics*. Edited by D. Ihde. Evanston, IL: Northwestern University Press, 1974.

————. "L'Écriture de l'histoire et la représentation du passé," *Annales, Histoire, Sciences Sociales* 55 (2000), 731–47.

————. *See* Changeux, Jean-Pierre.

Rivera de Ventosa, Enrique. *Presupuestos filosóficos de la teología de la historia*. Zamora: Edics. Montecasino, 1975.

————. *Visión cristiana de la historia y otros textos* [Suplementos. n. 26], Barcelona: Anthropos, 1991.

Sáenz Badillos, Angel. *La filología bíblica en los primeros helenistas de Alcalá*. Estella: Verbo Divino, 1990.

Salinas, Pedro. *Defensa del lenguaje* [1944]. Madrid: Amigos de la Real Academia, 1991.

Sapir, Edward. *Language. An Introduction to the Study of Speech* [1921]. New York: Harcourt, Brace & World, 1949.

Sartre, Jean Paul. *Existentialism and Humanism* [1946]. Translated by P. Mairet. London: Methuen, 1948.

Searle, John R. *Expression and Meaning: Studies in the Theory of Speech Acts*. Cambridge: Cambridge University Press, 1979.

Simmel, Georg. "On the concept and tragedy of culture" [1912], in *Georg Simmel The Conflict in Modern Culture and Other Essays*. Translated by K. P. Etzkorn. New York: Teachers College Press, 1968.

Snow, C. P. *The Two Cultures and a Second Look*. Cambridge, Cambridge University Press: 1983.

Steiner, George. *No Passion Spent: Essays 1978–1996*. London: Faber and Faber, 1996.

Stray, Christopher. *Classics Transformed: Schools, Universities, and Society in England, 1830–1960*. Oxford: At The Clarendon Press, 1998.

The Future of the Humanities. In *Daedalus: Journal of The American Academy of Arts and Sciences* (Summer, 1969).

The Search for Knowledge. In *Daedalus* (Spring, 1973).

Toffanin, Giuseppe. *La fine dell'umanesimo*. Torino, Fratelli Bocca, Editori, 1920.

Unamuno, Miguel de. *Obras completas*. Barcelona: Vergara, 1958. 16 volumes.

Vico, Giambattista. *The New Science of Giambattista Vico* [1744]. Translated by Th. Bergin and M. H. Fish. Ithaca, NY: Cornell University Press, 1984.

Villanueva, Darío, et al. *Curso de teoría de la literatura*. Madrid: Taurus, 1994.

White, Andrew D. *Autobiography*. New York: The Century Co., 1905, 2 vols.

◌ℬ Index

The Humanities in the Age of Technology was designed and composed in Dante with Cataneo display type by Kachergis Book Design, Pittsboro, North Carolina, and printed on 60-pound Glatfelter Natural and bound by Cushing-Malloy, Ann Arbor, Michigan.

☙